The Berlin Wall Today
Remnants, Ruins, Remembrances

THE BERLIN WALL TODAY

REMNANTS, RUINS, REMEMBRANCES

WITH AN INTRODUCTION BY

MICHAEL CRAMER

PHOTOGRAPHS BY EVA C. SCHWEITZER

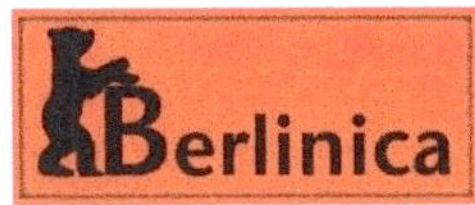

The Berlin Wall Today
By Eva C. Schweitzer, Ph. D. and Michael Cramer

Published 2011 by Berlinica Publishing LLC
Second updated edition in 2015
255 West 43rd St., Suite 1012, New York, NY, 10036; USA
© Berlinica Publishing UG
Editor: Eva C. Schweitzer
Translator: Cindy Opitz
Printed in the United States by LightningSource

Illustrations
Opposite page: East Side Gallery, Jolly Kunjappu, Dancing to Freedom
Andreas Schoelzel: Page 12
Landesarchiv Berlin: Page 16, 24, 32, 38, 44, 50, 54, 62, 68, 72, 80; 84, 94, back cover; all other photos: Eva C. Schweitzer

Maps: Open Street Map

Cover photo: Eva C. Schweitzer; the original painting is by Thierry Noir, at the East Side Gallery in Berlin.

ISBN Print: 978-1-935902-10-2
ISBN ebook:
978-1-935902-12-6
978-1-935902-08-9
978-1-935902-07-2

LCCN: 2011907211

www.berlinica.com

BERLIN PARTNERS, the City's Tourism Agency, has created an interactive map to explore where the Berlin Wall has been. To see it step by step, click on the map (in the ebook) or on the link at http://www.berlin.de/mauer/verlauf/index/index.en.php

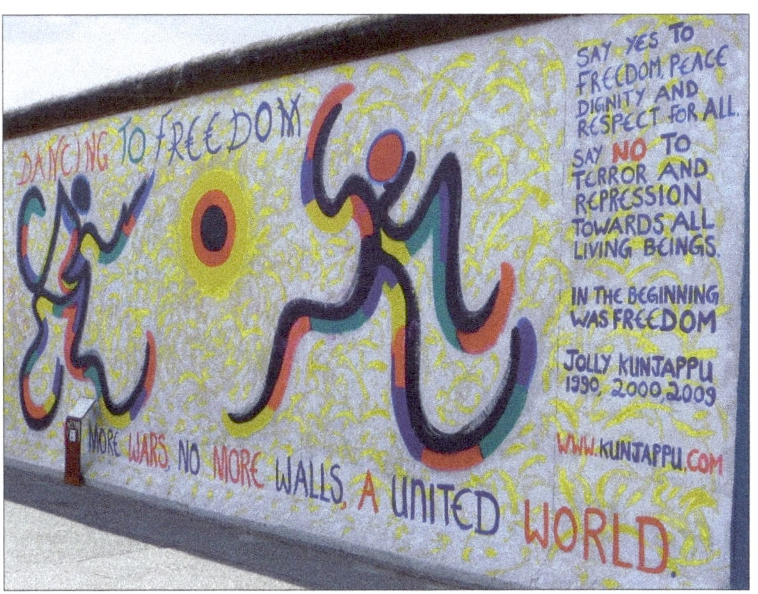

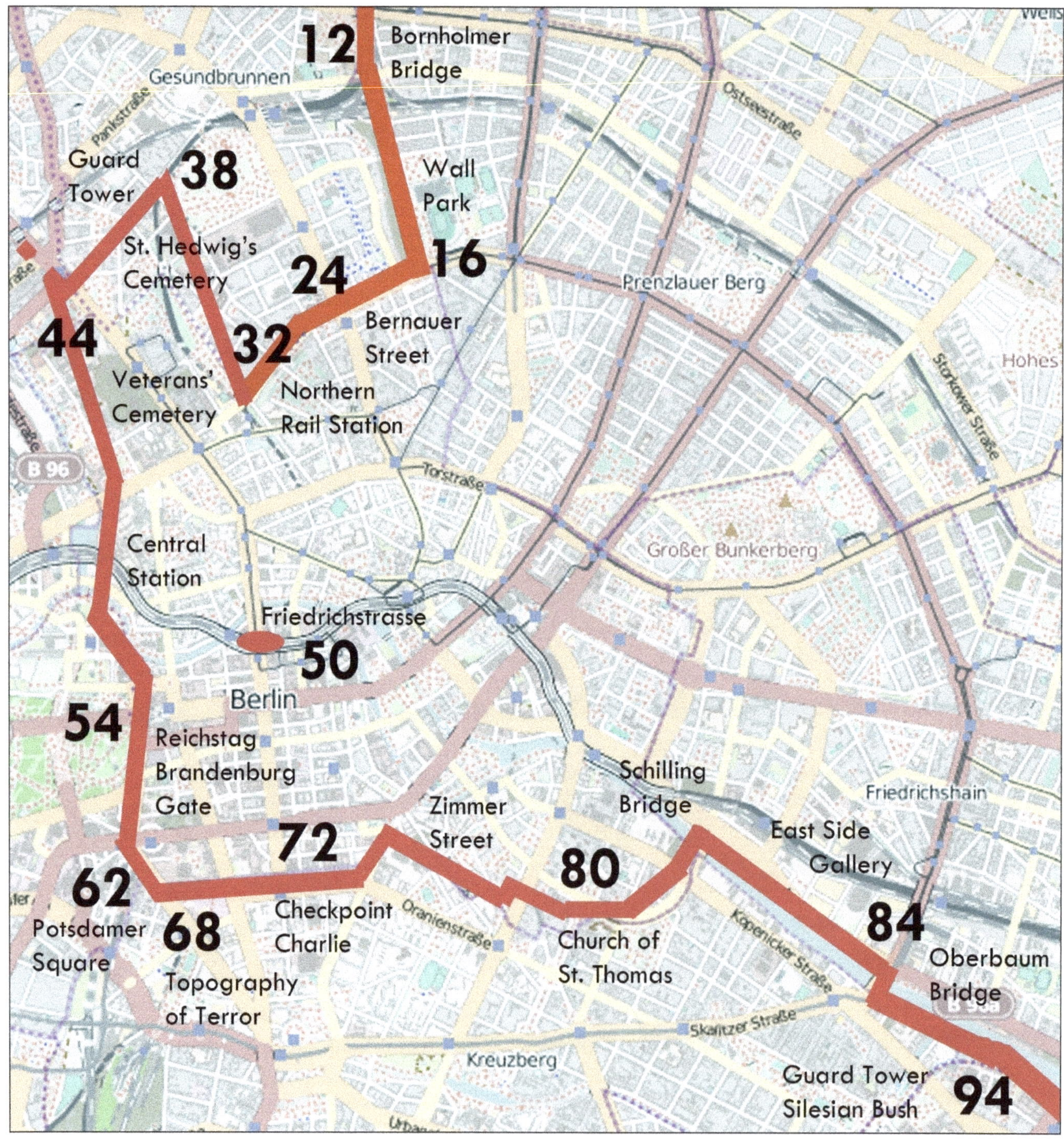

12
Bornholmer Bridge
Gesundbrunnen
Guard Tower
38
Wall Park
St. Hedwig's Cemetery
24
16
44
32
Bernauer Street
Veterans' Cemetery
Northern Rail Station
Prenzlauer Berg
B 96
Torstraße
Hohes
Central Station
Großer Bunkerberg
Friedrichstrasse
50
Berlin
54
Reichstag
Schilling Bridge
Brandenburg Gate
Friedrichshain
Zimmer Street
East Side Gallery
72
62
80
84
Potsdamer Square
68
Checkpoint Charlie
Oranienstraße
Church of St. Thomas
Oberbaum Bridge
Topography of Terror
Köpenicker Straße
Skalitzer Straße
Kreuzberg
Guard Tower Silesian Bush
94
Ostseestraße
Pankstraße
Storkower Straße
Wells

Contents   Page

"Where Was the Berlin Wall?"

by Michael Cramer

"Where was the Wall?" is a question that many visitors to Berlin ask, since there are only a few remnants left of the Wall. Immediately after its fall in November 1989, the *Berliner Mauer*, the Berlin Wall was taken down so thoroughly that almost all traces of the inner-city border were erased. And in the years after the *Wende* (turn-around, the expression Germans use to refer to the fall of the Wall), the city of Berlin changed so dramatically that even Berliners can barely remember the exact location of the Wall. Teenagers now know of the era before 1989 only from history books.

But meanwhile, many people think removing the Wall was a mistake, and there are organizations and initiatives that want to make the twenty-eight-year division of the city visible for future generations. This book, which traces the remnants of the Wall with more than one hundred color photographs, is a guide for Berliners and visitors alike to what is left of the Wall, to the last concrete slabs, the guard towers, the lampposts, the graffiti-covered back portions of the Wall—the so-called *Hinterland Mauer*, a second security wall bordering the eastern part of Berlin—and the memorial sites that remember the persecuted and the dead.

Even though most of the Wall was demolished, some parts of the original construction have remained, mostly at the Wall Museum at Bernauer Strasse, and at Niederkirchner Strasse, near the Berlin Parliament and the Topography of Terror Museum. But there is more. The course of the Wall that cut through the inner city—twenty-five miles altogether, and twelve feet high—is marked by a double-row of cobblestones with copper plaques at regular intervals bearing the words *Berliner Mauer 1961–1989*, even running through some subway and S-Bahn stations. The *Hinterland Mauer* has been preserved at Nordbahnhof, Mauerpark, and, most importantly, at the famous East Side Gallery. Most of it is covered in graffiti today.

The entire Wall around West Berlin was a lot longer than the inner-city Wall; it was one hundred miles long. Its appearance and location have changed over time, also as a result of numerous territorial exchanges. The original barbed-wire fencing of 1961 was replaced by pre-manufactured Wall segments a few months later, which were reinforced in some places with metal-grid fences. To the initial "outer border wall" *(äußere Grenzmauer)* facing west, with its trademark bulky top, the *Hinterland Mauer* was eventually added, the "inner border wall" *(innere Grenzmauer)* facing east.

Between the two lay the notorious *Todesstreifen* (death strip), a sandy wasteland more than a hundred yards wide, with the *Kolonnenweg*, or patrol road, in the middle. There the armed border troops of the German Democratic Republic (GDR) guarded the frontier with their fierce German shepherd dogs. On the West Berlin side, there was a *Zollweg* ("customs path"), built for the police and the Allied patrol vehicles. Only rabbits thrived in this urban desert.

Victims of the Wall

After the Wall was built, only government-approved people were allowed to live in the apartments directly behind the Wall in the eastern part of Berlin. Their friends and relatives had to be registered before any visits and were required to obtain special permits. More than three hundred guard towers, floodlight systems, signal and alarm fences, dog-runs, and tank traps were installed to prevent East Germans from escaping to West Berlin. Before the construction of the Wall, about four million people successfully escaped the GDR. Even afterward, Easterners, especially young ones, kept trying to cross the barricades, despite the danger. Between 1961 and 1989, the West Berlin police registered a total of 5,075 successful escapes at the Berlin Wall, 574 of which were desertions of GDR border troops. According to recent research, at least 128 people lost their lives at the Berlin Wall during such attempts, and even more at the border between East Germany and West Germany. Eighty border guards responsible for these deaths were identified after the end of the GDR and brought to court. Seventy-seven of them received a suspended sentence, but no jail time.

The first victim of the Wall who was killed by GDR boarder guards died on August 24, 1961. It was twenty-four-year-old Günter Litfin. He was shot when he attempted to swim to the West Berlin side of the Humboldthafen. A memorial plaque at the Sandkrug Bridge in the Western part of Berlin is dedicated to him. The final fugitive to be shot dead at the Wall was twenty-year-old Chris Gueffroy. He was killed on February 5, 1989, in a rain of bullets, as he attempted to swim across the Britzer Canal to Neukölln, in West Berlin. On June 21, 2003, on what would have been his thirty-fifth birthday, a monument was put up at the site. The stories of all the murdered fugitives have been researched and published at www.chronik-der-mauer.de.

Immediately after the fall of the Wall, many environmental and transportation initiatives began with the aim of developing the former Wall area as a bicycle trail and tour. In order to win support for their initiative, supporters put up bike pictograms in many places along the eastern patrol road. Unfortunately, GDR border guards, who were still responsible for the Wall until October 2, 1990 (the reunification of Germany), removed many of the signs and tore up the paved road. They got the order: "You built the Wall, now you have to take it down," and they did it with Prussian-Socialist effiency.

Some time later, the governments of Berlin and the surrounding state of Brandenburg failed to take steps to preserve the right of way. As a result, parts of both the *Zollweg*—which was being used as a cycle and walking trail by Berliners in search of recreation—and the *Kolonnenweg* were lost. For instance, the rail tracks of the railway line to Dresden interrupt the Wall trail, along with many plots of land that were sold after reunification and are now housing developments. Nevertheless, it is still possible to cycle along the entire length of the former border today on the former *Zollweg* and *Kolonnenweg*.

Already shortly after the Wall came down, there has been heated debate over what to do with the remnants. The media as well as the politicians in Berlin wanted to erase all traces of the Wall and this terrible time as quickly as possible. Only a small minority thought "beyond the day" (according to the title of a book by former Berlin mayor Willy Brandt) and fought to preserve at least some authentic parts of the Wall and the border strip. It was mostly individuals, representatives of landmark preservationists, and citizens' initiatives who prevented this important part of history from being forgotten. One famous supporter of the movement was Willy Brandt himself, who governed Berlin from 1957 to 1966, at the time of the construction of the Wall, and later the first Social Democrat to serve as German chancellor after 1945. He was also awarded the Nobel Peace Prize for his policy of reconciliation towards Poland.

Tracing the Wall after 1989

On November 10, 1989, in front of the Schöneberger Rathaus at John F. Kennedy square, which then served as the seat of the West Berlin city government, Brandt proposed that Berlin should "keep a part of that dreadful construction ... as a reminder of a historic monstrosity, just as we made the conscious decision in our city years ago, after heated debates, to let the ruins of the Gedächtniskirche stand" (the bombed-out shell of a church that became one of West Berlin's best-known landmarks after World War II). Michaele Schreyer, from the Green Party, who served as Berlin's chief official for urban development and the environment during the fall of the Wall, also defied popular opinion at the time, even though people were accusing her of wanting to erect the Wall once again. Early on, she placed the remnants of the Wall at Niederkirchner Strasse under landmark status.

At the time, she was treated with hostility, but today, everyone is grateful for the authentic remains of the Wall, especially in that place. On May 10, 2001, the Berlin City Council voted in favor of developing a bicycle and walking trail along the former border. The idea was brought up by the Green Party and its new political partner Bündnis 90, an East German civil rights group; and it was a movement I myself was a part of. The establishment of the Mauermuseum (Wall Museum) in Bernauer Strasse also generated numerous angry debates. It owes its existence to the efforts of former chancellor Helmut Kohl (CDU), who supported the museum in the face of resistance from members of his own party, who instead wanted to turn Bernauer Strasse into a six-lane inner-city highway.

But memories have to be made visible. We know that there is still no common collective memory between the West and the East. East and West Germans remember the border differently, partly because the official politics in both states interpreted it completely differently. The SED in the East—the reigning Socialist Unity Party—had declared it to be an "antifascist protection wall." For the West, it was a symbol of the lack of freedom in Socialism. In March 1996, a competition entitled "Crossings" was launched to generate proposals for memorials at the former border crossings, of which there were seven in 1961. Additionally, the *Geschichtsmeile Berliner Mauer* (Berlin Wall History Mile) was established. It is a permanent exhibition within the streets of Berlin, consisting of thirty plaques that provide information about the history of the division of the city as well as the construction and fall of the Wall. The plaques contain photos and short texts in four languages (German, English, French, and Russian), which describe events that occurred at specific locations along the Wall.

The first plaque was installed on November 9, 1999, on the tenth anniversary of the fall of the Wall. One such plaque at Bernauer Strasse, for instance, documents the escape of Conrad Schumann, an East German policeman whose leap across the barbed-wire fence on August 15, 1961, was recorded on film by Peter Leibing, a photo that became famous all over the world. Another plaque is dedicated to Ida Siekmann, the first victim of the Wall. She was a fifty-eight-year-old woman who died on August 22, 1961, of injuries sustained while jumping from her fourth-floor apartment at 48 Bernauer Strasse in East Berlin onto the pavement below, which belonged to West Berlin. Other plaques mark successful—and unsuccessful—escapes through secret tunnels under the Wall.

Berlin Wall History Mile

The main Berlin Wall memorial was dedicated at Bernauer Strasse on the Wall's 50th anniversary, in August 2011. It includes an information pavilion and a "Window of Remembrance", which was designed to look like a wall of funeral urns and features black-and-white photos of those known to have died at the Wall. Otherwise, the space is empty. A green lawn is now where the former border strip used to be. The *Kolonnenweg* was preserved as a walkway. Rusted Steel beams represent the Wall, recalling the "Iron Curtain". About 120 copper plaques or "Points of Remembrance" mark successful and failed attempts to flee, as well as political stunts or rallies. About ten escape tunnels are marked in the grass, and twenty-two information pillars complete the memorial site.

The Berlin Wall History Mile continues on the outskirts of the Wall Trail with seventeen information pillars. Historical photos and texts in German and English direct the attention of passers-by to certain places. Due to their former usage, specific development, or other special events, they highlight in some way the different aspects of the city's former division. The pillars—just like the Berlin Wall Trail signs—are twelve feet tall, just like the Wall once was. In addition to the information boards, there are also pillars and commemorative crosses for the slain fugitives, in order to remind the public of their fate. There are plans to put up such crosses for all of the known one hundred twenty-eight fugitives who were killed.

With all of these markers, it is now possible, twenty years after the Wall came down, to follow its path on the Berlin Wall Trail. The trail, which can be followed by bike and subway as well as by foot—and by foot is especially recommended in the inner city—is an interesting combination of history workshop and tourism, of recreation and culture. The Berlin Wall Trail between Bornholmer Strasse and the Schlesischer Busch, which is also the part this book covers, is especially informative and historically significant.

The Berlin Wall Trail has become part of Berlin's tourism program, and it has developed into a tourist highlight in the last few years. Today, some five-star hotels even advertise the route and offer bikes and guides to their guests. Tracing the path of the former Berlin Wall is an exciting route full of history. It takes cyclists past many important and famous landmarks. There are also many names that serve as reminders of past events: Checkpoint Charlie, Potsdamer Platz, Brandenburger Tor, Invalidenfriedhof (Veterans' Cemetery) or Bernauer Strasse. The route also passes the Bornholmer Brücke, which became famous on November 9, 1989, when the first East Berliners crossing the border were greeted with cheers and champagne.

The Oberbaumbrücke, the legendary East Side Gallery, or the remaining Wall segments at Niederkirchner Strasse or Nordbahnhof are also worth a visit. Another interesting site is the *Parliament of Trees against War and Violence*, by Berlin artist Ben Wagin. His work was integrated into the new buildings of the Bundestag, near the Reichstag, on the eastern bank of the Spree River, after the fall of the Wall. All these spots are covered and pictured extensively in this book, which marks the 50th anniversary of the Berlin Wall's construction.

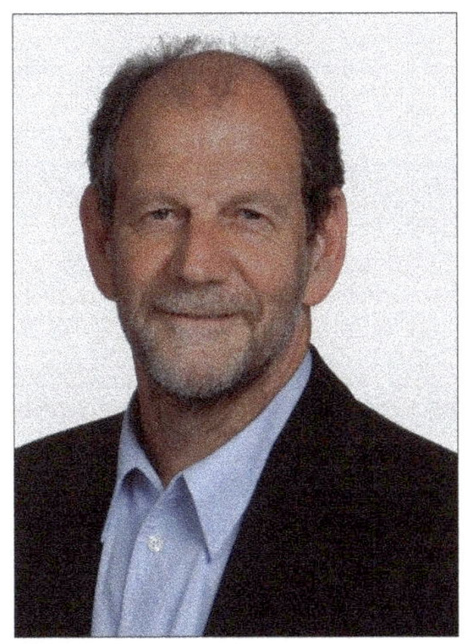

Michael Cramer has lived in Berlin since 1974. He worked as a grammar school teacher in the district of Neukölln until 1995. Early on, he joined the newly founded Alternative Liste, known today as Bündnis 90/ Die Grünen (Green Party) and became the party's go-to politician for transportation issues and sustainable environmental policy. He was a member of the Berlin City Council, the Abgeordnetenhaus. In 2001, he published *Berliner Mauer-Radweg,* and *Europa-Radweg Eiserner Vorhang* in 2009. Since 2004, he has been a member of the European Parliament. He is a member of the committee on transportation and tourism. Cramer was born on June 16, 1949, in Gevelsberg, Germany, and he studied education, music, and sports in Mainz.

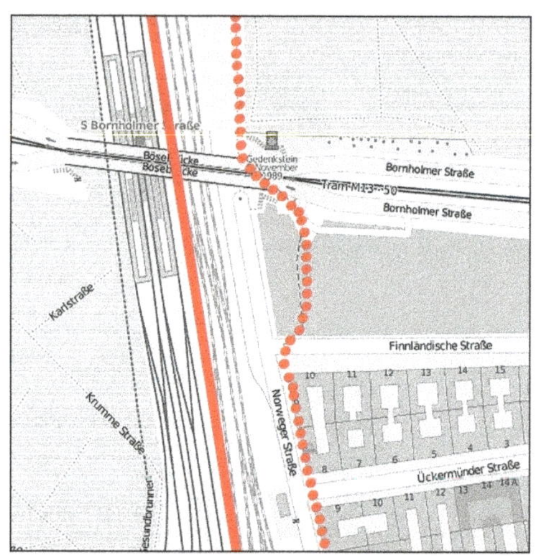

BORNHOLMER STRASSE
BÖSEBRÜCKE

BORNHOLMER STREET
BOESE BRIDGE

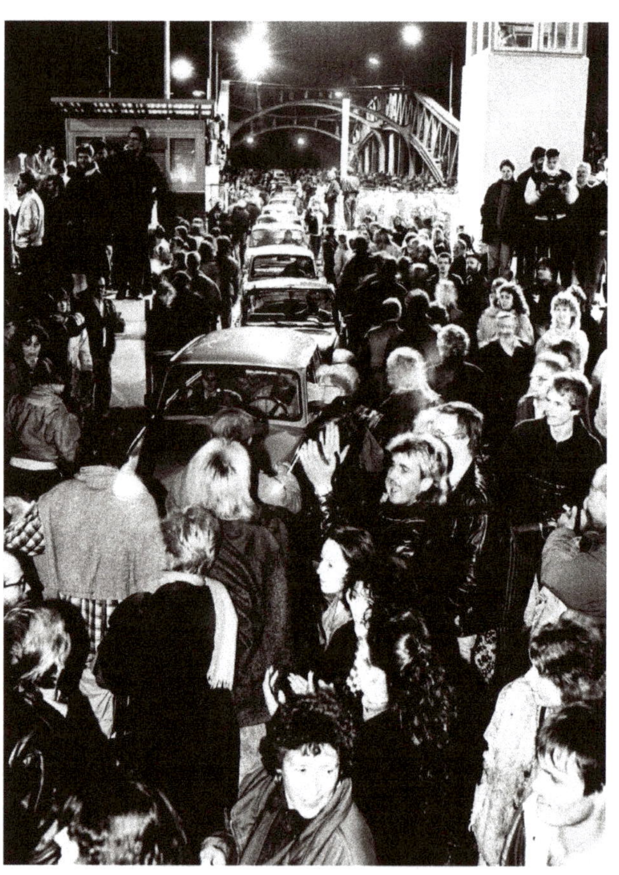

On a cold and foggy night, November 9, 1989, the Berlin Wall came down, twenty-eight years after it was built in August 1961. It was 7:30 p.m. when Günter Schabowski, an operative of the Communist Party, the SED, told live on camera that citizens of the GDR would be permitted to leave. Less than an hour later, hundreds and soon thousands of people went to the checkpoints and demanded to cross the border, growing louder and louder. Finally, at 10:30 p.m., nervous border guards at Bornholmer Bridge made the call: they opened the gates, and droves of happy people, along with a lot of honking cars, poured into West Berlin. Berliners from the West and the East hugged each other. During the next one and a half hours, all checkpoints opened. Berlin celebrated one long, happy night.

Today, Bornholmer Bridge, which was divided right in the middle, connects East and West, Pankow and Wedding, again. The bridge, a steel construction from 1913, was originally named after German president Paul von Hindenburg. In 1948, East Berlin authorities renamed it Wilhelm-Böse-Brücke, after a resistance fighter executed by the Nazis. But Berliners still refer to it as Bornholmer Brücke, after the street. A fairly long piece of the Hinterland Wall remains, beginning on the north side of Bornholmer Street (the dotted line on the map; while the actual Wall is marked by the straight line). A memorial with 23 trees, a time line, quotes on weathered steel plaques, and large photo tableaus remind passers-by of the moments right before and after the Wall came down. Starting on the northern side, visitors can relive the day from 9 a.m. to midnight.

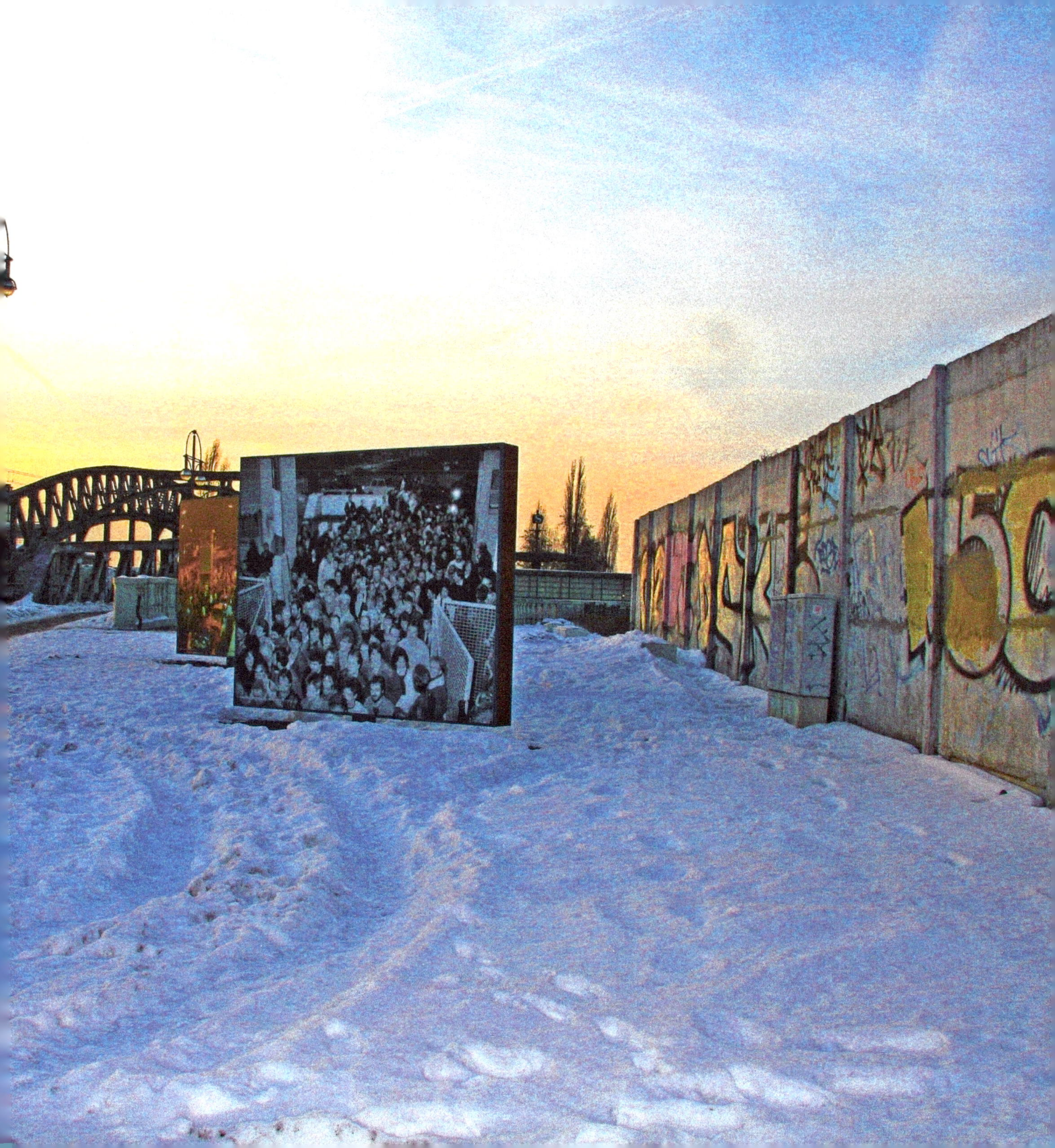

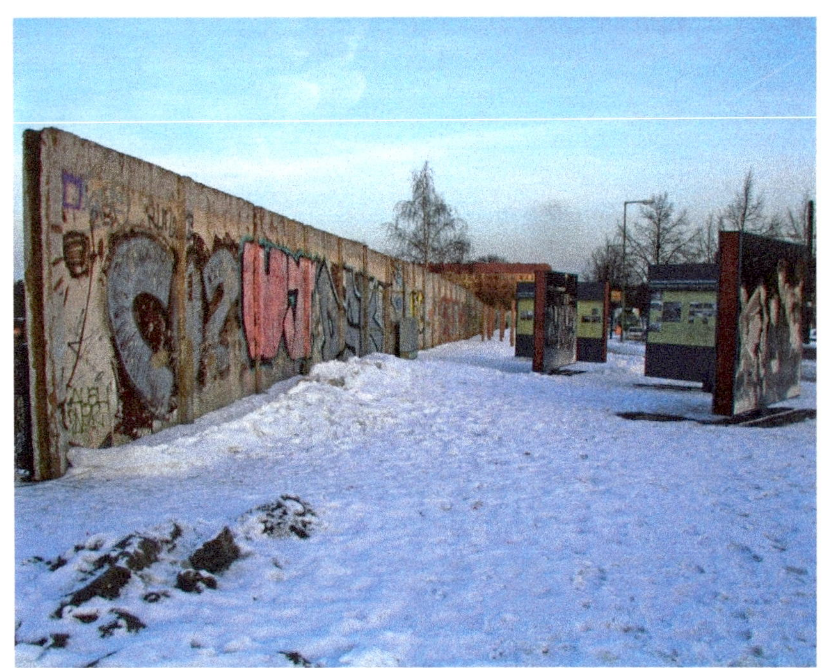

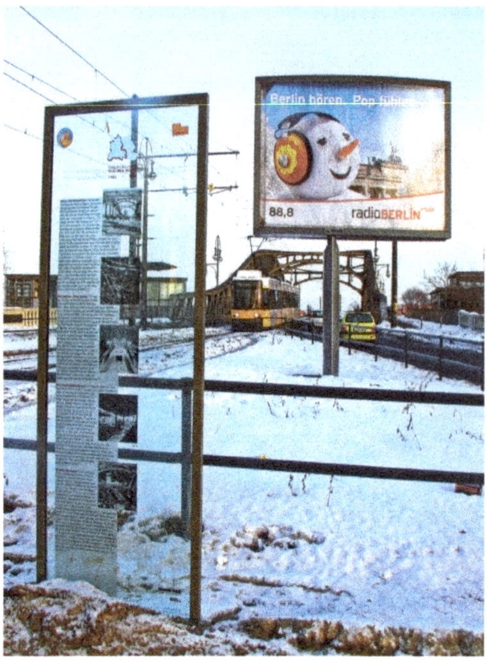

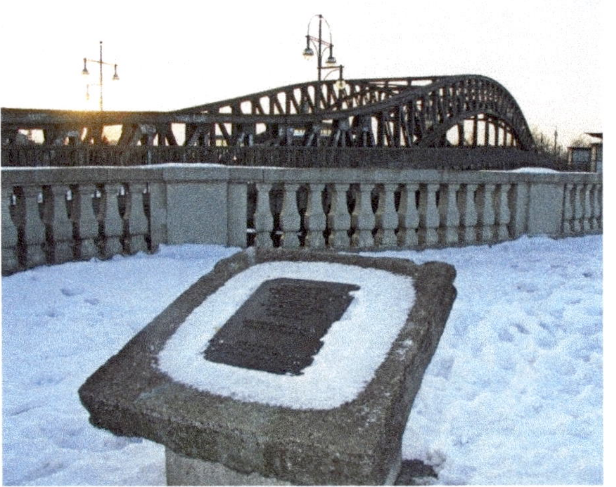

Upper left: The last Hinterland Wall along Bornholmer Strasse.
Left: The plaque quotes Willy Brandt, late Berlin mayor and German chancellor: "Berlin will live, and the Wall will fall." (1989).
Above: A streetcar crossing the bridge. In 1953, West Berlin outlawed female drivers; the East, however, did not. On January 1953, a woman in the driver's seat of a streetcar from the East tried to cross the bridge to the West and was turned back by western authorities. East Berlin took that as a provocation and divided the streetcar system eight years before the Wall was built. West Berlin subsequently shut down its streetcars. The last one ran in 1967, from Zoo to Spandau. Only after the Wall fell, did streetcars cross the bridge again.
Below: A quote from that night in 1989, on a memorial copper band embedded in the sidewalk: "'We're being overrun! We're opening everything now!' — Stasi Officer."
Opposite: View from Bornholmer Bridge of the city's center, with the *Fernsehturm* (TV tower) and the *Marienkirche* (Church of St. Mary).

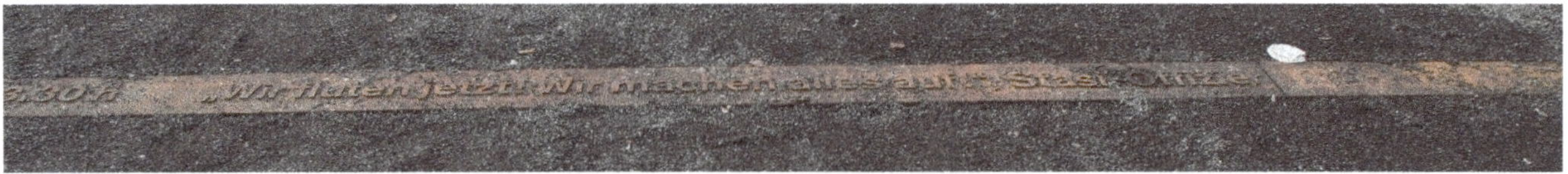

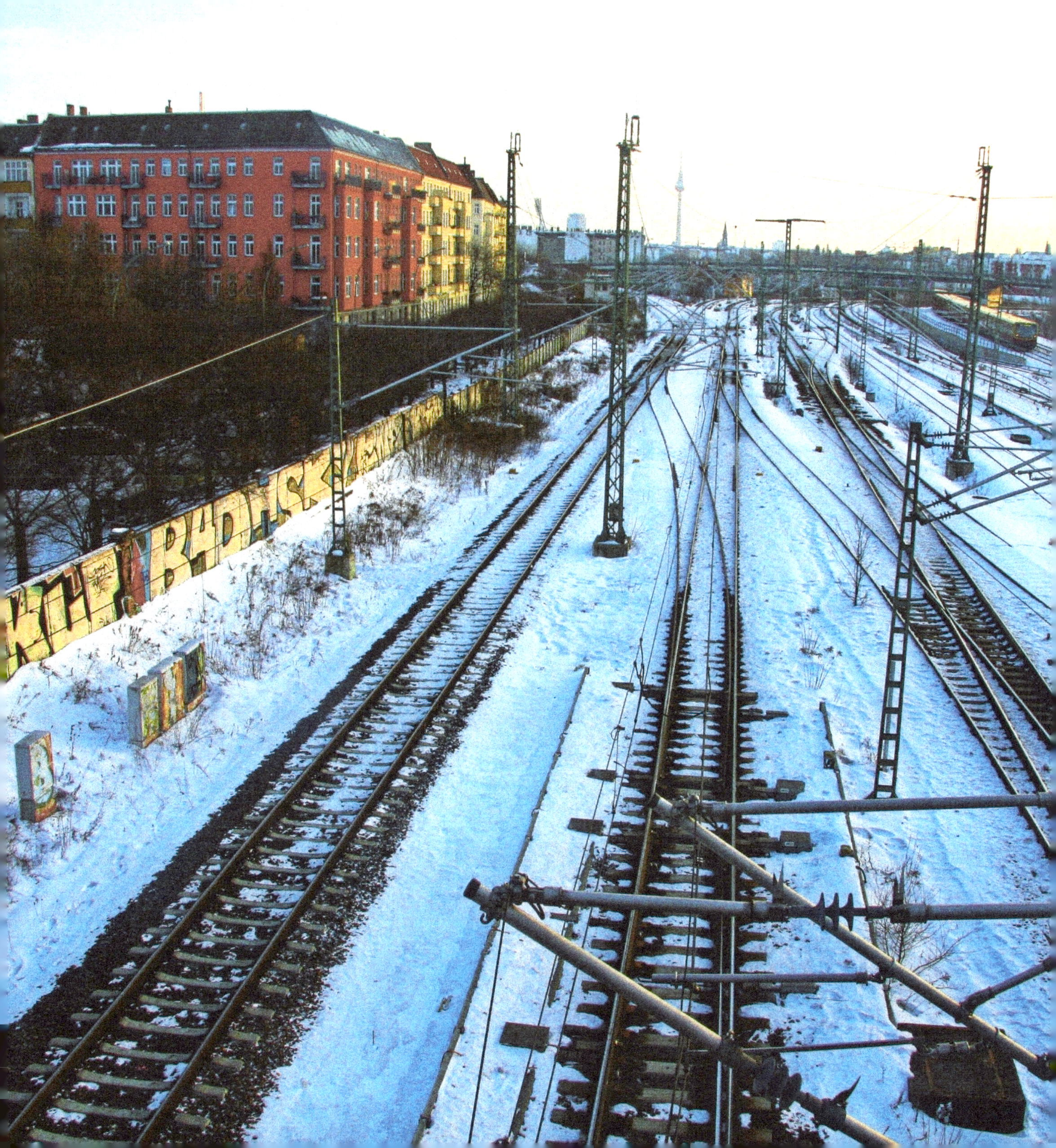

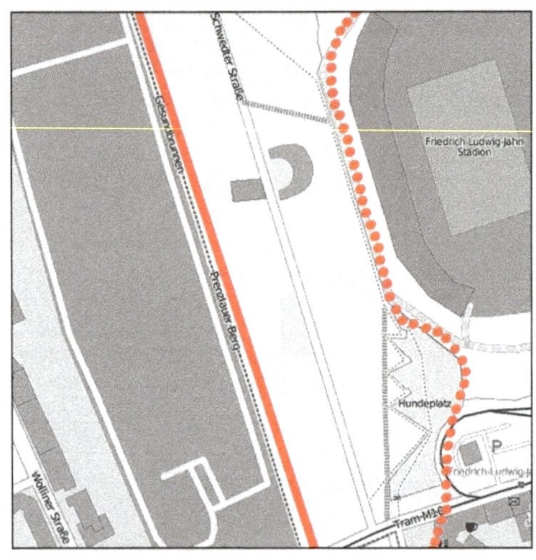

MAUERPARK
JAHN-STADION

WALL PARK
JAHN STADIUM

The area where Mauerpark is today used to be border wasteland, with guard towers, patrol roads, and guards with dogs, a lonely stretch along Schwedter Strasse and the old Eberswalder Freight Terminal. The Wall separated Wedding in the West from Prenzlauer Berg in the East, where buildings were cleared and the freight rails abandoned. The soccer stadium that was built for the traditional Berlin club Hertha BSC was in the East. Eastern authorities turned it into an arena for BFC Dynamo, a soccer club associated with the Stasi *(Staatssicherheit,* East German secret police), and renamed it Friedrich-Ludwig-Jahn-Stadium.

Today, the stadium, with its trademark floodlights, is accompanied by a tennis court and an area for beach volleyball. It is the second largest sports field in Berlin and used by quite a few clubs. Even Michael Jackson performed here in 1992. In addition, a new sports arena has been built, the Max-Schmeling-Halle, named after the famous German boxer. It is the home of the football team *Reinickendorfer Füchse* (Foxes from Reinickendorf). Rock and pop stars perform here as well.

A few hundred yards of the old Hinterland Wall are still left, now shielding the Max-Schmeling-Halle from trespassers. Also, the ancient cobblestones of Schwedter Strasse have mostly been restored, as well as some of the tracks.

Mauerpark has evolved into a huge international summer gathering place, with a basketball court, a boule area, an amphitheater with karaoke on the weekends—pictured opposite—and a flea market.

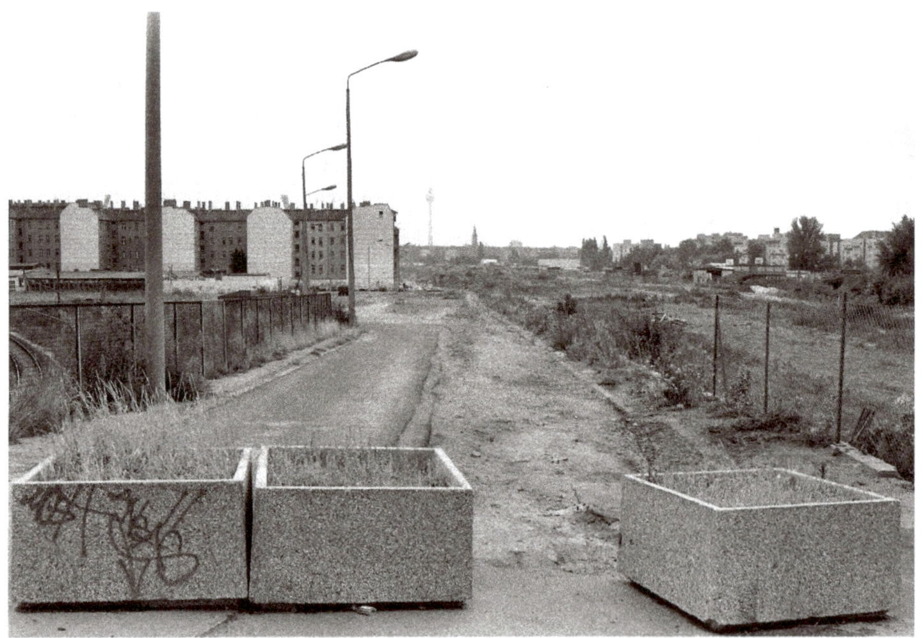

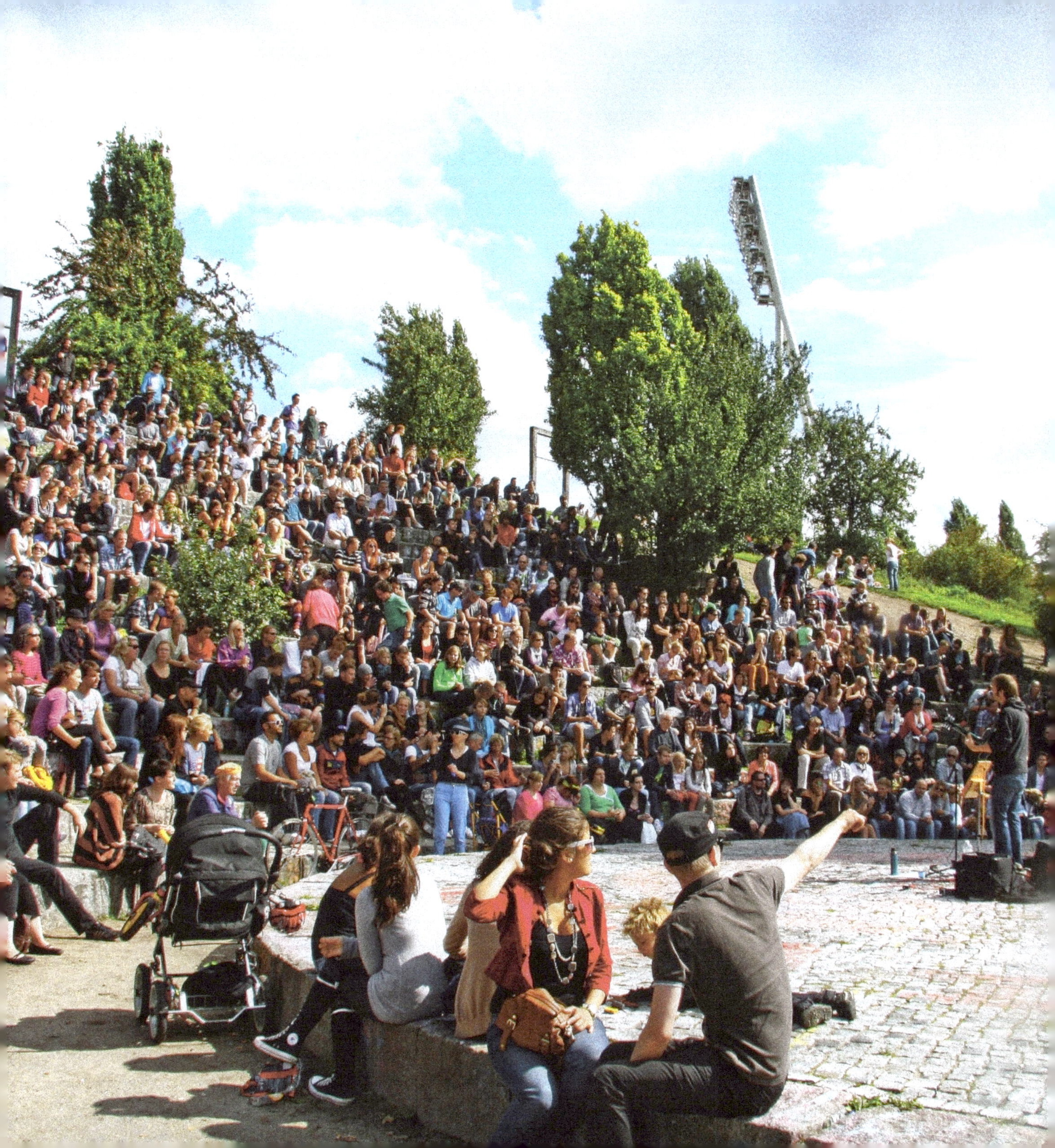

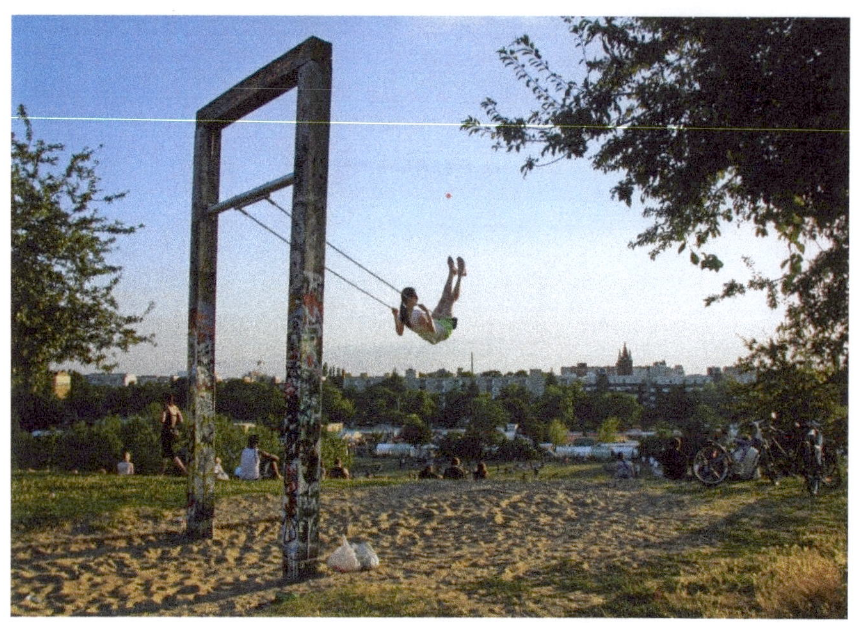

Left: Kids and grownups alike enjoy these swings, which offer a view over all of Wedding, a working-class district, now home to many Turkish and Arab immigrant families. Wedding was divided by the Wall from neighboring Prenzlauer Berg.

Below: These pianos are one of the city's many cultural arts projects. But there is also room for sports, such as boules.

Opposite: One of Berlin's largest flea markets sprawls throughout Mauerpark on the weekends. Many oddities, from homemade T-shirts and GDR medals to half broken china—or, as pictured, a former GDR border sign—can be found here.

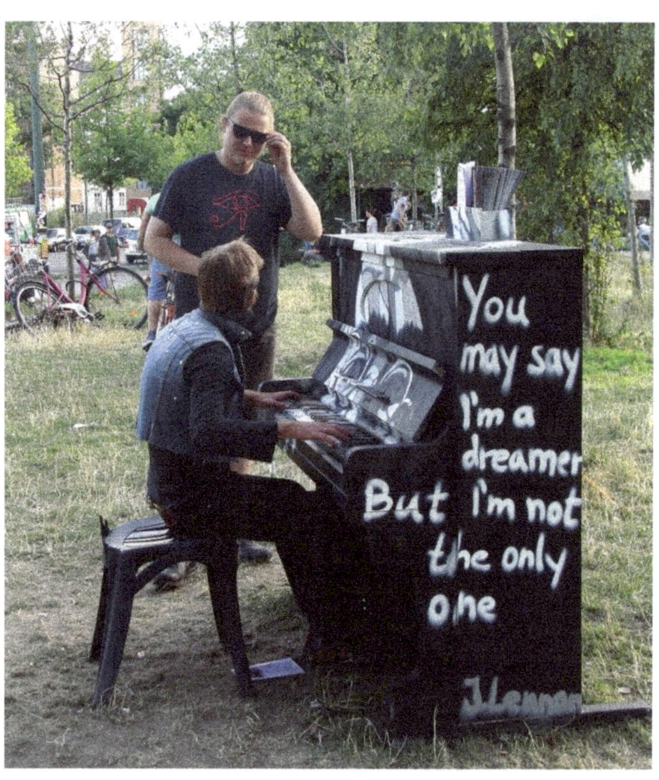

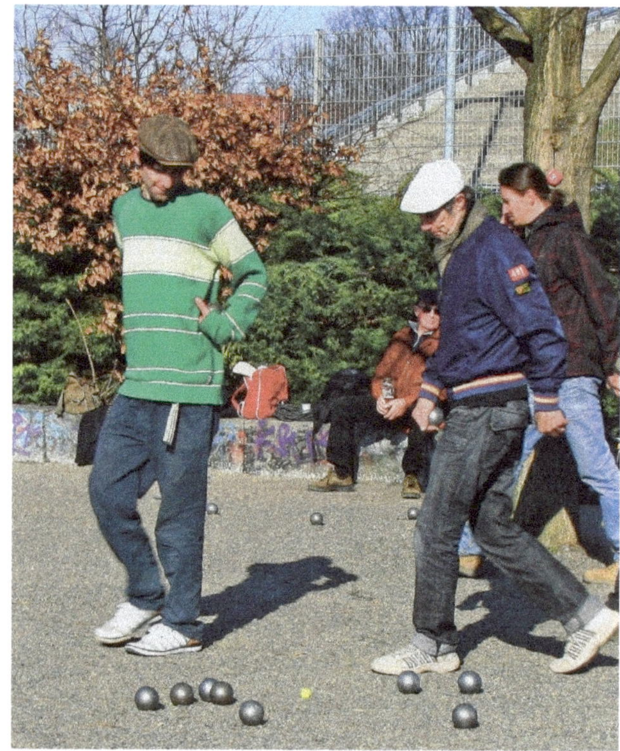

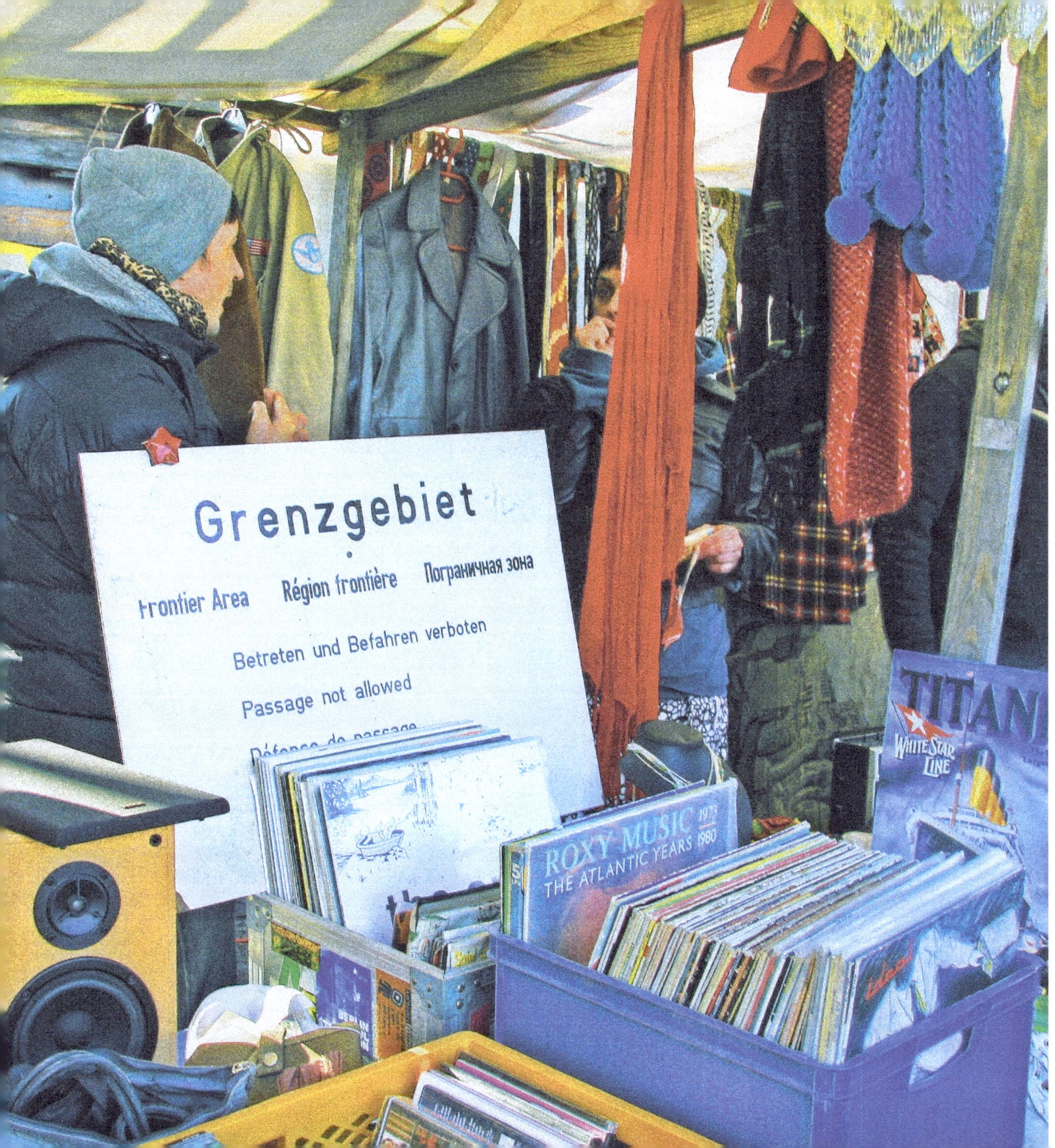

Grenzgebiet
Frontier Area   Région frontière   Пограничная зона
Betreten und Befahren verboten
Passage not allowed
Défense de passage
ROXY MUSIC 1973
THE ATLANTIC YEARS 1980
TITAN
WHITE STAR LINE

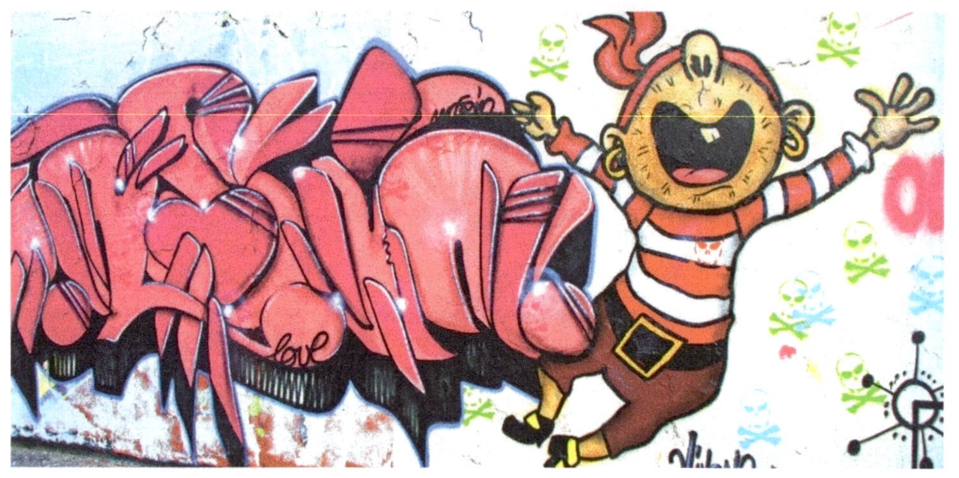

Graffiti is legal in Mauerpark, but only when confined to the former Hinterland Wall. The street art here never lasts, though, because the next painter is right in line.

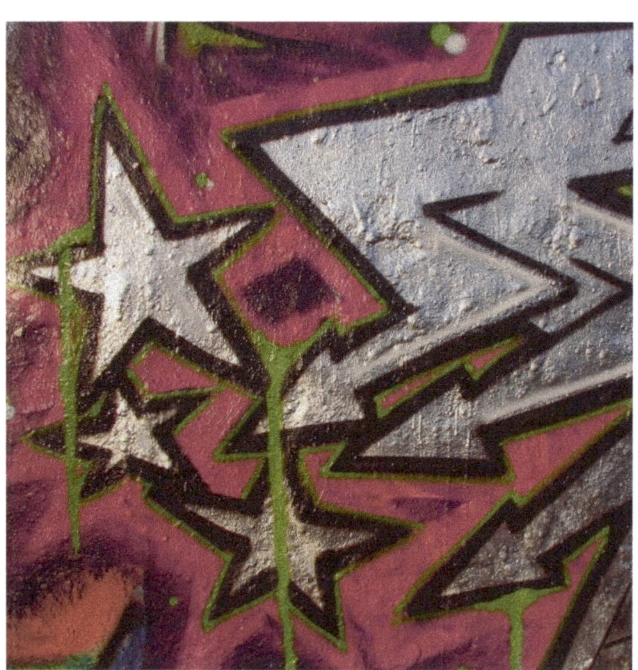

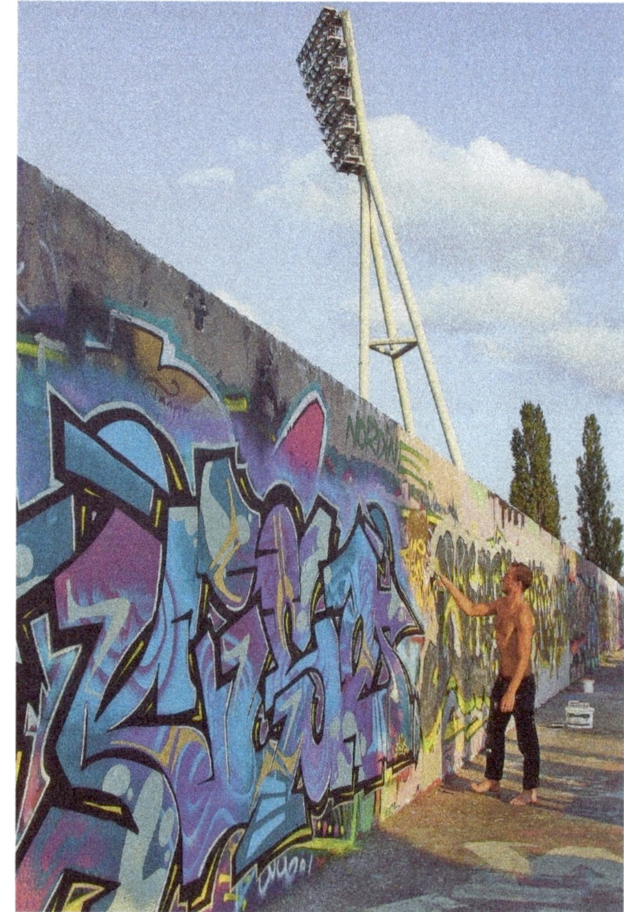

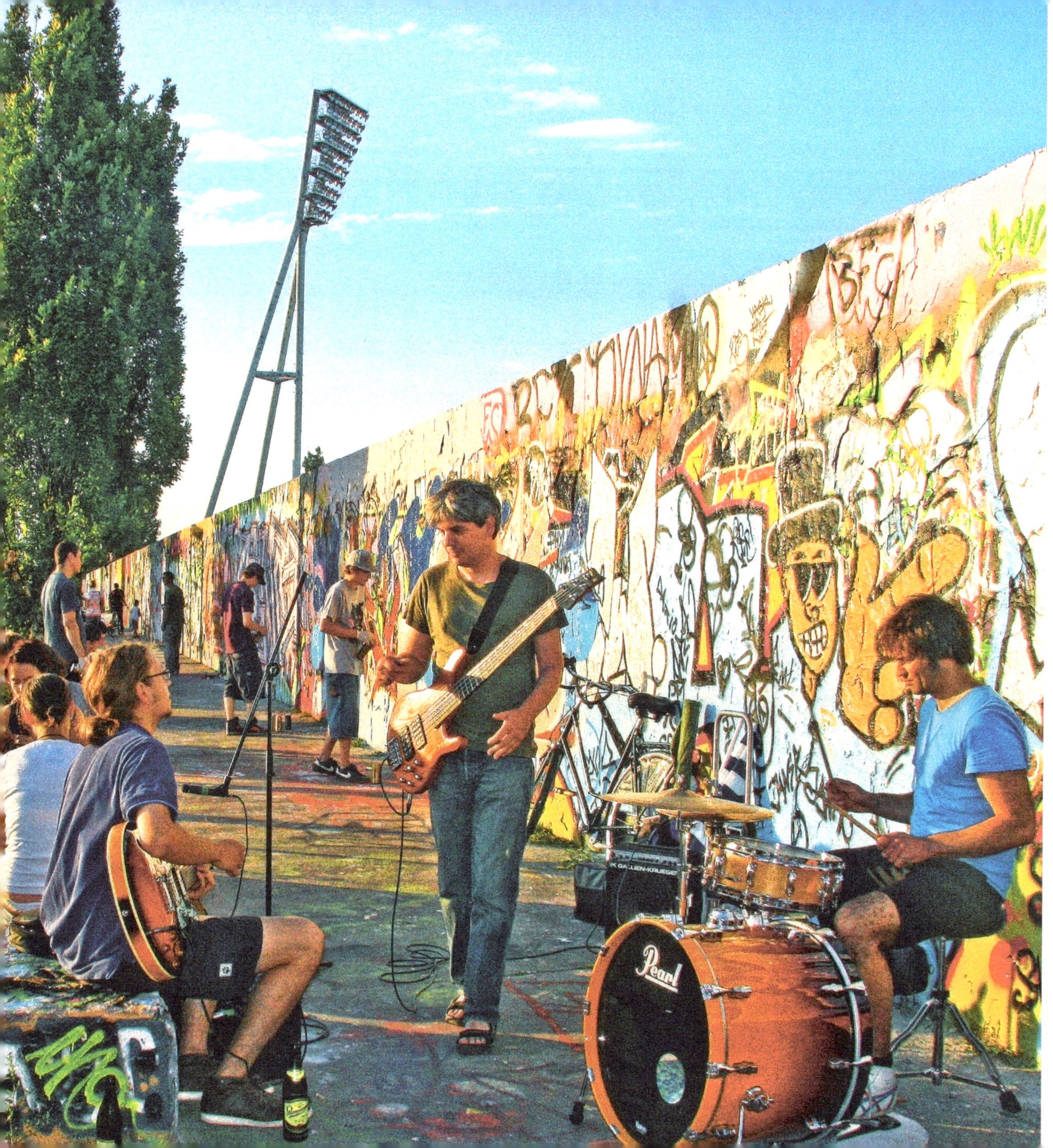

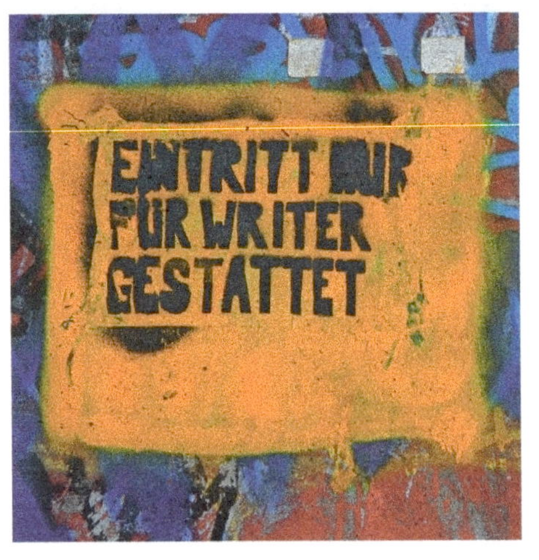

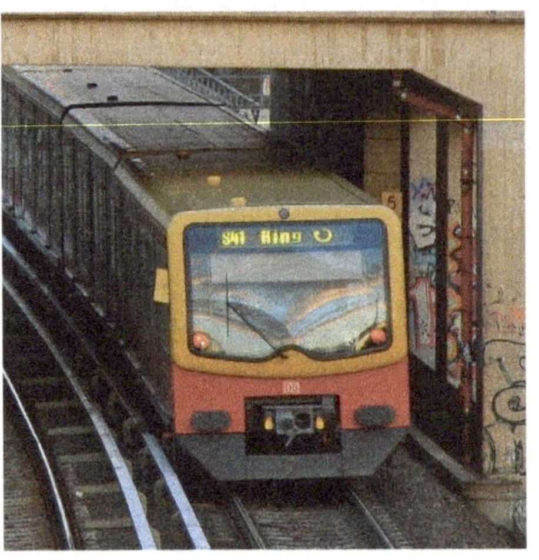

Opposite: The northern part of Mauerpark overlooks the extended S-Bahn rails all the way to Bornholmer Bridge. The park runs over Gleimtunnel, a tunnel that connected Prenzlauer Berg and Wedding, which was closed before 1989. Now stairs lead up to the park. **Far left:** "Access for writers only," according to this sign (or maybe not).

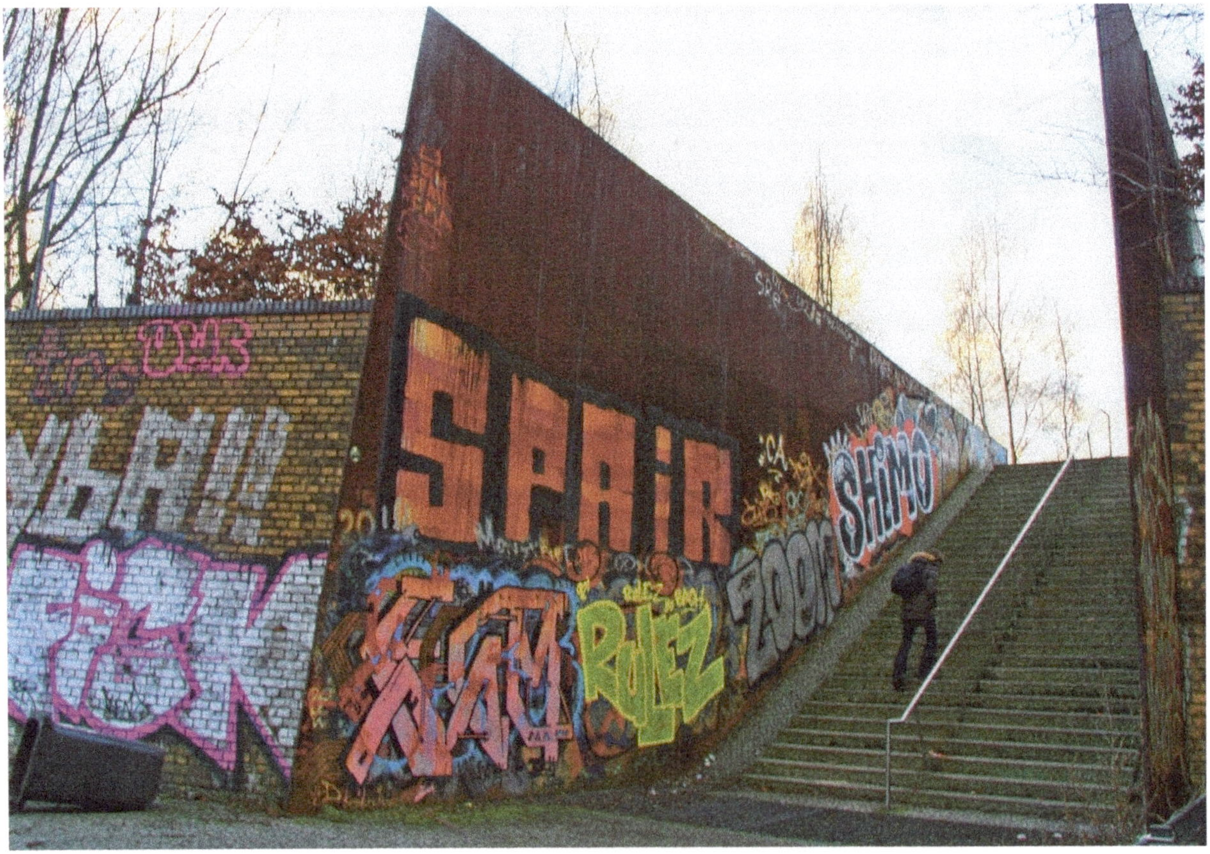

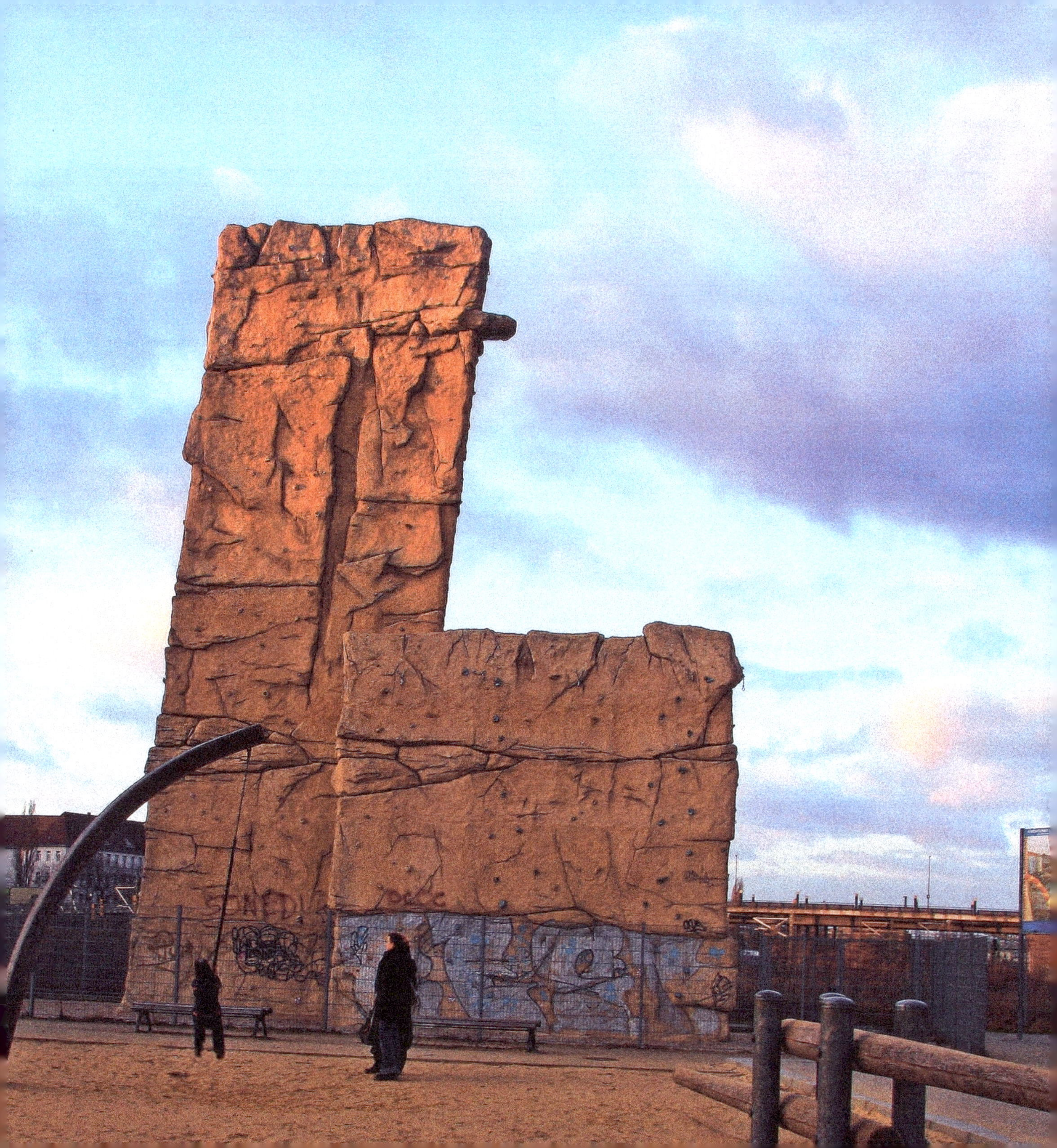

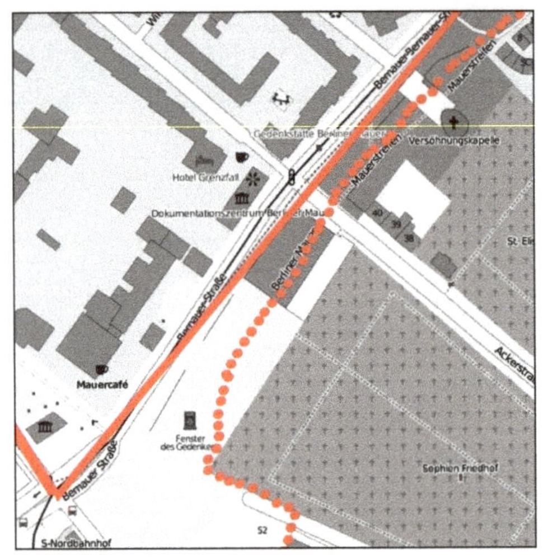

MAUER-GEDENKSTÄTTE BERNAUER STRASSE

BERLIN WALL MEMORIAL AT BERNAUER STREET

The first victim of the Wall resided at Bernauer Strasse, fifty-eight-year-old Ida Siekmann. On August 22, 1961, nine days after the Wall was built, she jumped from the window of her fourth-floor apartment. She had thrown cushions and a bedspread down to the sidewalk below, which lay in West Berlin, but she died anyway. A few days earlier, a border guard named Conrad Schumann jumped over the Wall while it was still being built and escaped.

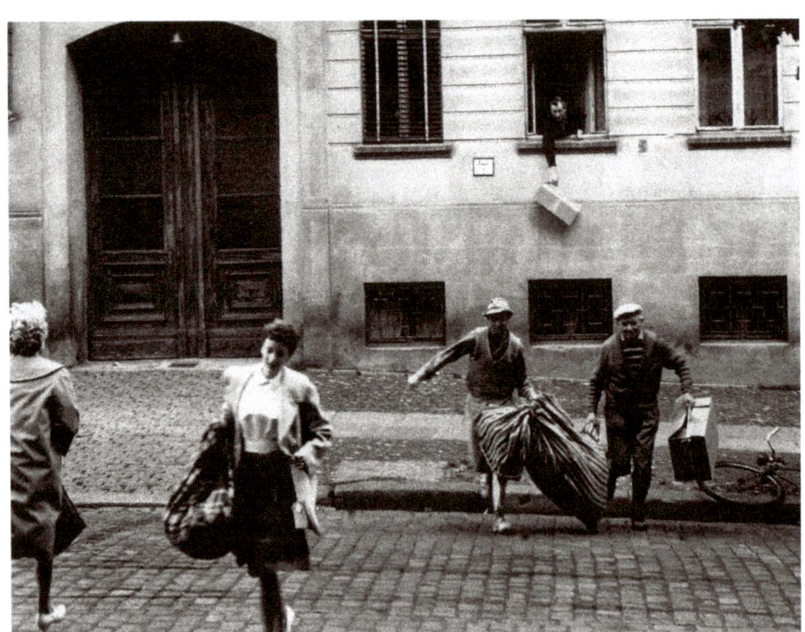

The Wall ran along the entire length of Bernauer Strasse, right up to the edge of the buildings in East Berlin. It ran from where Mauerpark is today all the way down to Nordbahnhof. The tenements that belonged to the East were boarded up and eventually cleared of tenants. Many residents tried to flee. Twenty-nine made it through an escape tunnel that was not discovered until 2000, and fifty-seven more fled through a tunnel at nearby Strelitzer Strasse.

Today, Bernauer Strasse is the only place where a mile-long stretch of the Wall has been preserved. The area has been turned into a memorial site with a museum and an outdoor exhibit. As shown in the opposite photo, the actual Wall is in the front, while the Hinterland Wall is in the back; between the two is the "death strip," with it's dark-gray patrol road, guard tower, "archaeological windows" with lampposts, border lights, remnants of tunnels, and a "Window of Remembrance" to the victims. An observation tower was built across the street.

The Wall Memorial Museum is open to visitors Tuesday through Sunday from 9:30 a.m. to 7 p.m. (until 6 p.m. in winter). The museum offers guided tours, as well as self-guided audio tours outdoors.

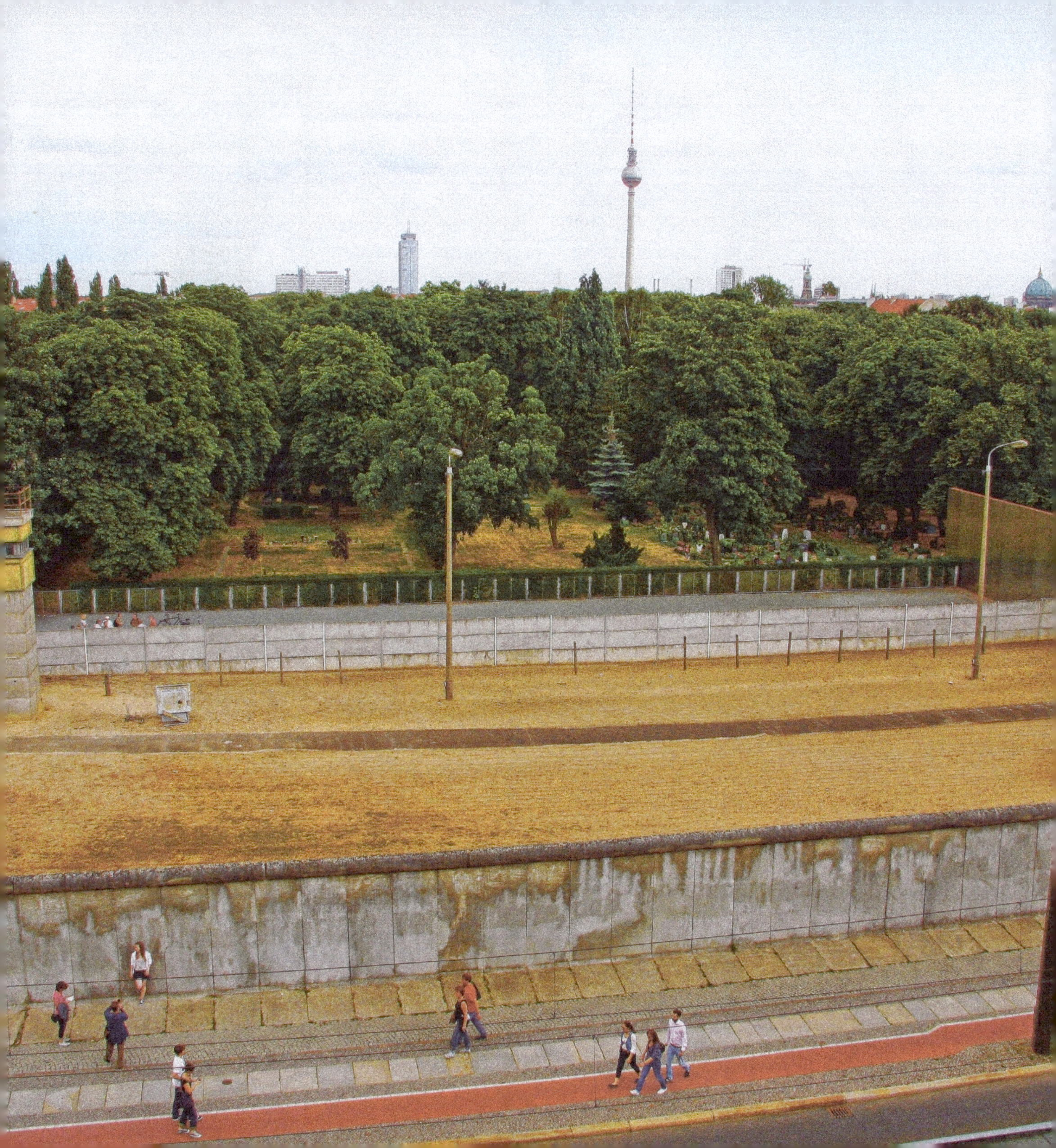

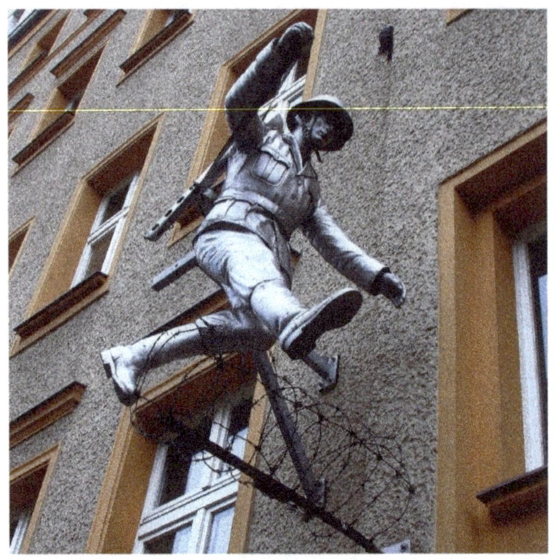

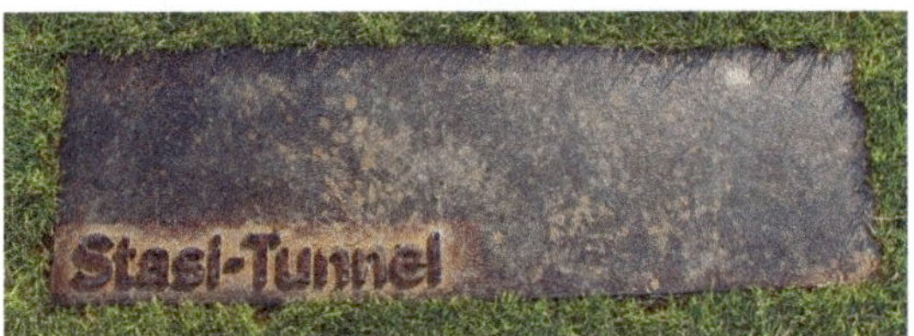

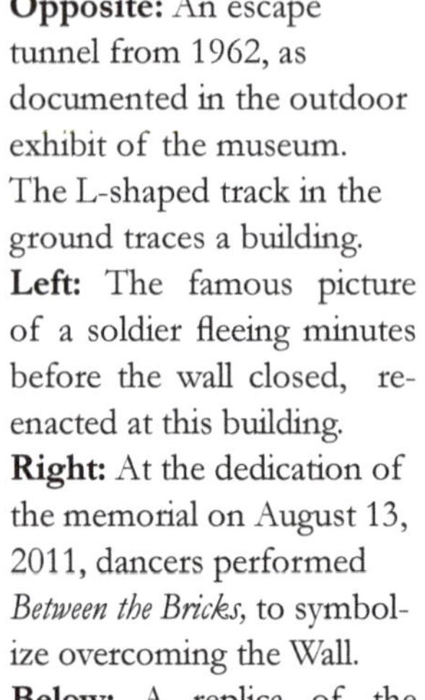

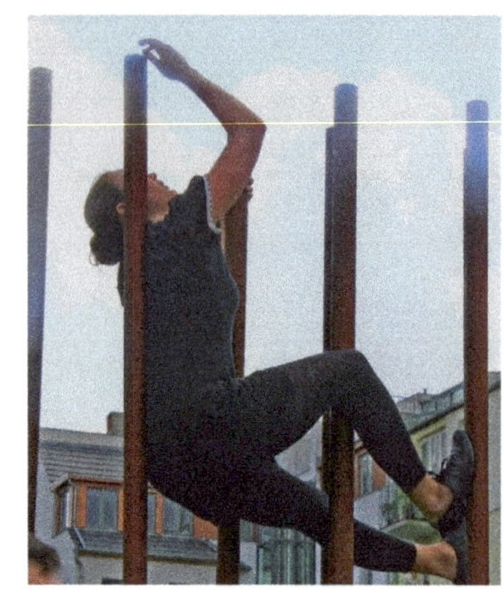

Opposite: An escape tunnel from 1962, as documented in the outdoor exhibit of the museum. The L-shaped track in the ground traces a building.

Left: The famous picture of a soldier fleeing minutes before the wall closed, re-enacted at this building.

Right: At the dedication of the memorial on August 13, 2011, dancers performed *Between the Bricks,* to symbolize overcoming the Wall.

Below: A replica of the basement of an apartment building is also part of the exhibit. This building, along with the other residential buildings on the south side of Bernauer Street, was torn down by East Berlin authorities after the Wall was built

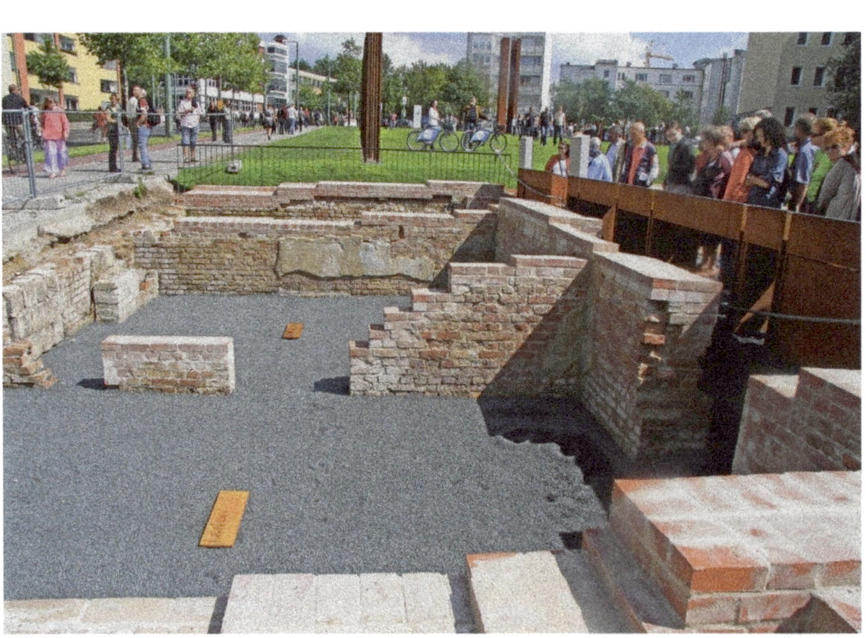

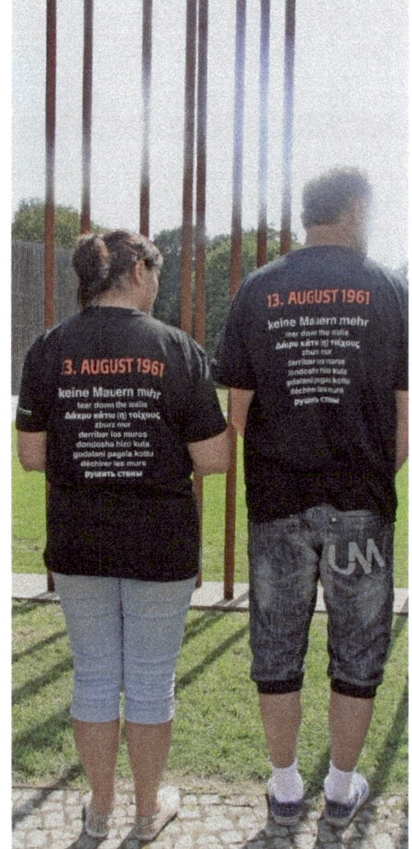

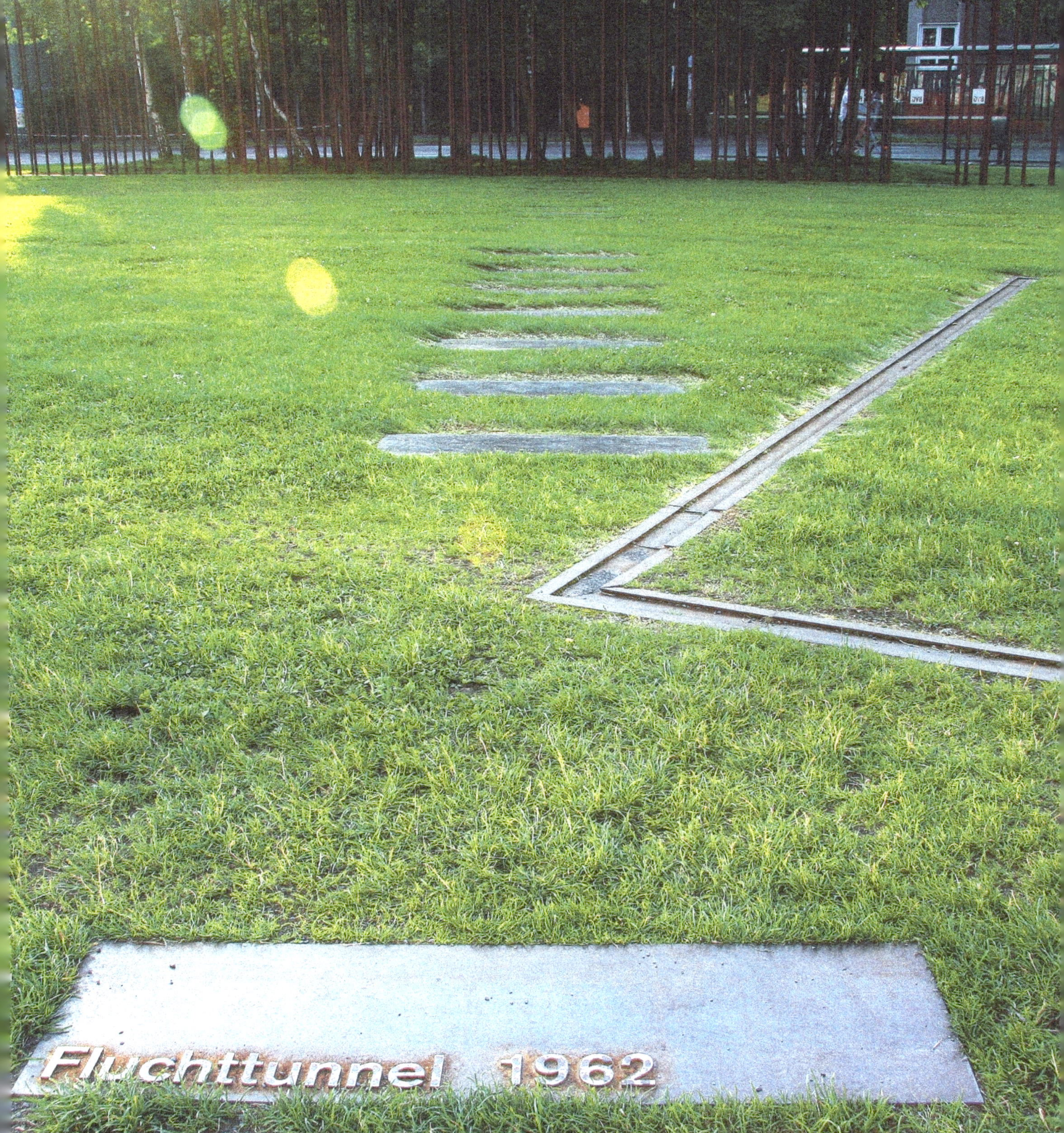

Fluchttunnel 1962

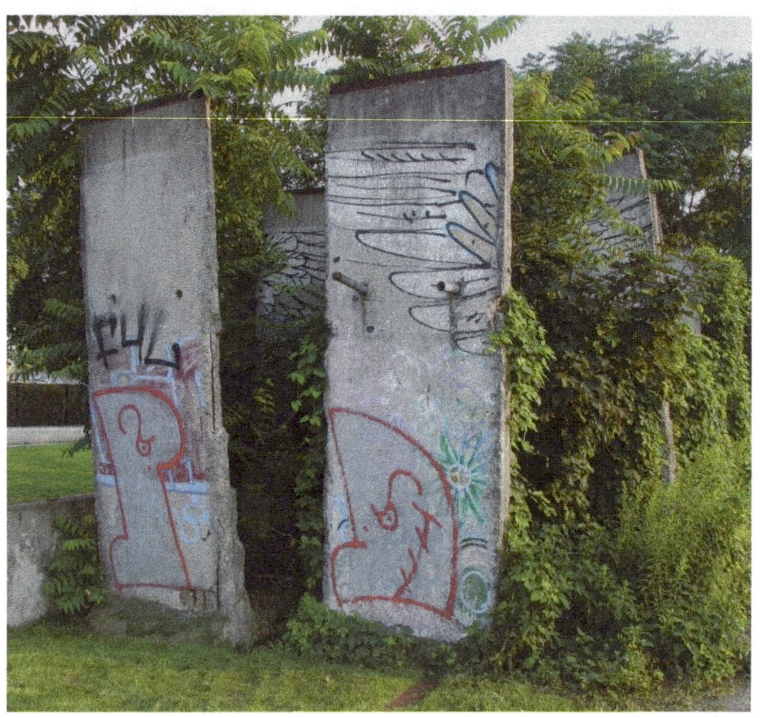

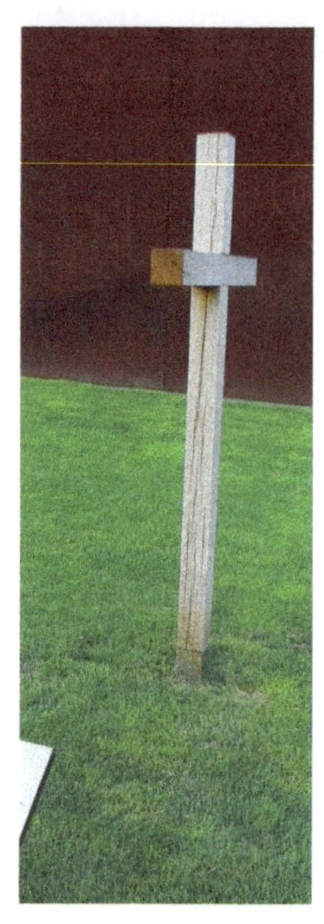

Opposite: This is what the Wall used to look like from most parts of West-Berlin.
Left: Original Wall slabs within the museum's outdoor exhibit.
Right: This cross is a memorial to the St. Sophie Cemetery. The Wall cut through one of the mass graves from World War II.
Below: The Church of the Reconciliation, destroyed in 1986 by the SED, was rebuilt as a chapel and is also part of the permanent exhibit. The lamb right next to it was saved from destruction.

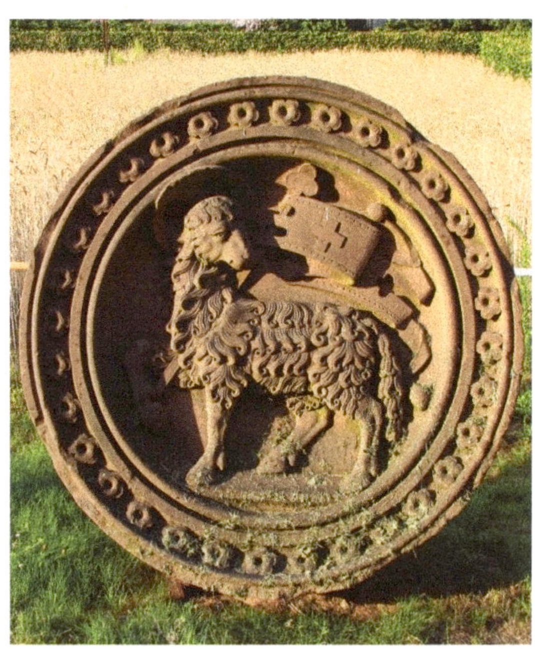

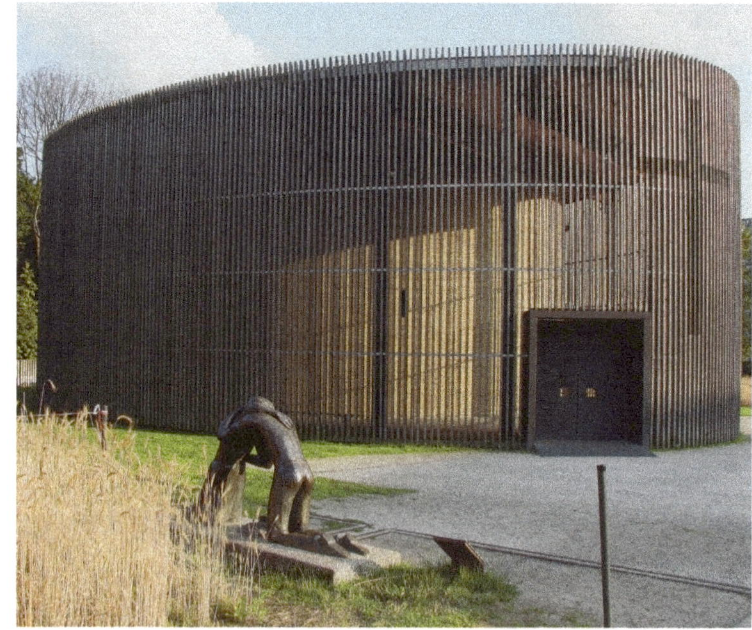

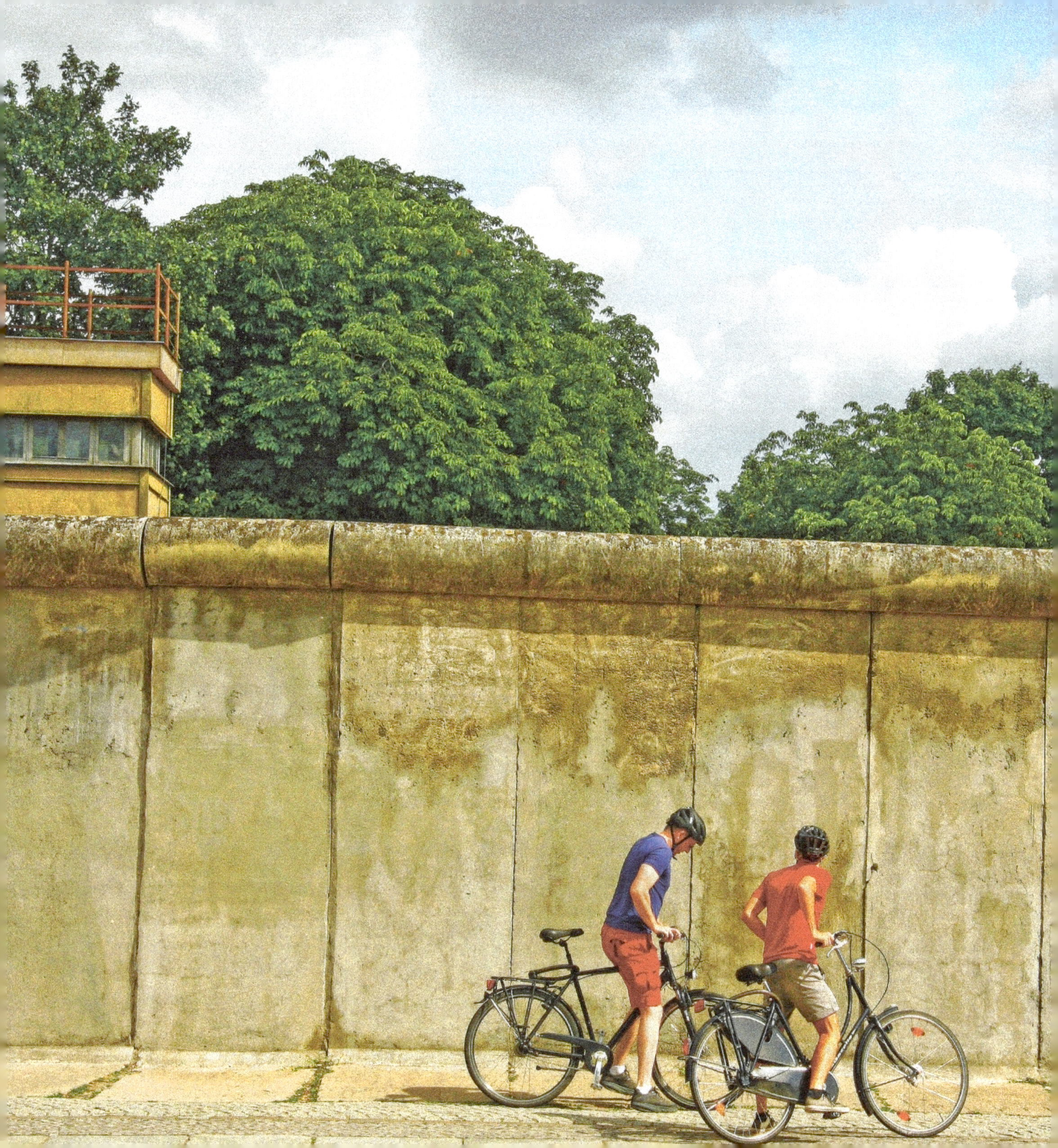

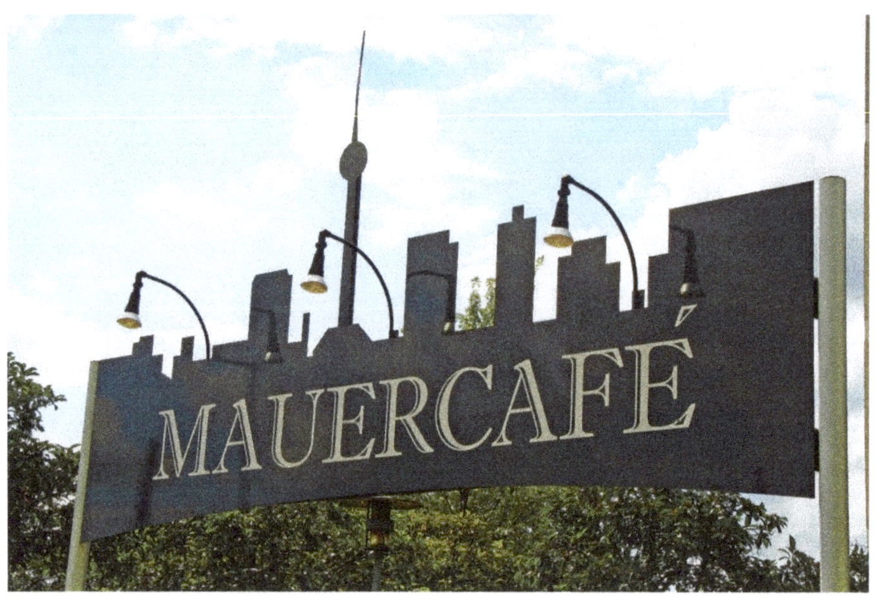

Above: The Wall Cafe serves refreshments to the many visitors of the memorial.
Below:: The "Window of Remembrance" for Germans killed at the Wall, featuring photographs of known Wall victims.

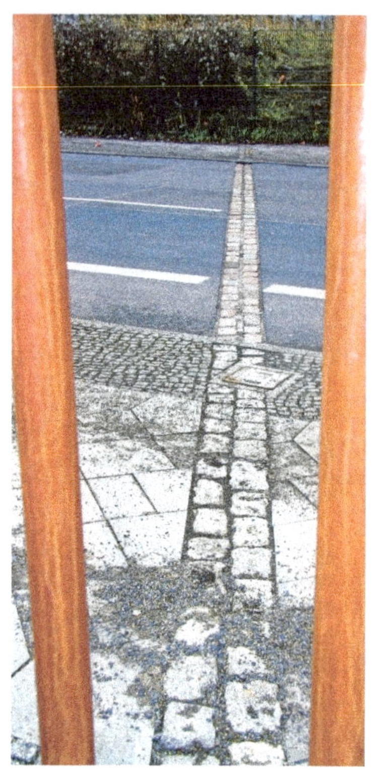

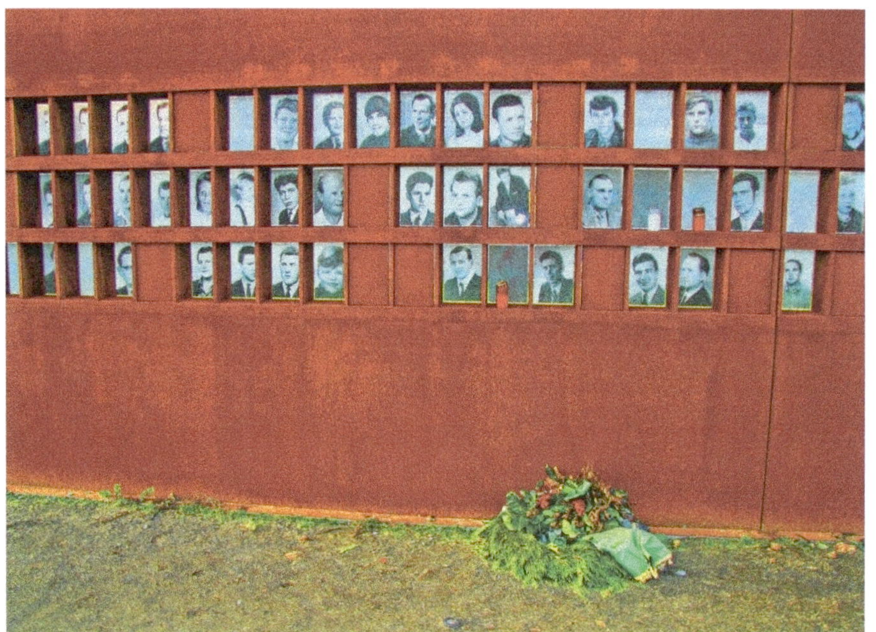

After the Wall fell, the City of Berlin commissioned a double-row of cobblestones (above) to document the path of the Wall, dotted occasionally with plaques reading *Berliner Mauer 1961–1989*. Pedestrians and bicyclists can follow the path through most of Berlin's inner city. At Bernauer Strasse, the path of the Wall is marked by rusted steel beams as high as the Wall had been. The beams are replaced by the row of cobblestones, starting at Gartenstrasse. Here is Nordbahnhof, Northern Rail Station..
Opposite: The Hinterland Wall at Bernauer Strasse at night.

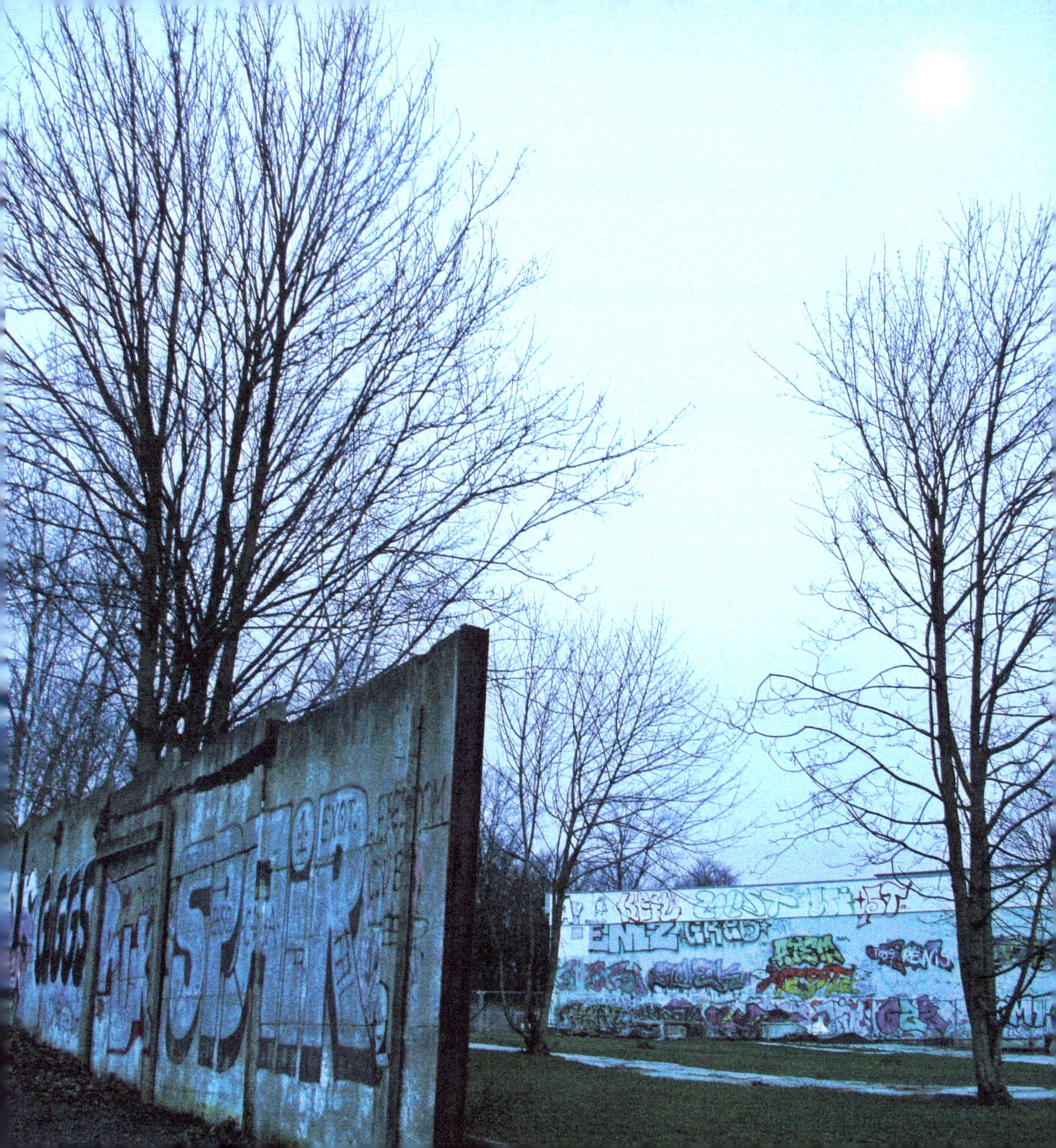

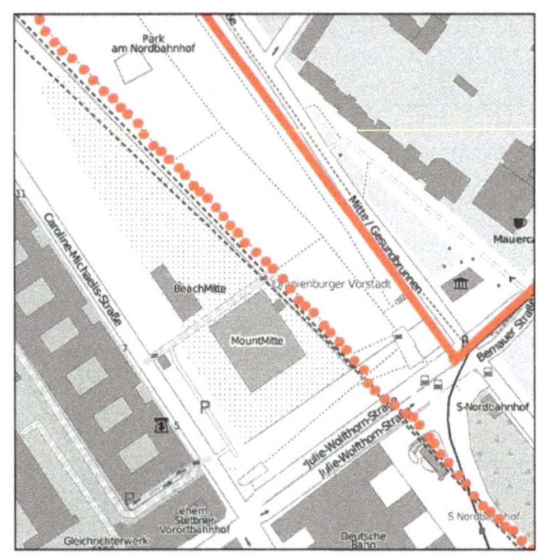

Nordbahnhof
Pflugstrasse

Northern Rail Station
Pflug Street

Nordbahnhof, the Northern Rail Station, used to be the destination of trains arriving in Berlin from Stettin and Danzig. The station, built in 1841 and enlarged in 1876, was originally named Stettiner Bahnhof, after a town on the Baltic Sea north of Berlin. It was heavily damaged during World War II. After the Wall was built, the station and the huge track area surrounding it lay in the no-man's-land between East and West-Berlin. In 1952, West Berliners were barred from entering the area. Soon after, the station was closed and the building torn down.

Today, only the S-Bahn Station is left, mostly underground except for a small, red-brick entrance building. The S-Bahn that runs from north to south and stops at Brandenburger Tor was constructed from 1936 to 1939. After the Wall, the S-Bahn ceased to stop at the underground stations, except Friedrichstrasse, which was a border crossing, but crawled past these "ghost stations" guarded by silent soldiers. Eventually, the S-Bahn in the West was shut down altogether.

Now, the tunnel has been refurbished and all stations reopened. An exhibit within the mezzanine commemorates the "ghost trains." The square in front of the station has been remodeled; engraved plaques bear the names of cities on the Baltic Sea to which trains used to travel from here.

Opposite: The track area has been turned into a park, including the Hinterland Wall. The S-Bahn sign is in the background.

Below: A brass sign on the stairs to the platform marks the Wall within the station.

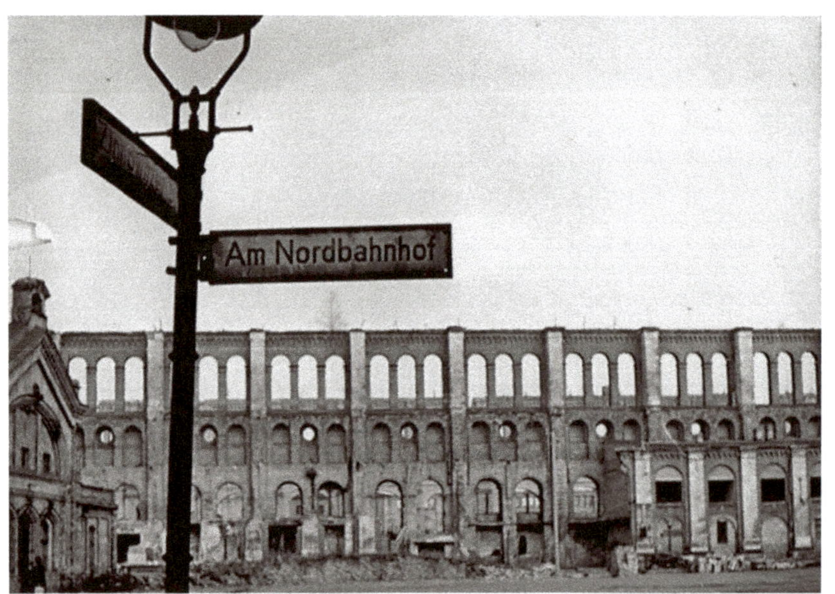

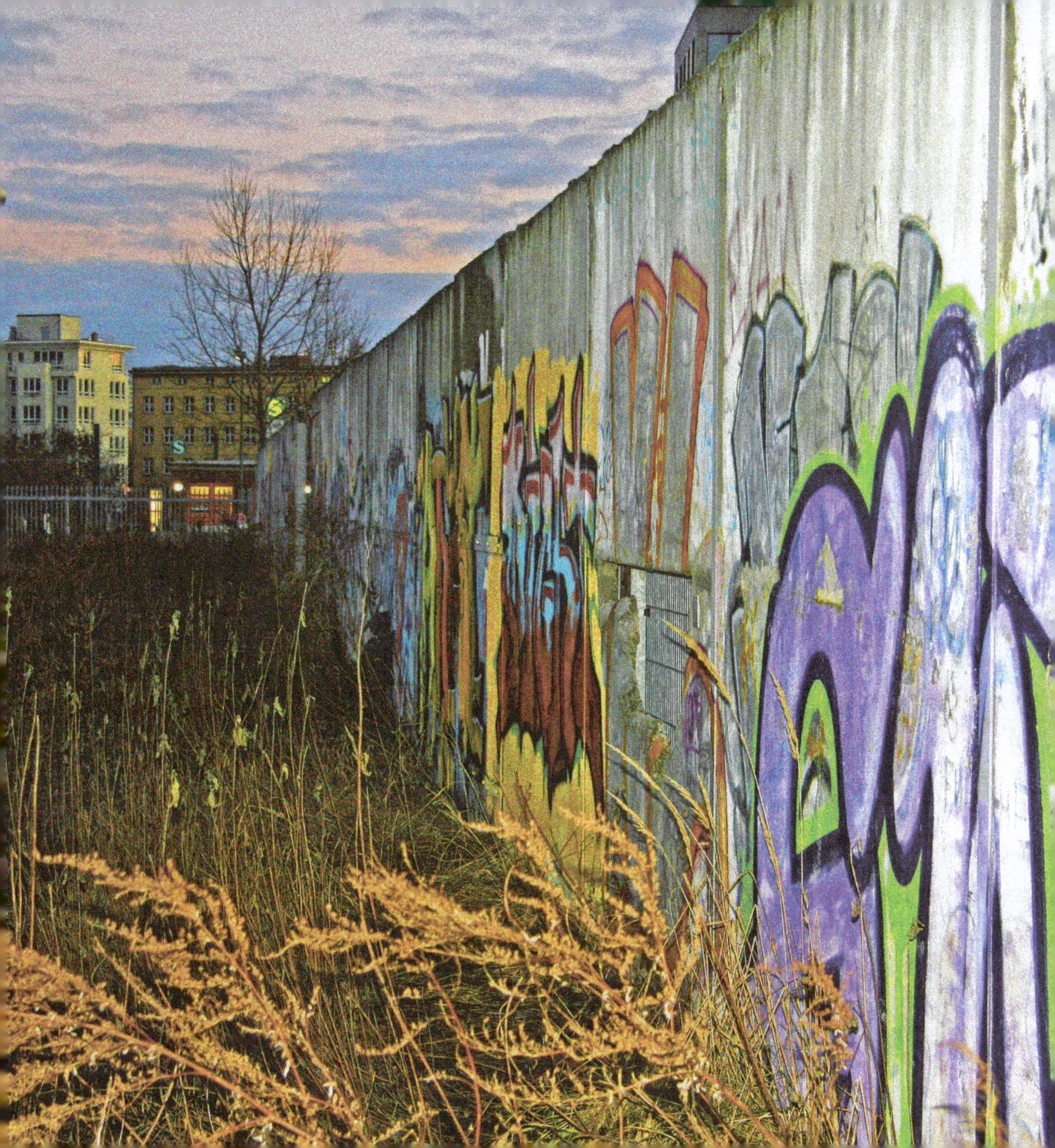

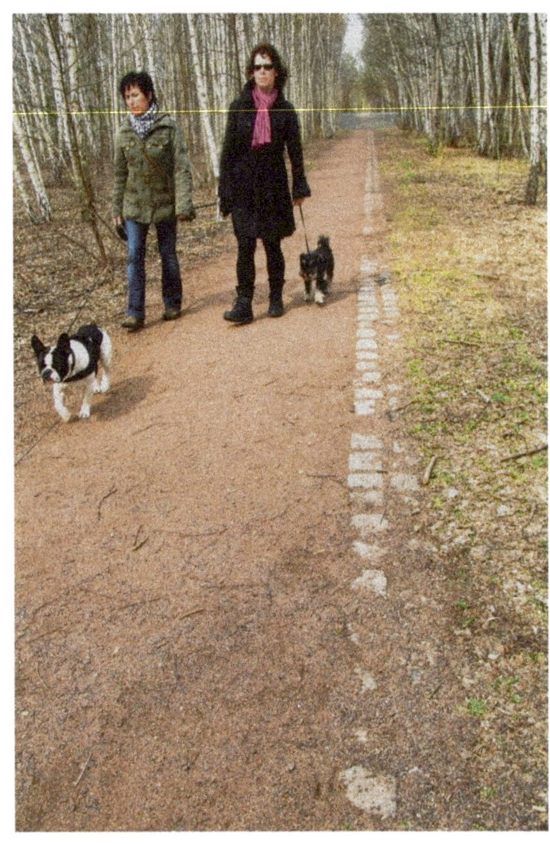

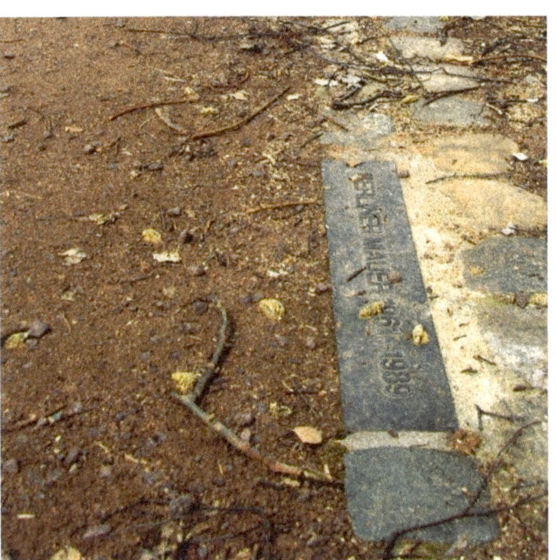

Opposite, above: This is "Mount Mitte," a recreational climbing facility six hundred feet high. It was put up in 2010, sponsored by the district of Mitte. It features some GDR-Trabants, a VW Beetle, and a beach chair.

Left: The row of cobblestones marks the former Wall in the park
Below: Nordbahnhof; the S-Bahnhof. The green sign can be seen from afar. Plaques among the cobble stones document where people fled.

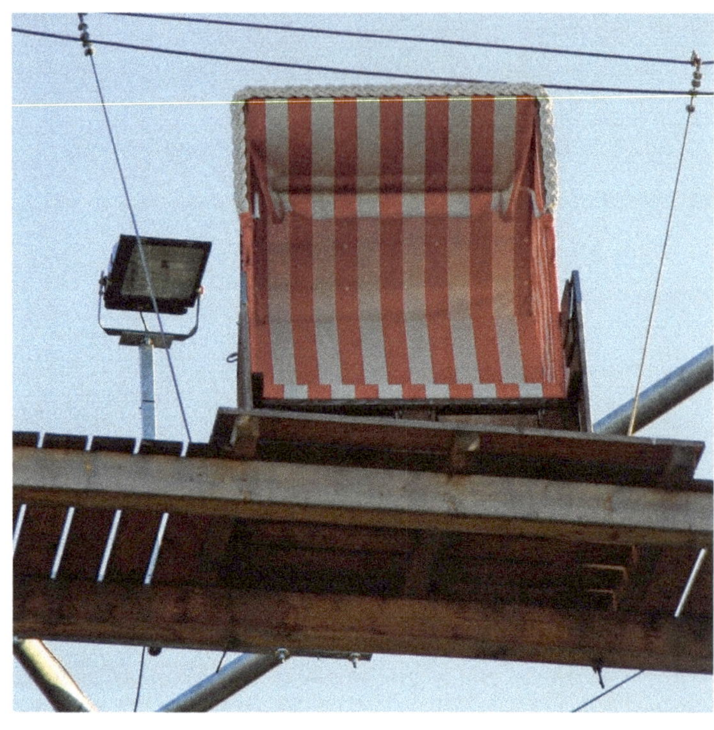

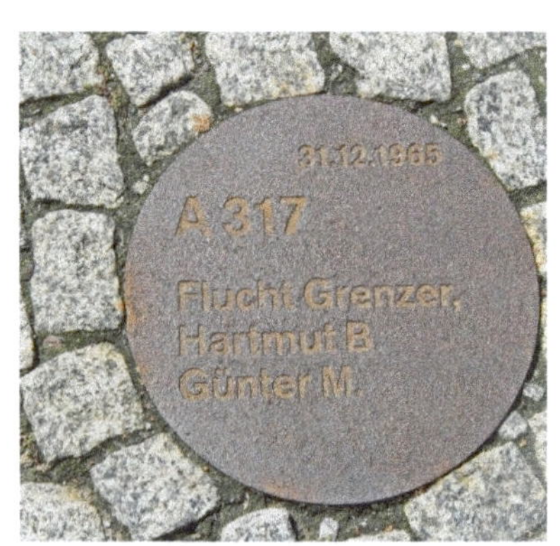

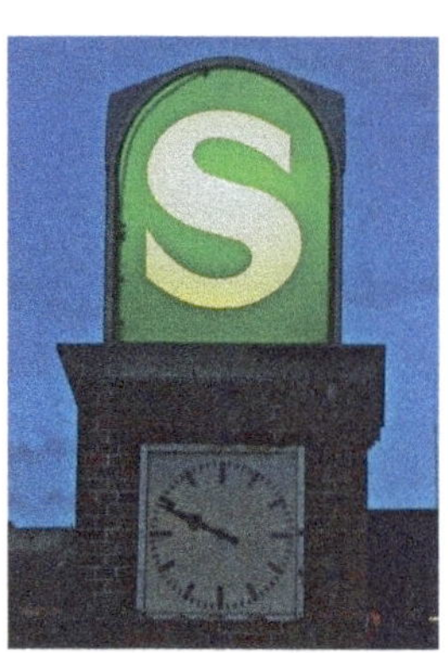

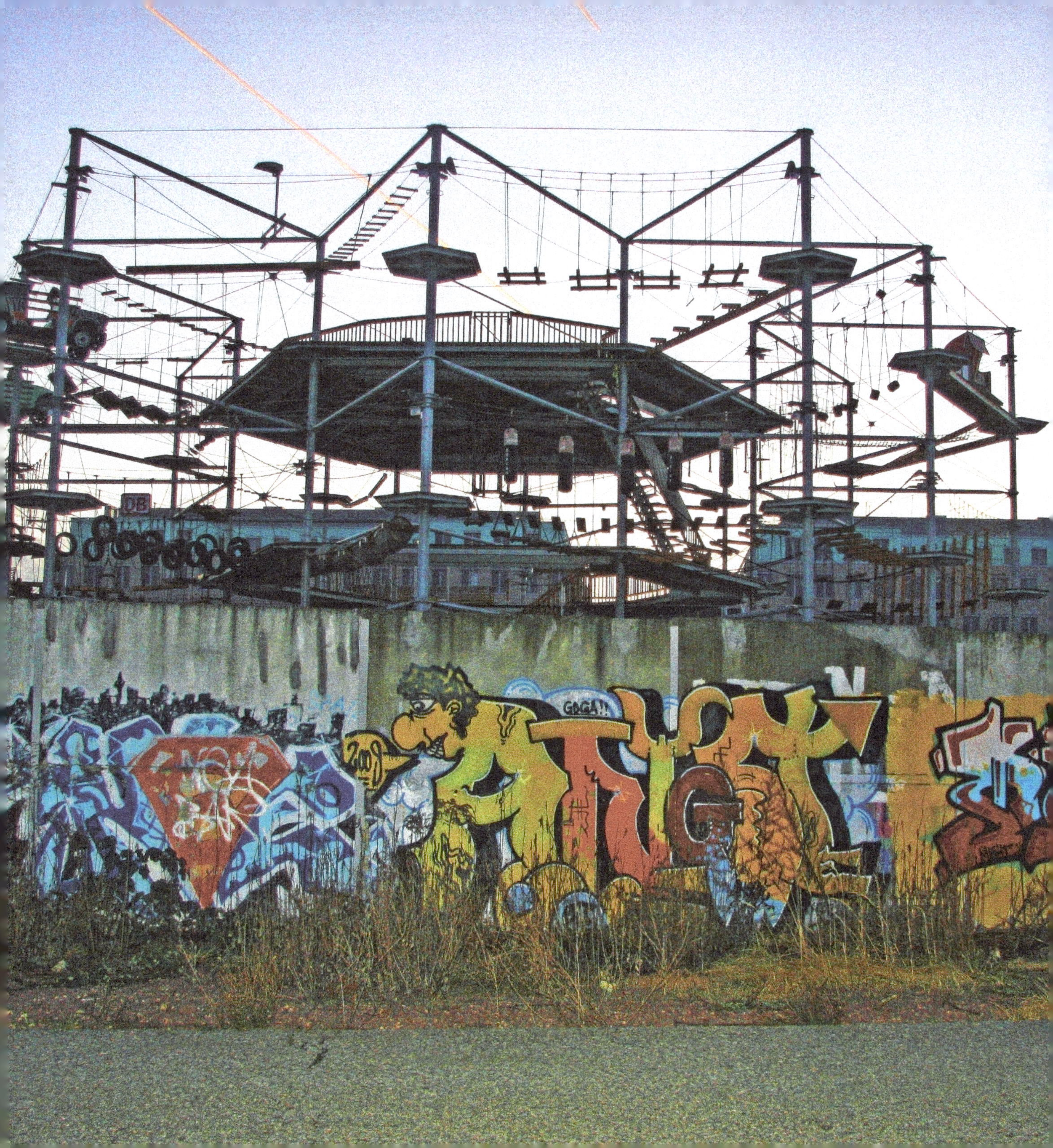

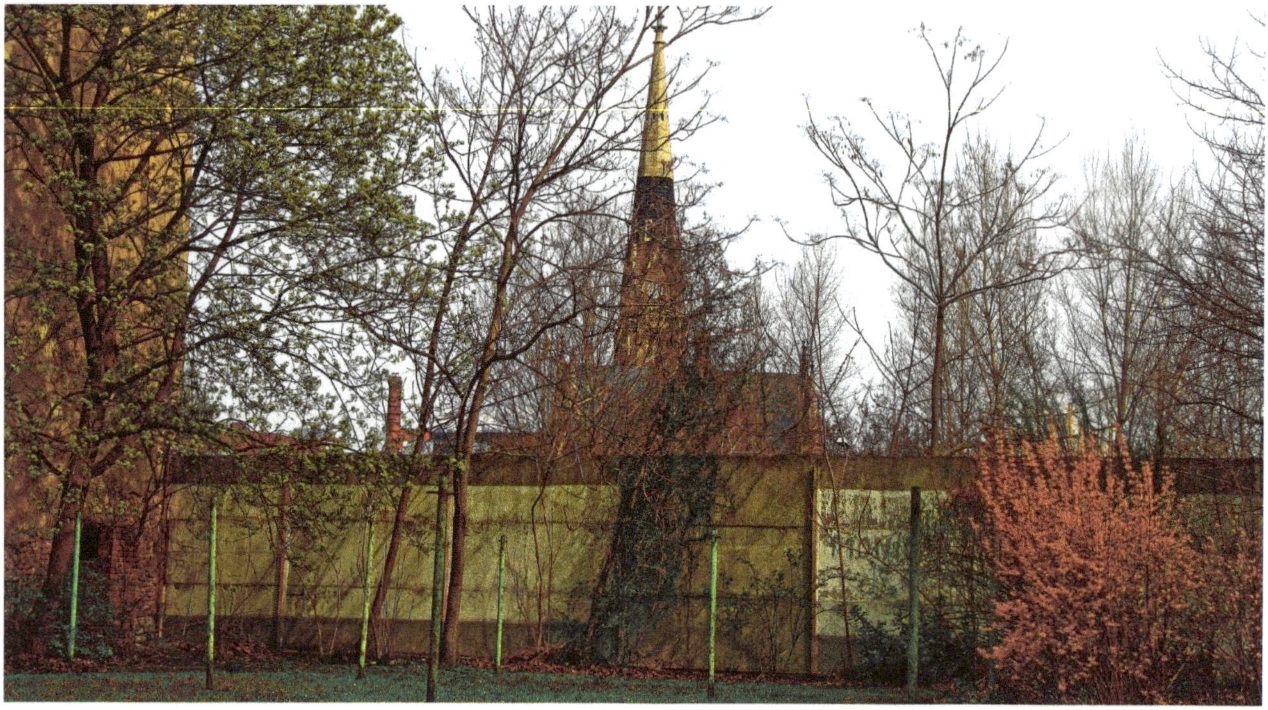

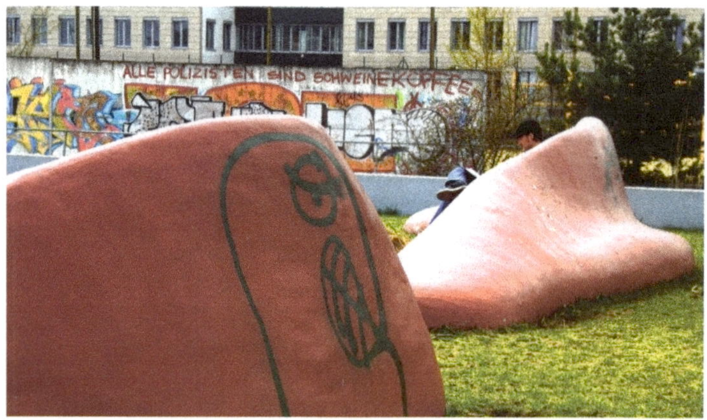

Above: The view from a row of apartment buildings in Pflugstrasse, Mitte. The lot was sealed off by the Hinterland Wall for decades. This part has been left intact, since it shields the buildings from the S-Bahn tracks. The Church of St. Sebastian stands in the background. Below left is the Wall from the Nordbahnhof park side where playgrounds, and sitting areas were built.

Opposite: Before the Wall was built, the track area of Nordbahnhof used to be accessible from the street level by a number of staircases. The GDR sealed off all of those staircases with brick walls to prevent people from even getting close to the Hinterland Wall. Today, these stairs have been opened again, except this one which was preserved as an "archaeological window" for visitors interested in Berlin's history. Though this "window" is guarded by a wire fence, graffiti artists still manage to sneak in.

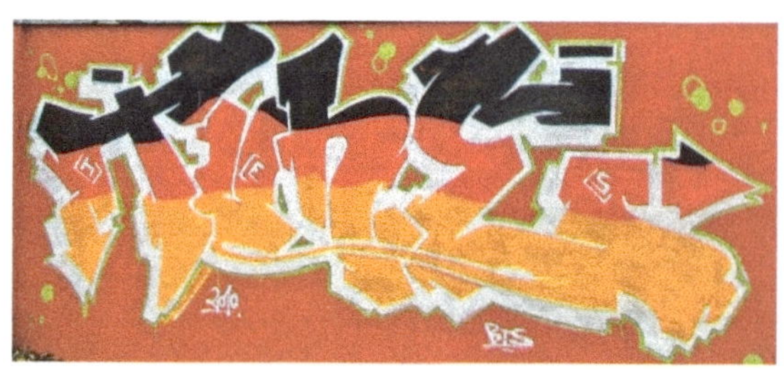

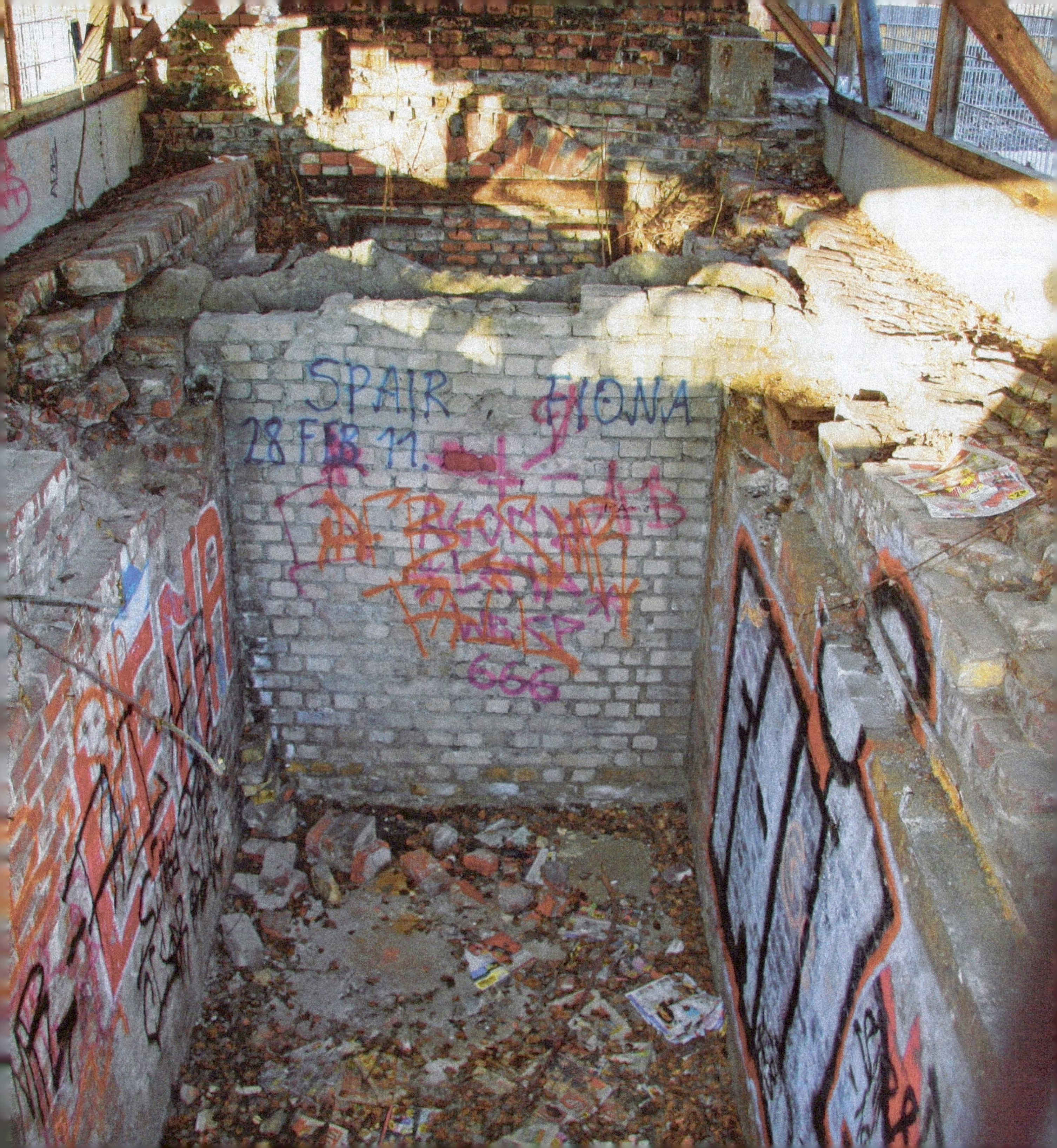

SPAIR   FIONA
28 FEB 11.
666

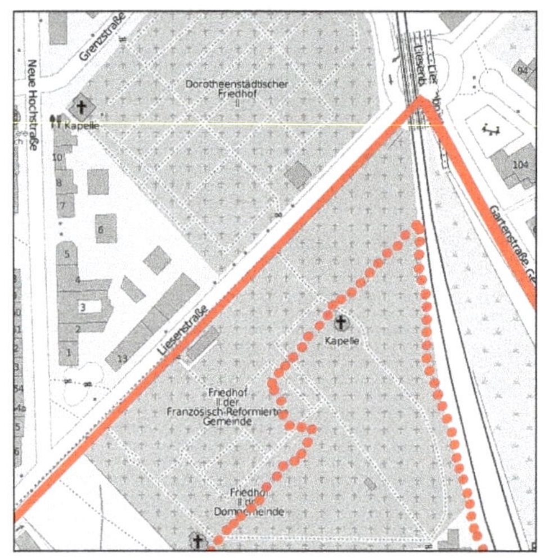

St.-Hedwigs-friedhof
Chausseestrasse

St. hedwig's Cemetery
CHaussee Street

The Wall ran right through the historic French, St. Hedwig's, and Cathedral cemeteries. The GDR closed the cemeteries and destroyed many graves after World War II had also taken its toll. The graveyard from 1834 is the oldest Catholic burial site in Berlin, with quite a few local celebrities laid to rest here, including Daniel Liszt, the son of composer Franz Liszt, Marianne Schadow, the widow of sculptor Johann Gottfried Schadow and Bernhard Lichtenberg, a priest who fought against the Nazis. One thousand and five hundred victims of a 19th-century cholera epidemic were buried in a mass grave here.

Opposite: About a hundred feet of the Wall are still intact at Liesenstrasse, bordering the cemetery, fairly high above street level. The S-Bahn runs between Nordbahnhof and the cemeteries, crossing Schwindsuchtbrücke and passing Humboldthain, a city park. During World War II, two anti aircraft towers stood here, one of which was demolished shortly after 1945. The other one is now a museum open to the public, run by the nonprofit *Berliner Unterwelten*.

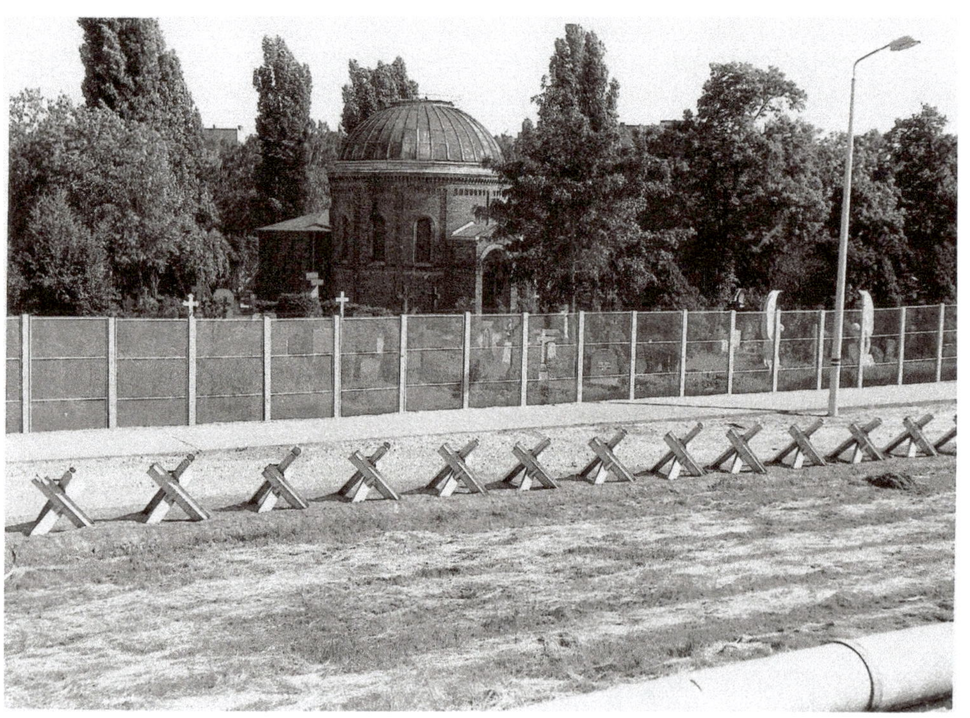

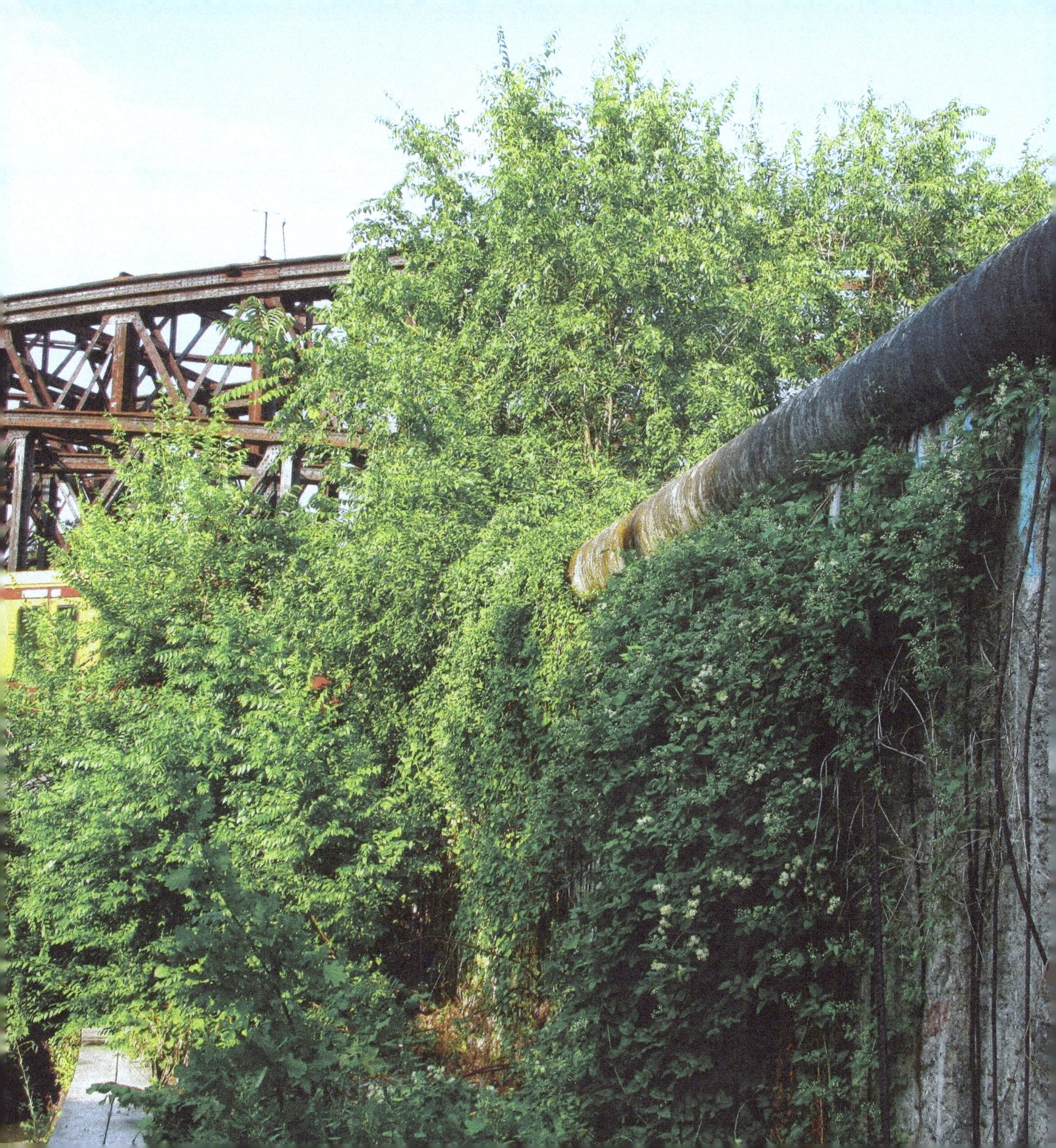

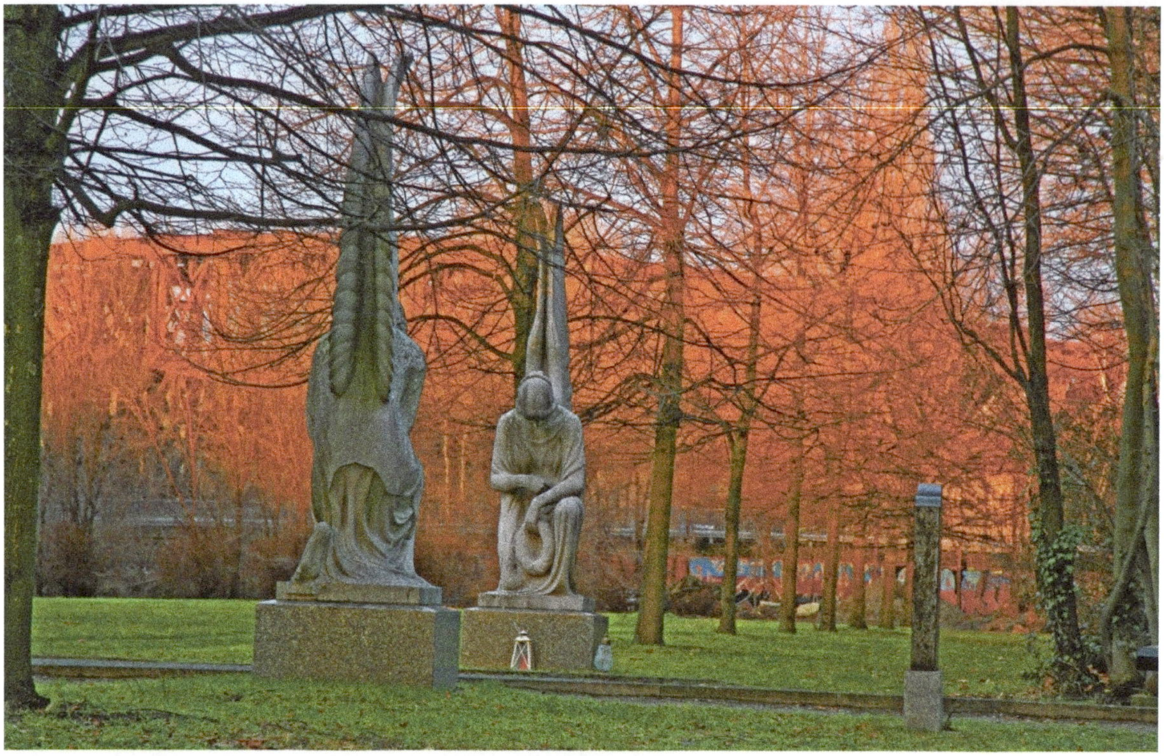

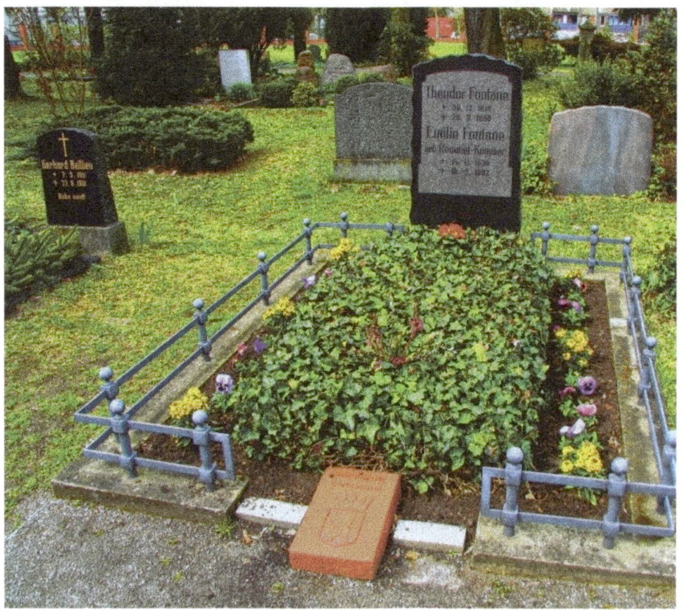

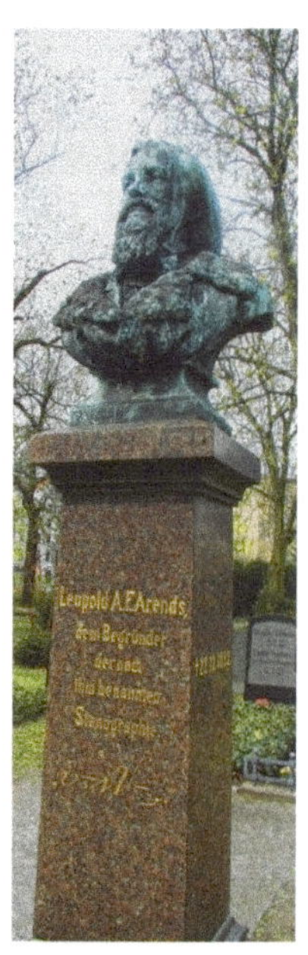

Above: The marble angels are back in their original places, here at sundown. In the background: the S-Bahn, Schwindsuchtbrücke, and the last remnant of the Wall.

Left: Theodor Fontane, the great Berlin journalist, novelist, and poet, who was a descendant of a Huguenot family, was buried in the French Cemetery with his wife, Emilie. His grave was destroyed in World War II. The tombstone has been restored, but their bones are lost. Leopold Arends, the inventor of stenography, is also laid to rest.

Opposite: A part of the Hinterland Wall that ran through the French and St. Hedwig's cemeteries has been preserved as a landmark.

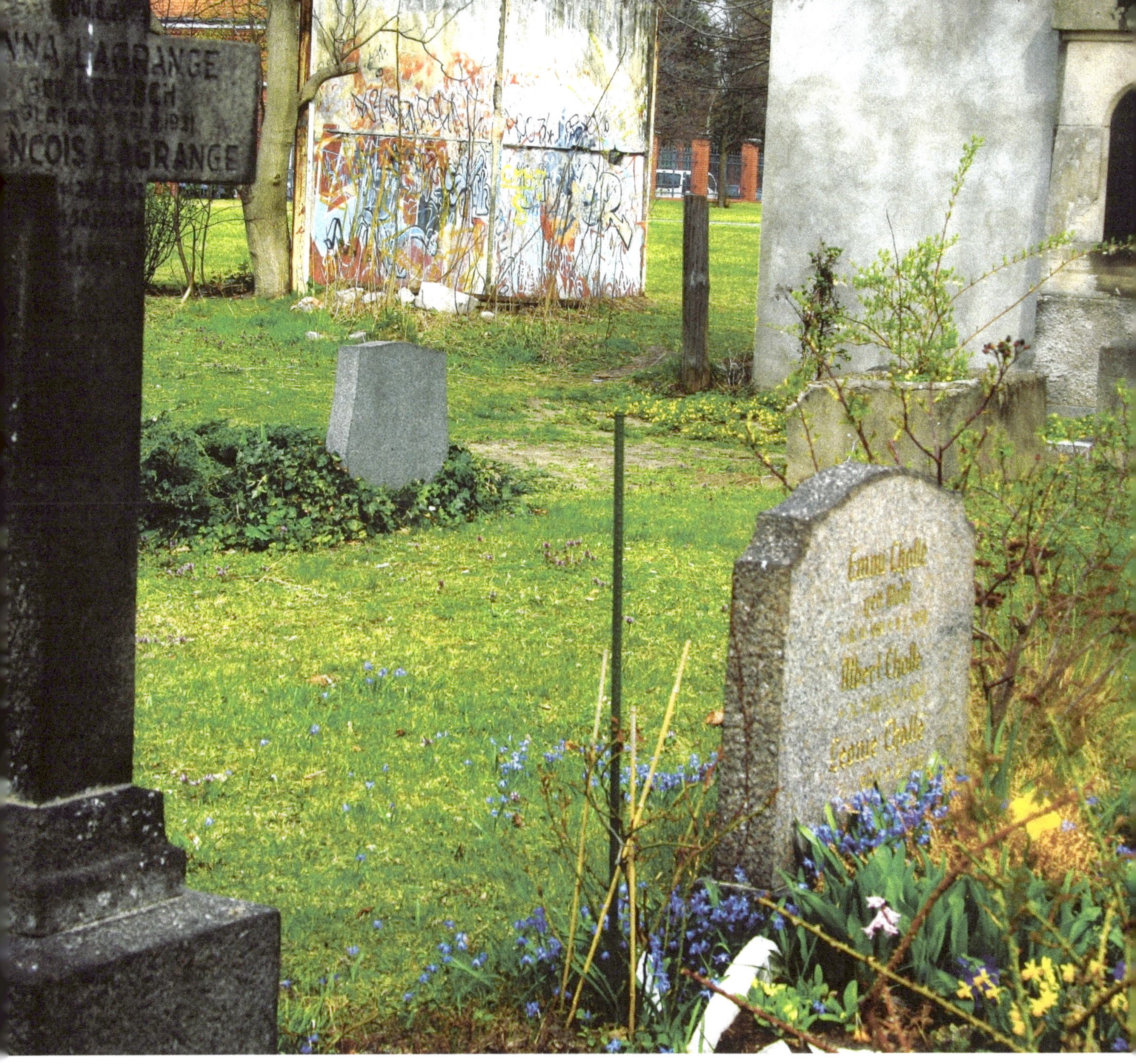

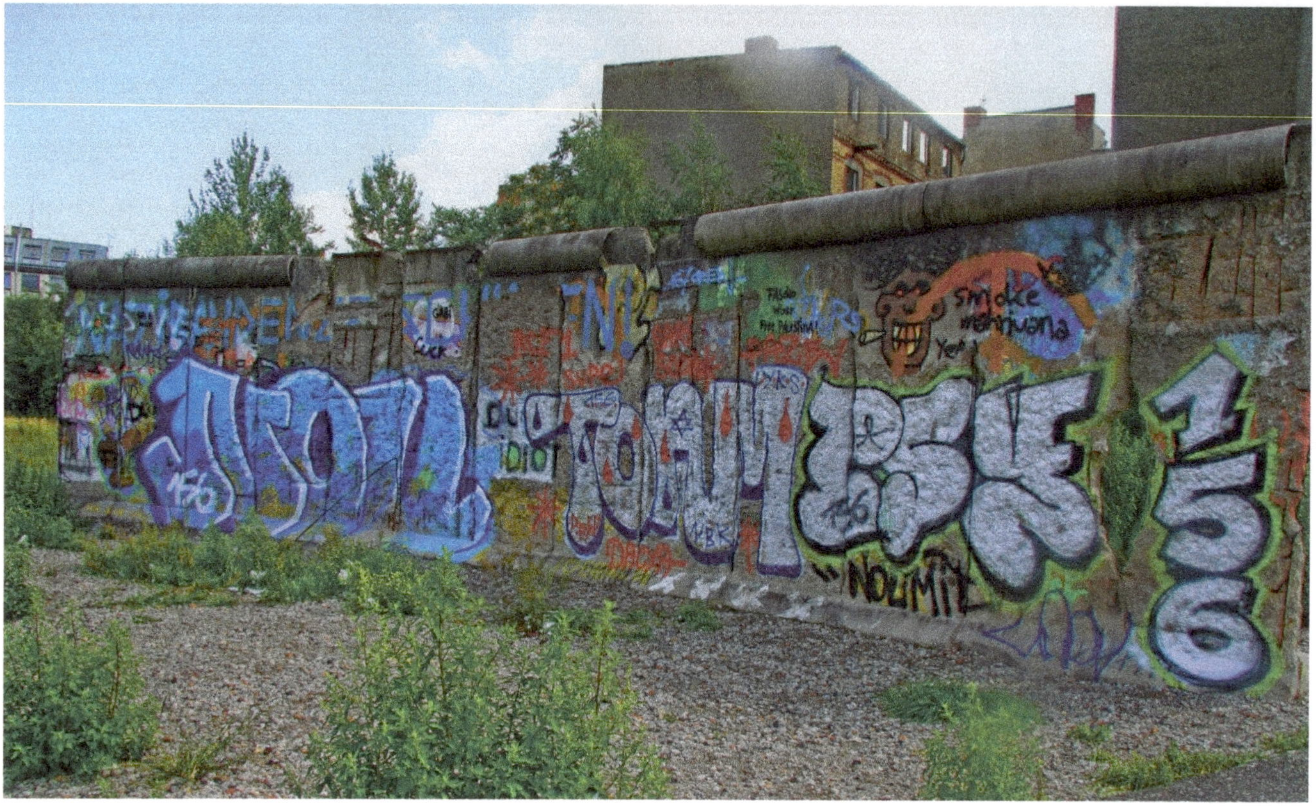

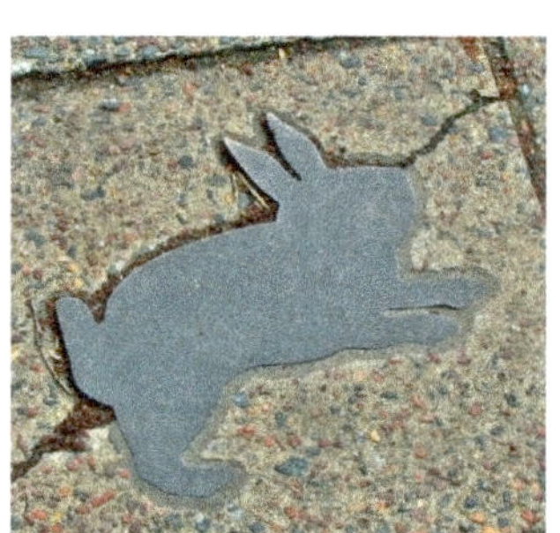

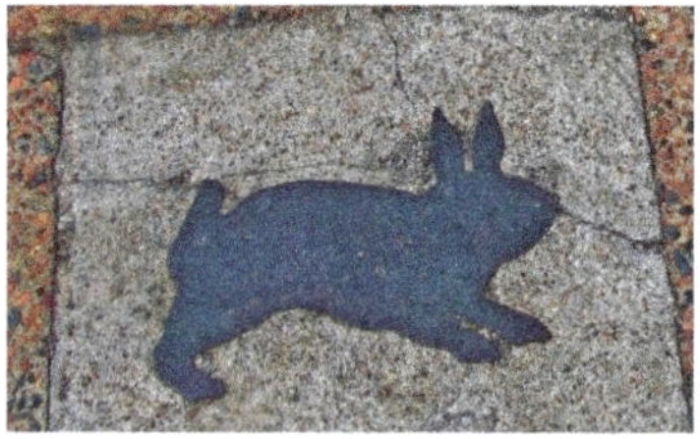

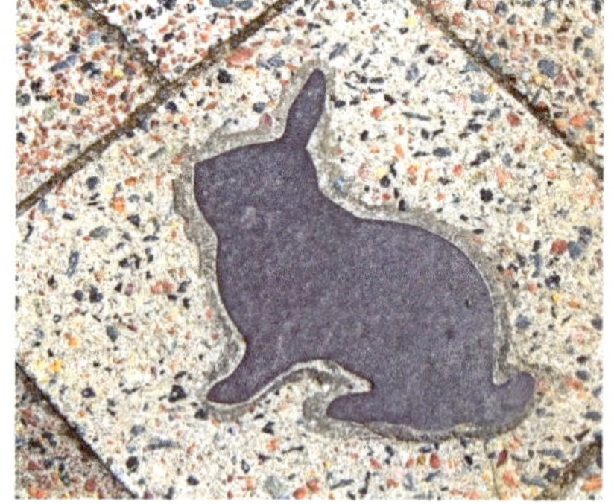

Left, Below: The rabbits on the sidewalk along Chausseestrasse are part of an art installation by Karla Sachse. 120 copper rabbits symbolize the only animals that lived in the "death strip".

Above and Opposite: If you thought that the Wall was vanishing, think again. The Wall was resurrected right here at Chausseestrasse—as a movie set of *Russendisco*, filmed here in 2011. The film is based on the bestselling book by Wladimir Kaminer. It is a short story collection about the adventures of the Russian-born author and his friends Mischa and Andrej in Berlin. The film, released in February 2012, features Matthias Schweighöfer as Kaminer. The Wall slabs are authentic, but they were placed here by the studio and left them right here at Chausseestrasse after the film's completion, for whatever reason. In the film, they were digitally extended, using a blue screen.

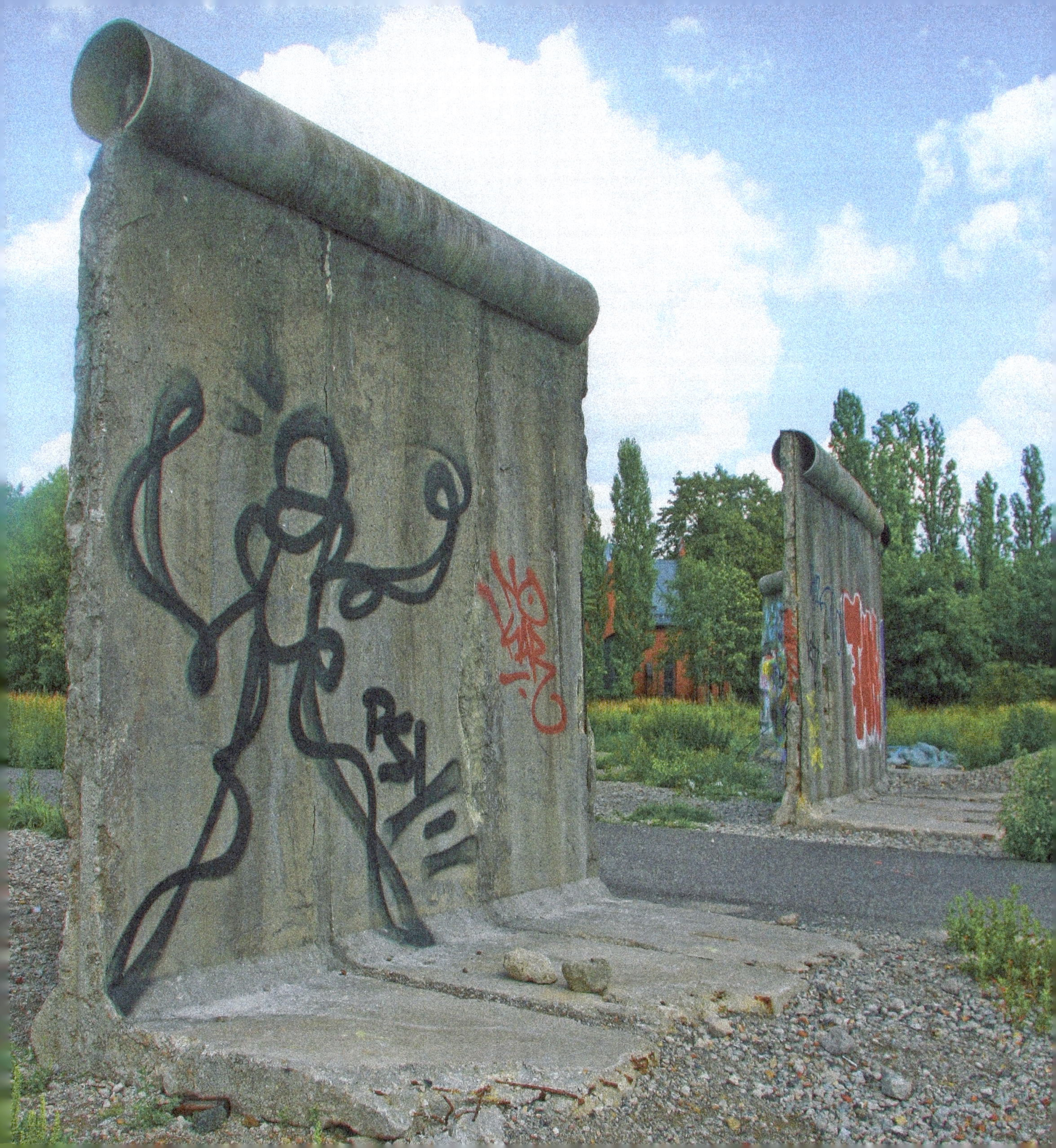

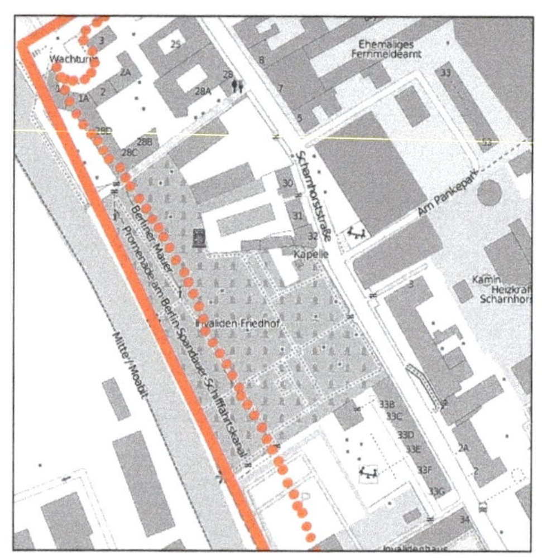

WACHTURM / INVALIDEN-FRIEDHOF / HAUPTBAHNHOF

GUARD TOWER / VETERANS' CEMETERY / CENTRAL STATION

Günter Litfin was the first refuge killed by gunfire at the Wall after it was built. On August 24, 1961, the twenty-four-year-old Litfin tried to flee by jumping into the Berlin-Spandau Schifffahrtskanal (Freight Canal), and was shot immediately by GDR border guards. His body was recovered later that day (below). A plaque on the guard tower (opposite page) commemorates his death.

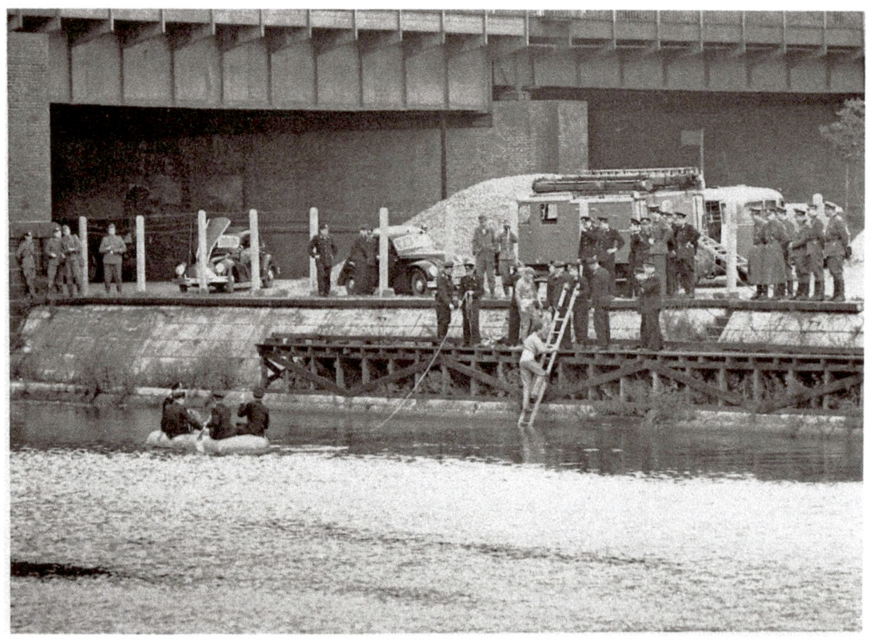

The former guard tower at Kieler Strasse, near the canal, has been preserved as a landmark. Today it is situated in the backyard of newly built apartment buildings. The flag of the GDR was left on the top floor. The tower, which is owned by Litfin's brother, is a museum, it can be visited by appointment.

The Wall ran from near Nordhafen (North Haven), along the Berlin-Spandau Schifffahrtskanal, a canal for freight ships, and continued southward to Humboldthafen, a city harbor—today the location of the new Central Station. The Wall passed the old Hamburg train station, now a contemporary art museum, the Museum of Natural History, and Sandkrug Brücke (Sandkrug Bridge). In May 1963, twelve young people tried to escape here. They attempted to drive a van through the checkpoint at high speed but were stopped by border guards, who shot and wounded them.

Today, bikers and pedestrians can walk or ride along the canal on the Wall Trail. Apart from some memorial plaques and pillars, however, not much is left.

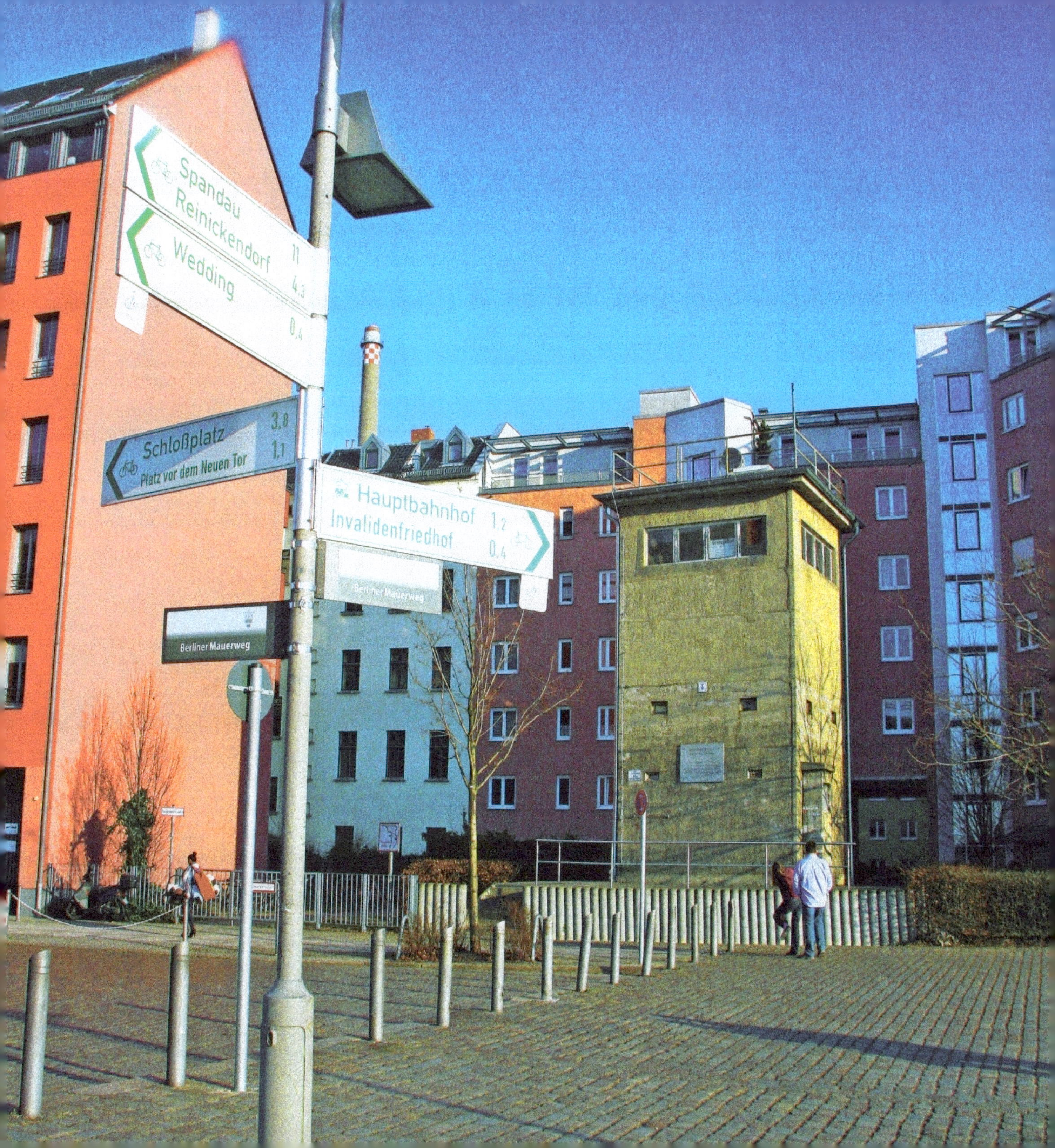
Spandau
Reinickendorf 11
Wedding 4,3
0,4
Schloßplatz 3,8
Platz vor dem Neuen Tor 1,1
Hauptbahnhof 1,2
Invalidenfriedhof 0,4
Berliner Mauerweg
Berliner Mauerweg

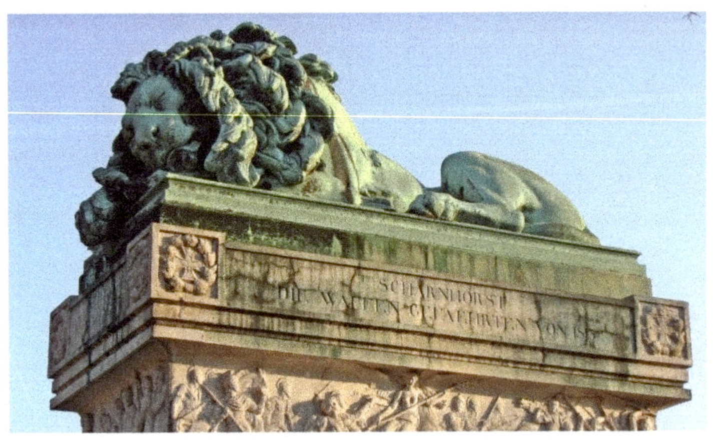

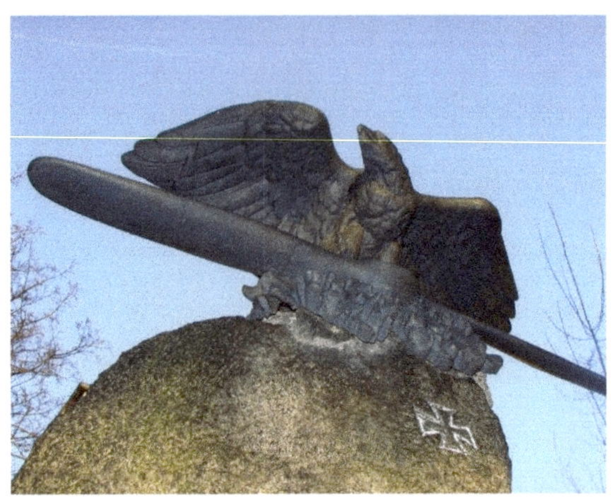

South of Kieler Strasse, the Wall cut right through Invalidenfriedhof, a veterans' cemetery from 1748, one of the oldest cemeteries in Berlin. Many Prussian soldiers who fought in the Wars of Liberation against Napoleon were laid to rest here, most notably Gerhard Gen-

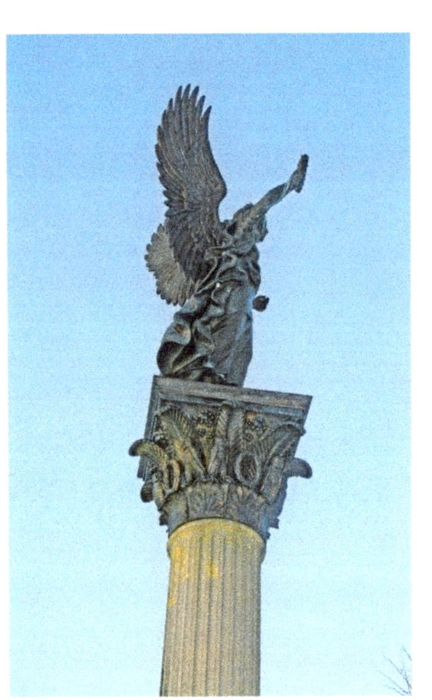

eral von Scharnhost (above left) and Friedrich Graf Tauentziehn von Wittenberg. World War I fighter pilots were buried here as well—which is why the grave pictured above right is adorned with a propeller. Among the last to be laid to rest here were Manfred von Richthofen, known as the Red Baron, and Marga Wolff, one of the first women to fly long-haul in 1930. She killed herself at the age of twenty-five, after her plane was damaged when she landed in Syria. Both graves are gone today.

The Nazis first wanted to close the cemetery but then decided to use it—Reinhard Heydrich, the leader of the SS, was buried here after he was killed by Czech insurgents. Members of the anti-Nazi resistance of July 20th were also laid to rest at Invalidenfriedhof. During the final days of World War II, fighting took place in the cemetery. At least thirty-one civilians were buried in a mass grave; they and other war dead are memorialized by a plaque (right).

After 1945, the Allies confiscated the cemetery with the intent to level it, considering its German military heritage. This didn't happen after all, but when the Wall was built, many of the 250 gravestones that remained were destroyed or removed by the GDR. After reunification, only some of them could be restored. Today, a stretch of the Hinterland Wall in the middle of the cemetery is preserved as a memorial.

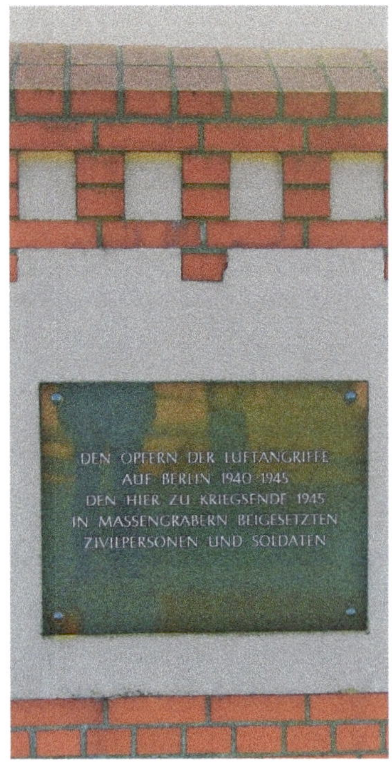

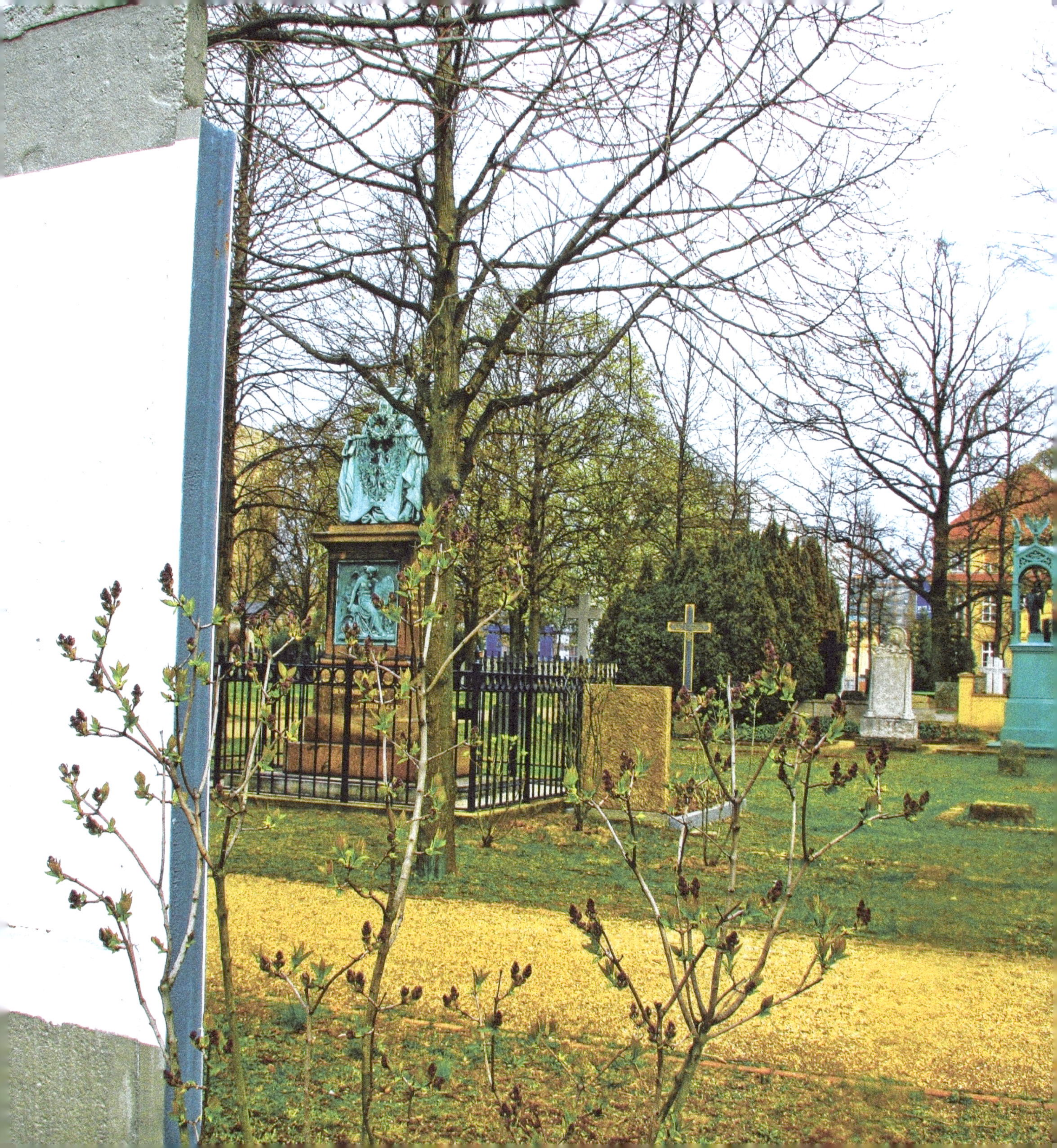

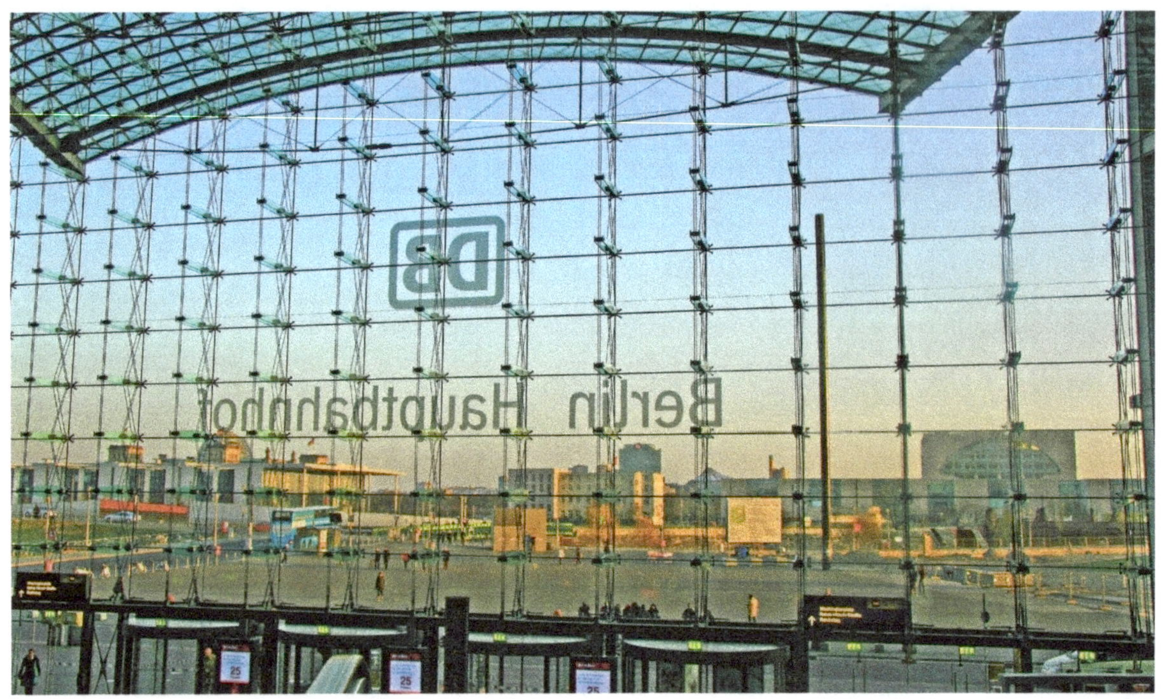

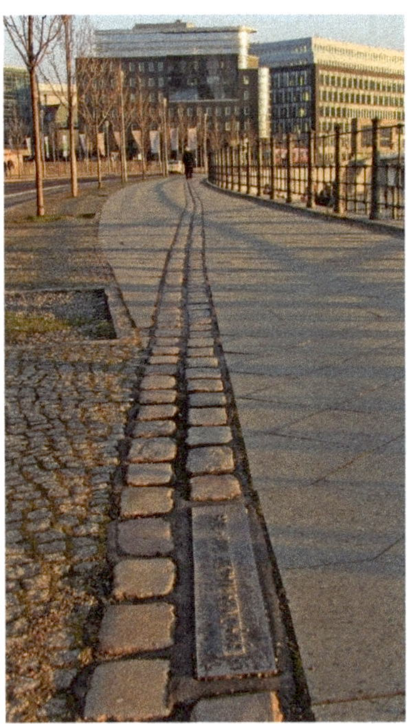

The Wall Trail runs close by the new Central Station that has replaced most of the old train stations destroyed during World War II. The huge glass hall, designed by architects Gerkan & Marg, covers the tracks from east to west, as well as stores and cafés. Below are underground tracks for trains running from north to south.

Now, high-speed trains from Paris and Warsaw stop at a platform overlooking Potsdamer Platz, the new chancellery, and the restored Reichstag. A new subway line connects the station with the Reichstag and the Brandenburg Gate. All that's left of the Wall near the Central Station is the cobblestone path with the plaque *"Berliner Mauer 1961-1989"* (opposite). **Right**: An ICE, the German high-speed train, on its way to Amsterdam.

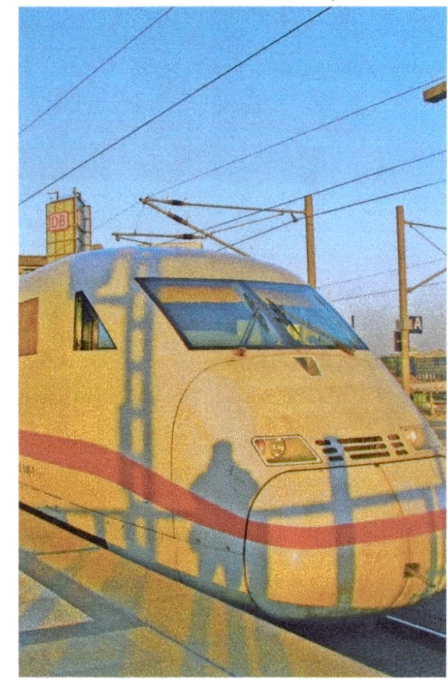

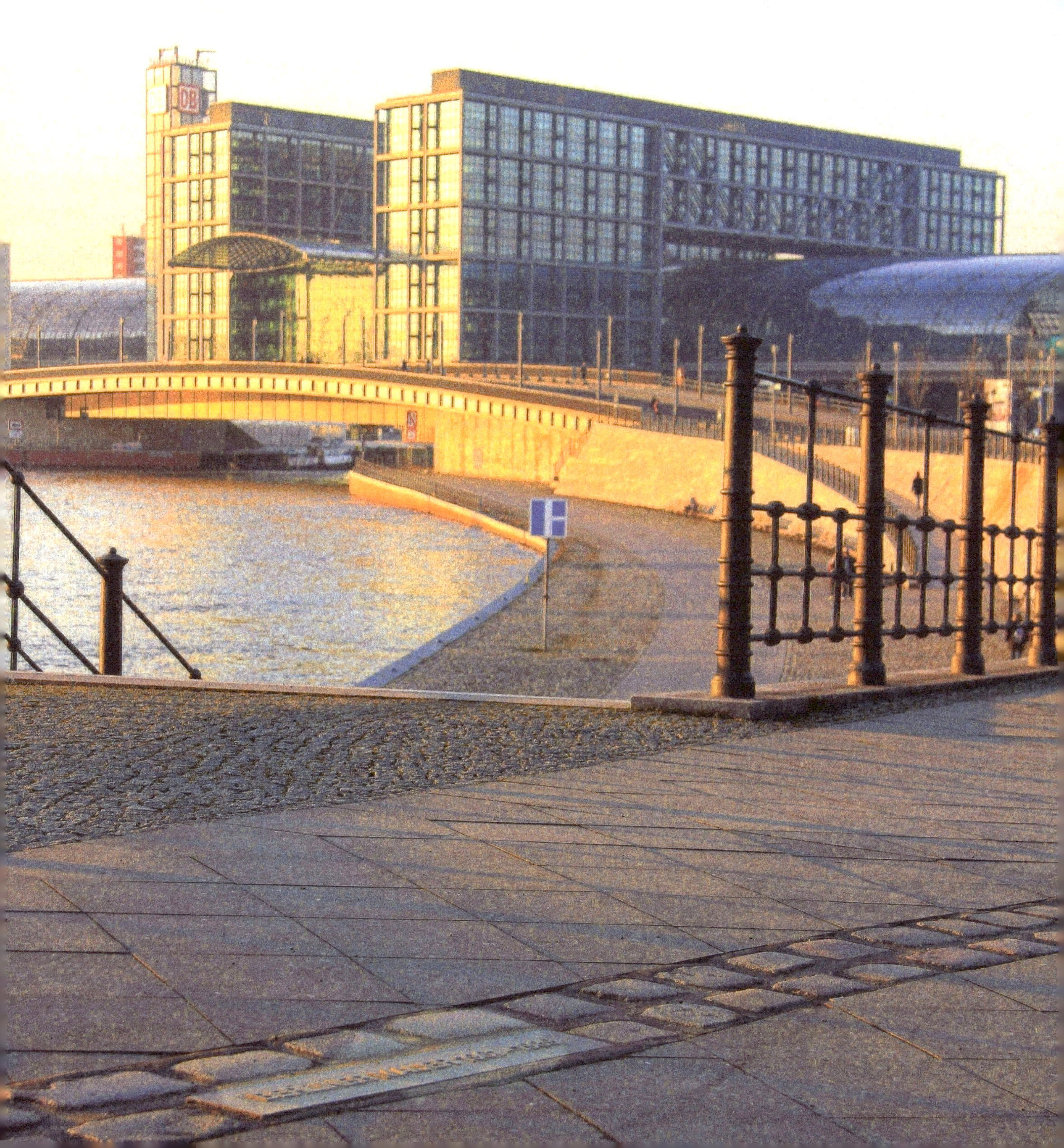

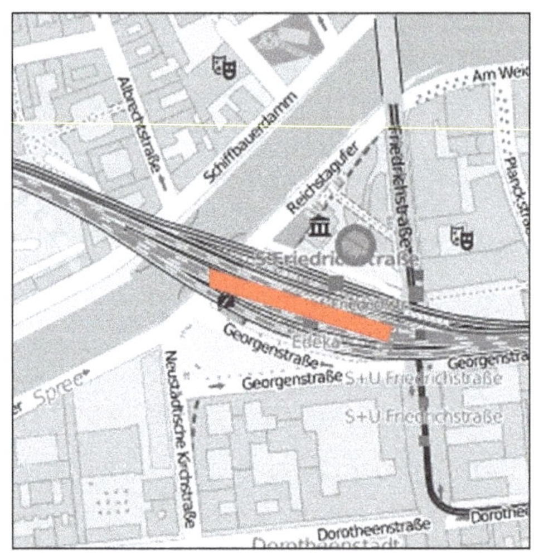

FRIEDRICHSTRASSE/ TRÄNENPALAST

FRIEDRICH STREET / PALACE OF TEARS

Friedrichstrasse was a Cold War border crossing in the middle of East Berlin, a train station where the S-Bahn and the U-Bahn from West Berlin stopped underground. Passengers from West Berlin, West Germany, and foreign countries would disembark and pass through control booths before entering the Eastern part of the city. The platforms above ground were divided by a metal wall, so passengers from the East could not access the track to the West. There was also a secret "agent door," where terrorists from the West German RAF vanished into the East in 1976, with the help of the almighty Stasi.

The building that formed the entrance to the train station—which was built in 1882 as part of the East--West S-Bahn —was called Tränenpalast, Palace of Tears. Here, East Berliners said goodbye to their relatives and loved ones who had to return to the West by midnight.

Opposite: Today, the Palace of Tears is a (free) museum devoted to the former border crossing. It is run by the Haus der Geschichte, the German equivalent of the Smithsonian. It features passport booths, border signs, and suitcases of East Berliners who managed to escape before 1989, video footage from East German times, pieces of the Wall, and a depiction of an "Intershop," a store that used to be located on the underground U-Bahn and S-Bahn platform. Intershops sold duty-free liquor and cigarettes for western currency, a major source of income for the GDR regime.

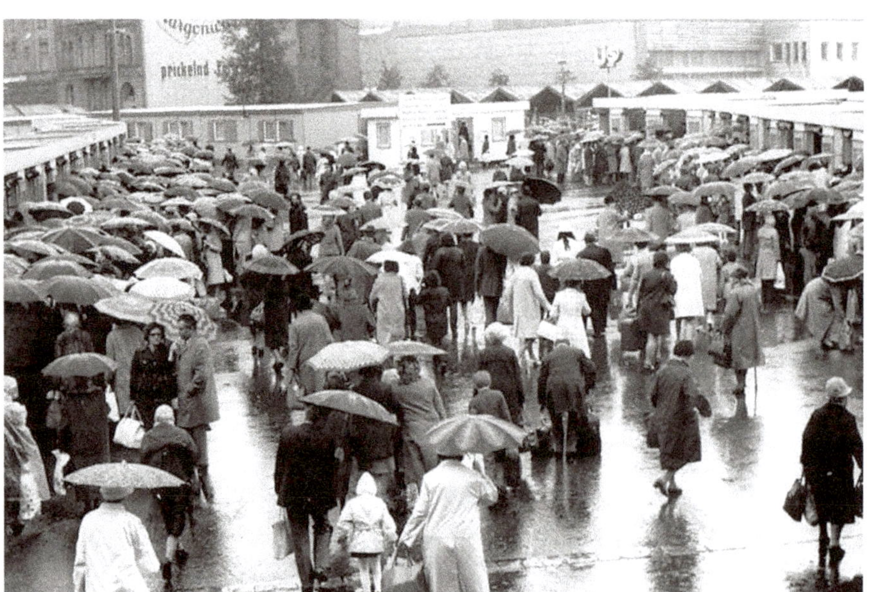

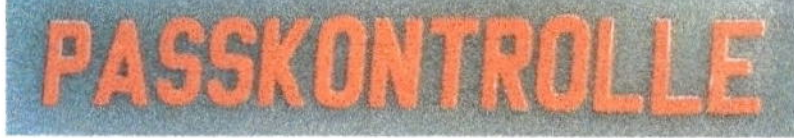

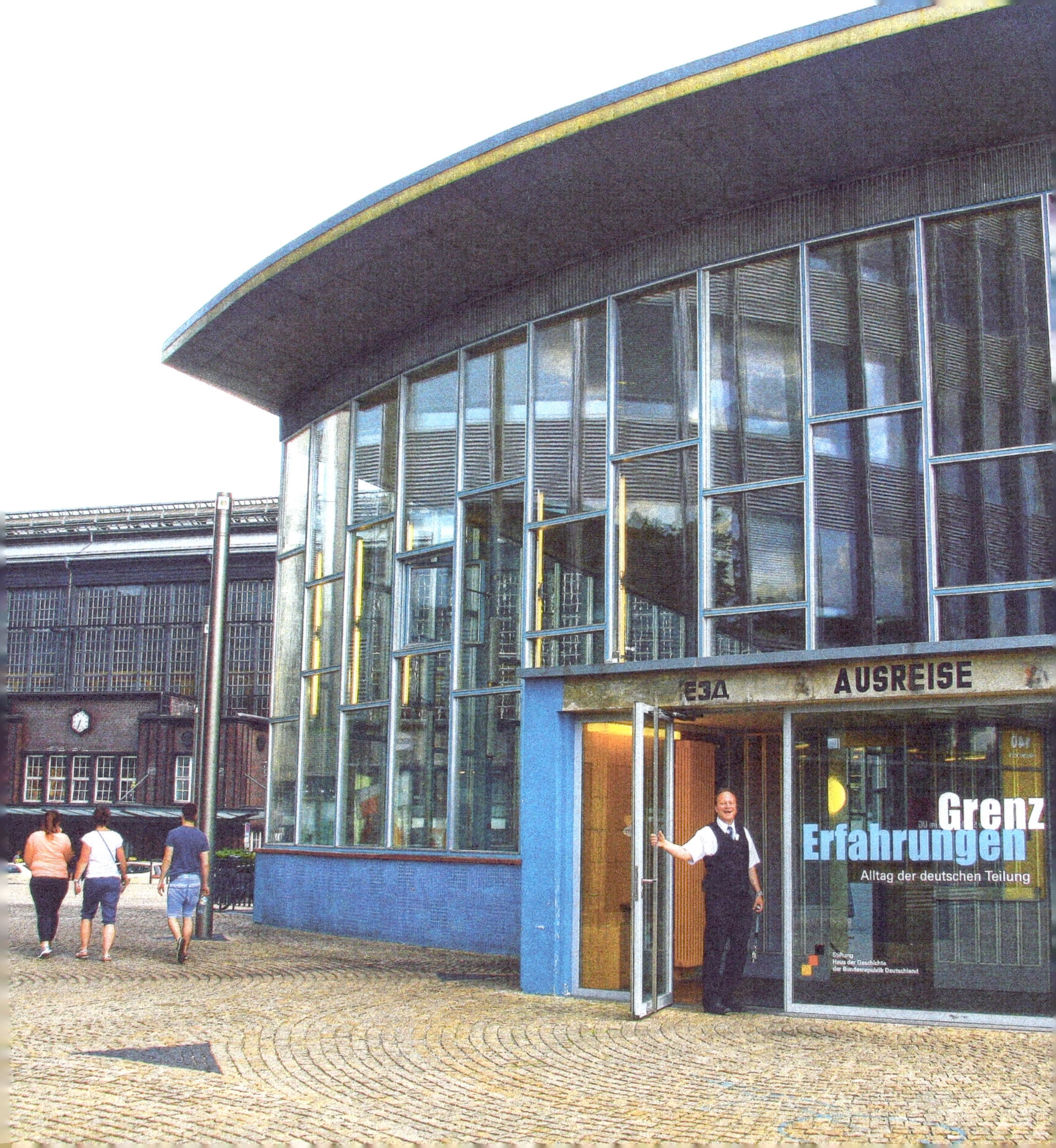
AUSREISE
Grenz
Erfahrungen
Alltag der deutschen Teilung
Stiftung
Haus der Geschichte
der Bundesrepublik Deutschland

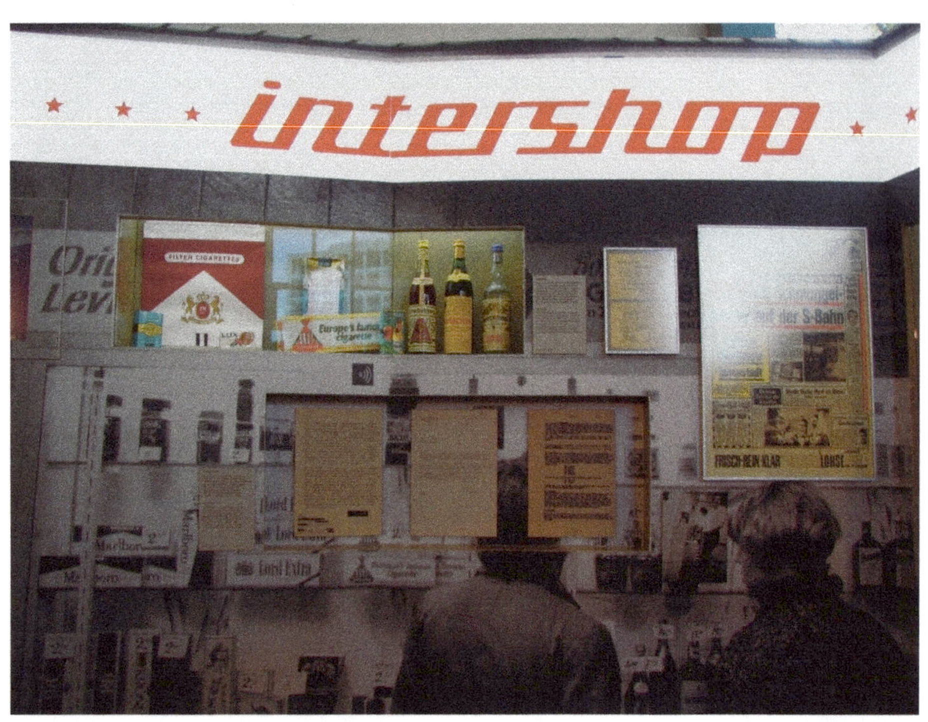

Left: The exhibit at the Tränen-palast Museum features a depic-tion of an "Intershop" with Western merchandise.

Below: A booth to show your passport to the border guard is also in the museum. The sign points to the long-distance train, the S-Bahn, and the U-Bahn. The museum at the Friedrich-strasse train station is open Tuesday to Friday, from 9 a.m. to 7 p.m., and Saturday/Sunday, from 10 a.m. to 6 p.m..

Opposite: This piece of the Berlin Wall stands right in front of the Westin Hotel at Fried-richstrasse, near the former bor-der station.. Tourists, like this young man from out of town, use it to pose for pictures.

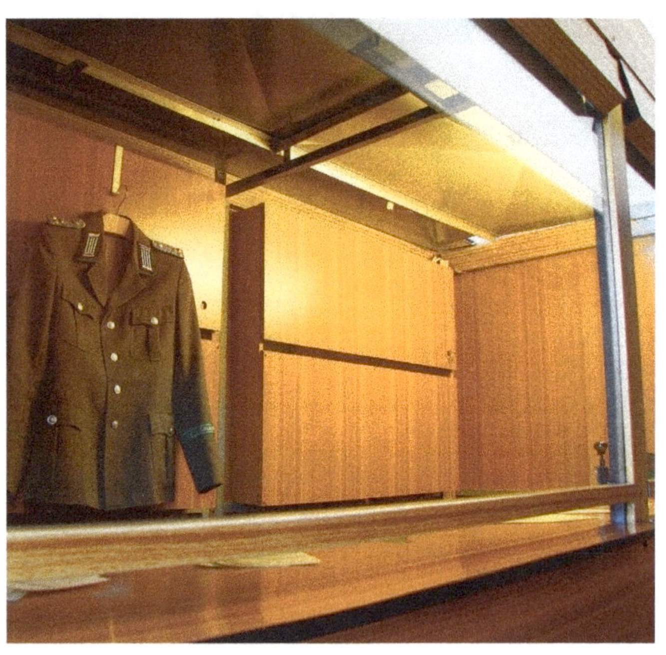

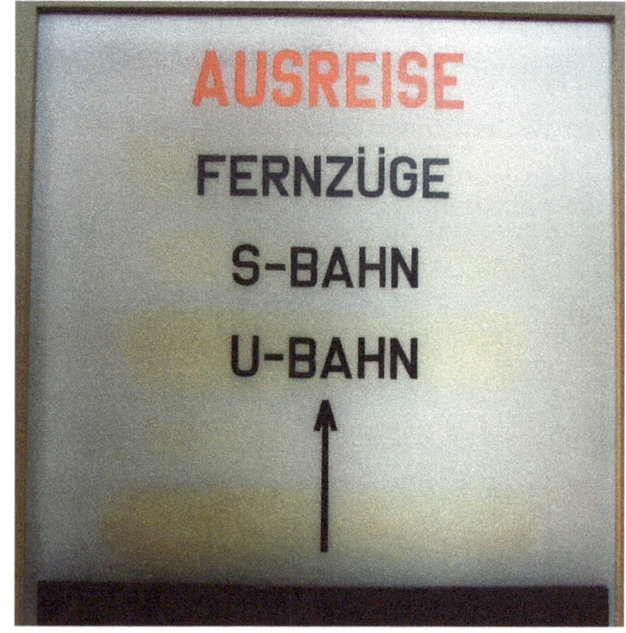

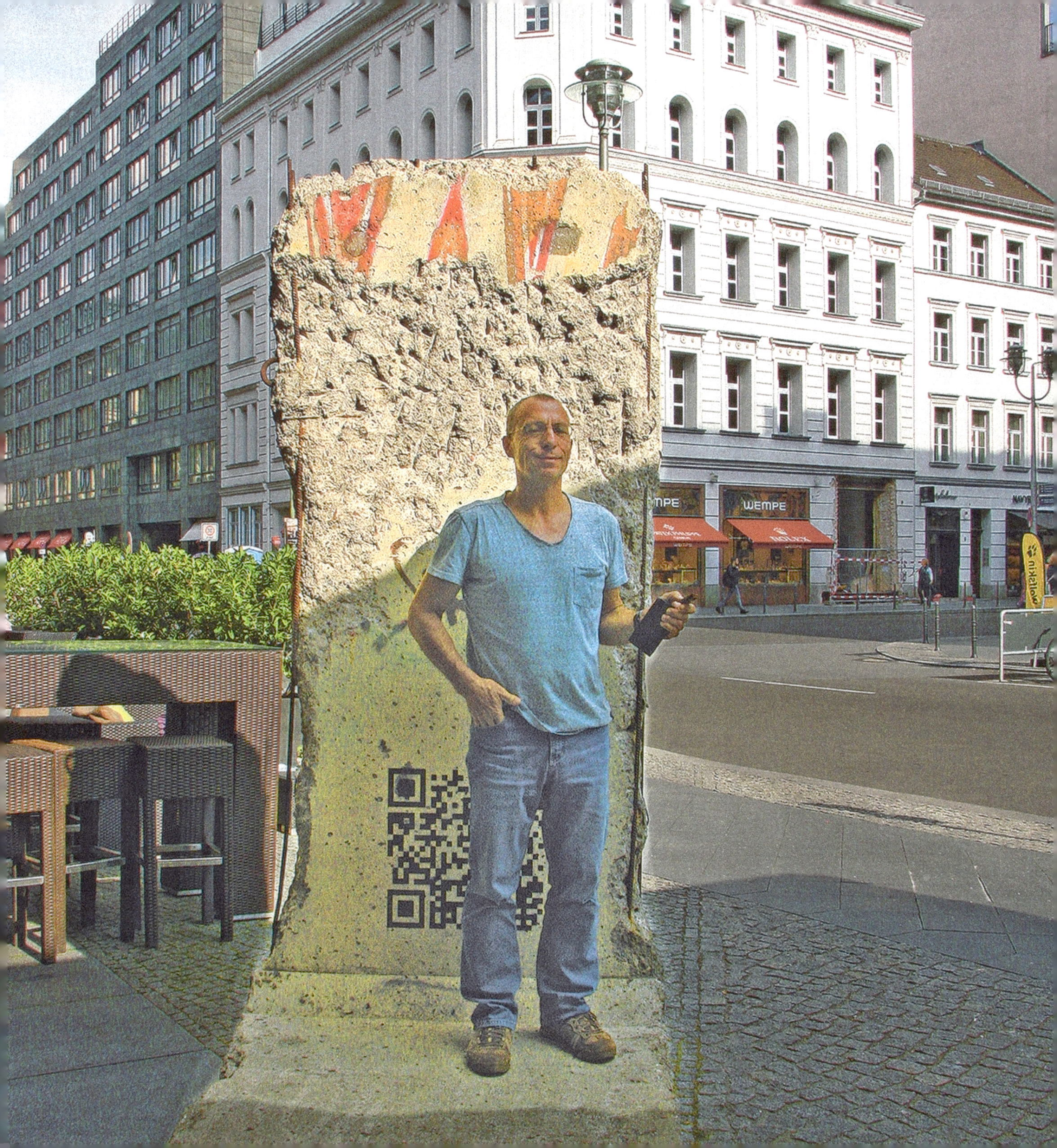

WEMPE

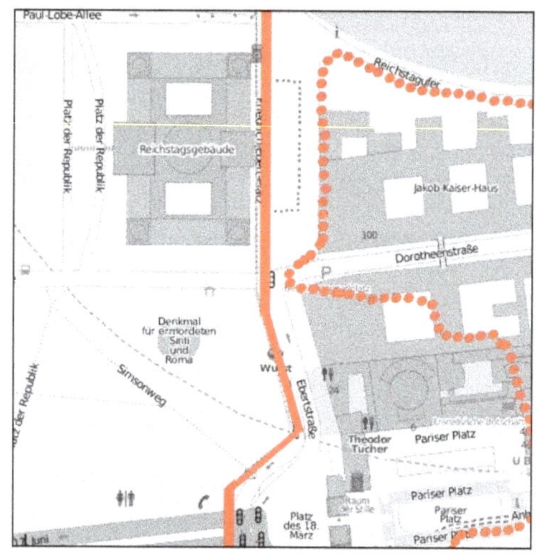

Deutscher Bundestag
Brandenburger Tor

Reichstag Building
Brandenburg Gate

For decades, the Reichstag was cut off from the former city center by the Wall. Built in 1841 by Paul Wallot, the Reichstag housed the first German parliament. In the infamous fire of 1933, presumably set by the Nazis, the Reichstag burned. In 1945, after the fall of Berlin, the Red Army hoisted its flag over the building's bombed-out shell. When the city was divided, the Reichstag sat on the edge of West Berlin, useless and empty. In 1954, the last remnants of the glass dome were taken down. Ten years later, the building was renovated, but without the dome. Occasionally, the German parliament would pay a visit from Bonn. Only after reunification was the Reichstag rebuilt state-of-the-art, by architect Sir Norman Foster, including a glass dome that offers a spectacular view. Some of the bullet holes from the war were intentionally left in the walls.

Today, only the cobblestone path between the Reichstag and the restored mansion of the Reichstag president commemorates the Wall, along with a dozen crosses bearing the names of victims that were shot or drowned trying to flee. Nearby is a memorial of the ninety-six Weimar parliamentarians murdered by the Nazis.

Opposite: the Paul-Löbe-Haus, a new office building for parliamentarians. It was named after a Social Democratic politician who was imprisoned by the Nazis. After 1945, Löbe became the first elder president of the new German Bundestag (German Federal Parliament). All political parties have offices in the vicinity of the Reichstag.

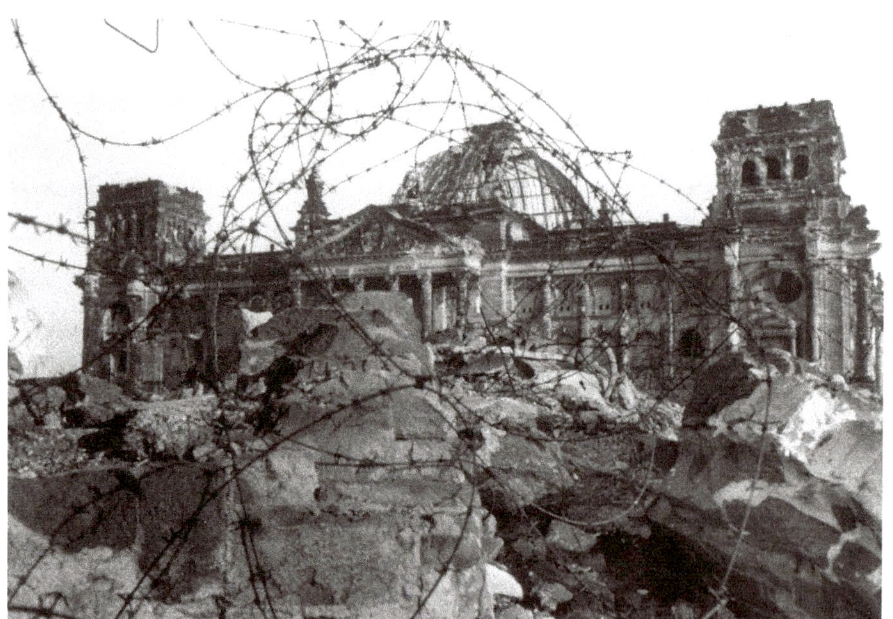

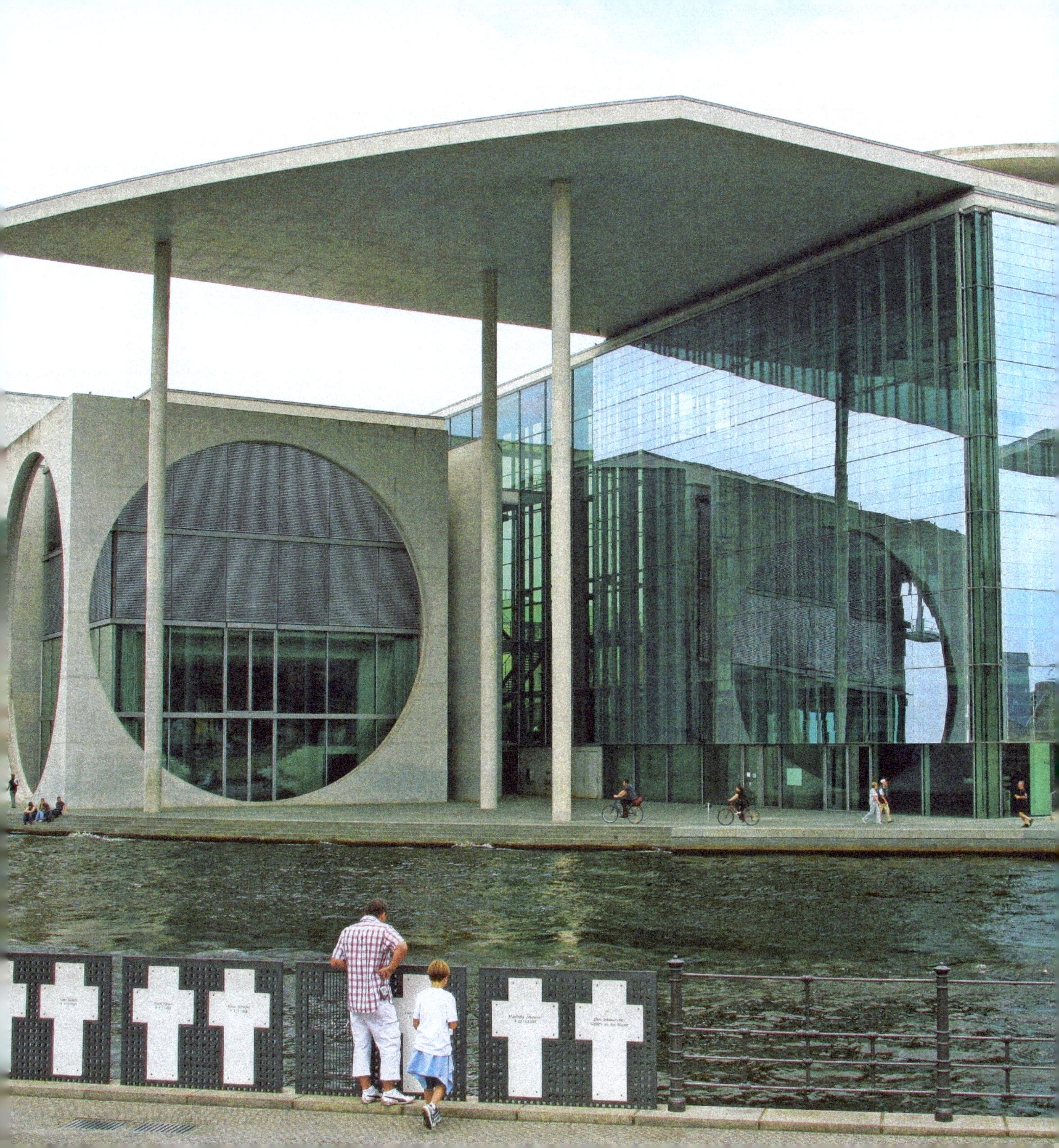

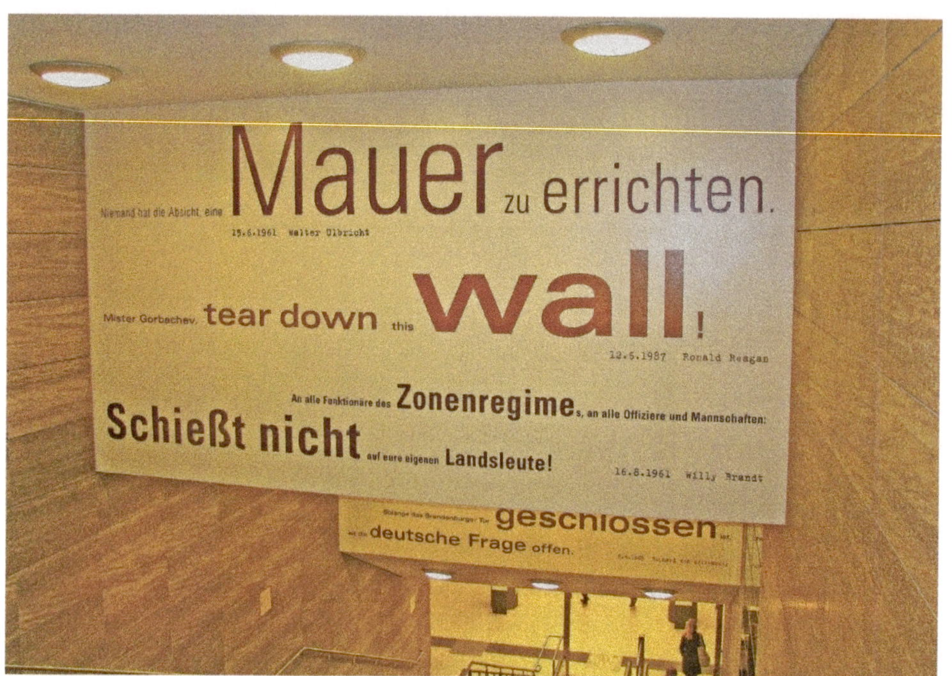

People from all over the world visit the Reichstag and climb all the way up to the dome for the view or simply hang out in front of the building.

Left: Two new subway stations, Reichstag and Brandenburger Tor, also serve as small museums, with historic photos and famous quotes from that era.

Below: This was the path of the Wall between the Reichstag and the Paul-Löbe-Haus, marked by the row of cobblestones.

Opposite: These crosses memorialize victims of the Wall in the Tiergarten, Berlin's central park, right across from the Reichstag. The crosses were hung by private organizations who want these people to be remembered.

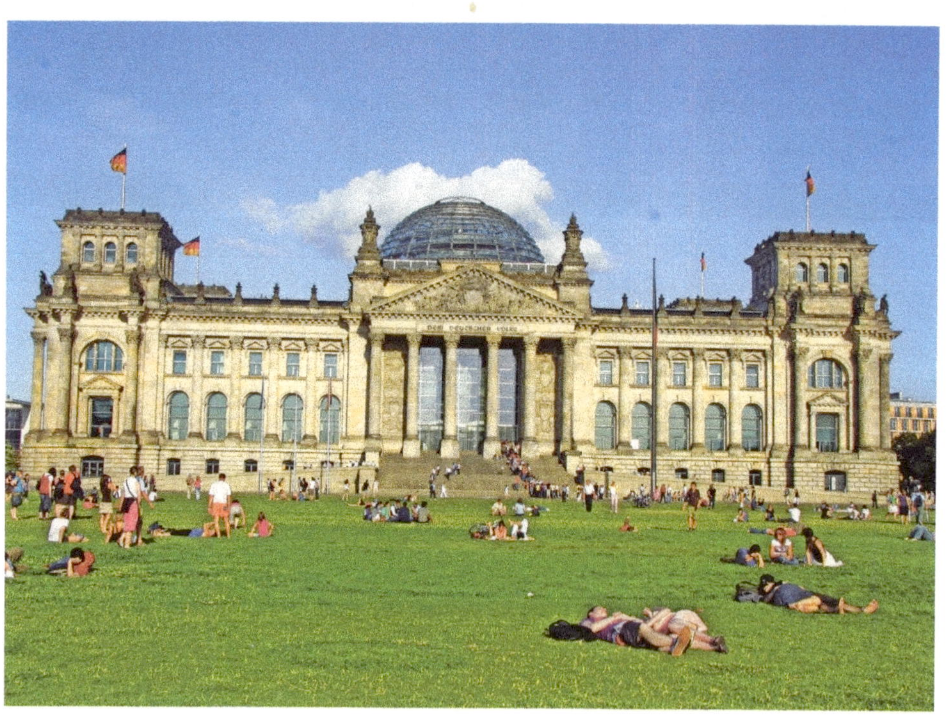

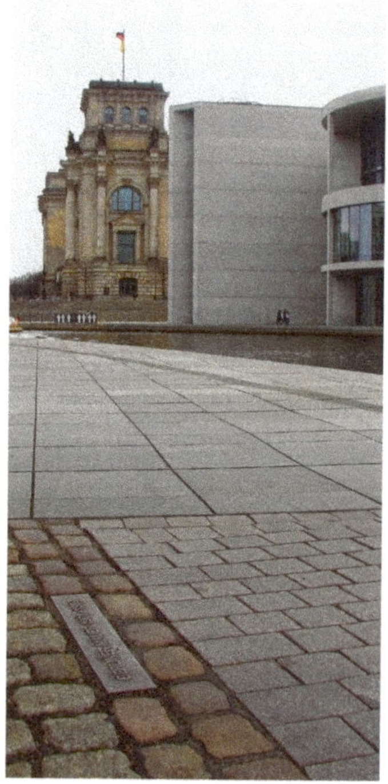

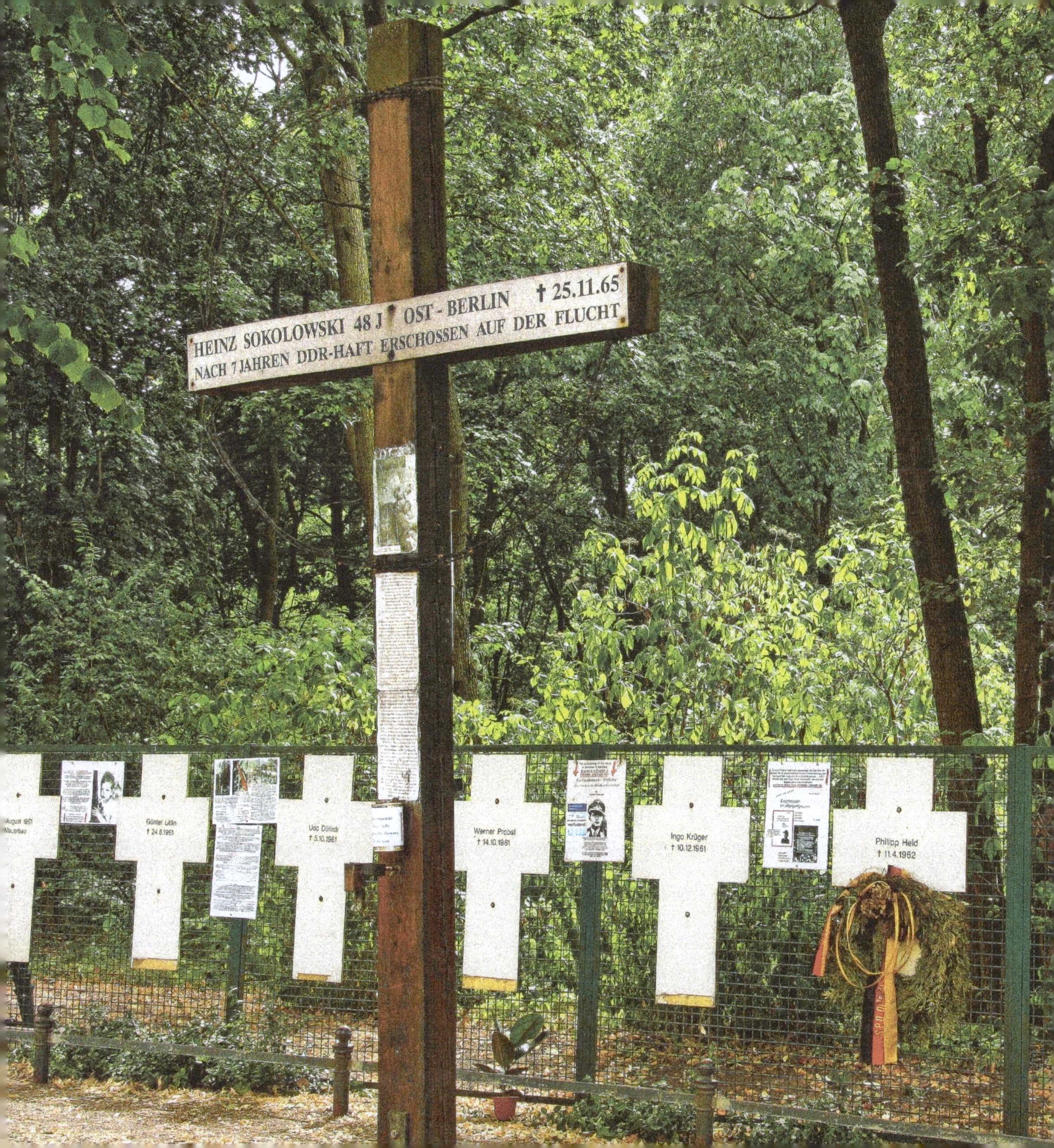

HEINZ SOKOLOWSKI 48 J   OST - BERLIN   † 25.11.65
NACH 7 JAHREN DDR-HAFT ERSCHOSSEN AUF DER FLUCHT
Günter Litfin
† 24.8.1961
Udo Düllick
† 5.10.1961
Werner Probst
† 14.10.1961
Ingo Krüger
† 10.12.1961
Philipp Held
† 11.4.1962

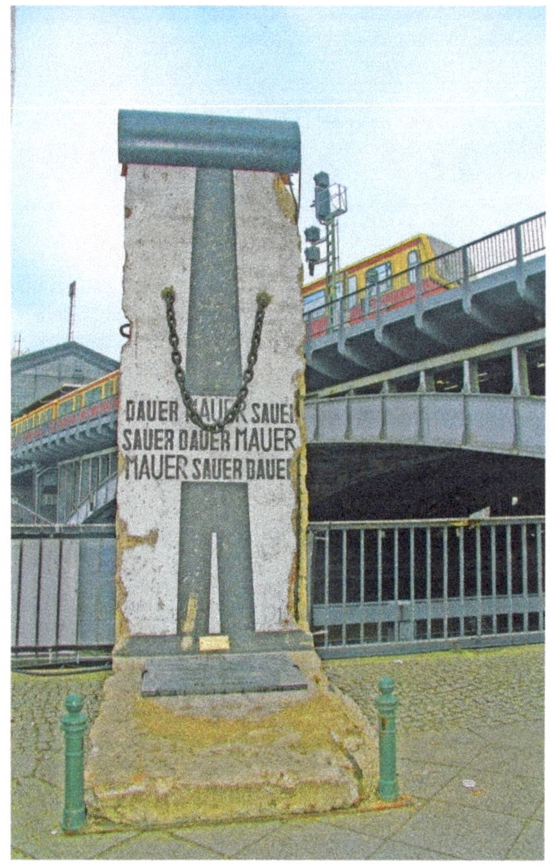

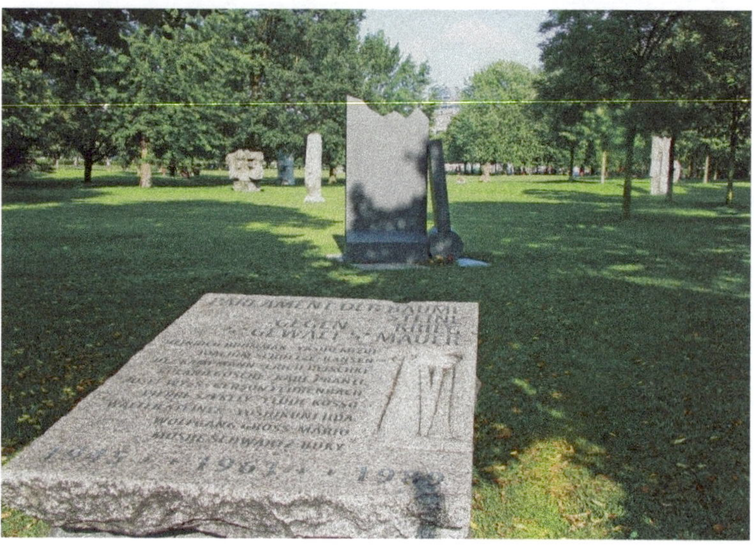

Behind the Reichstag is the *Parliament of Trees against War and Violence*—a Wall memorial designed by Berlin sculptor Ben Wagin. Originally, the memorial consisted of three parts: sixteen trees symbolizing the sixteen German states (after reunification), a green monument dedicated to Mother Earth that was removed for the National Press building, and 400 additional trees planted by government officials from East and West Berlin and federal parliamentarians. Of those, only hundred are left, along with 116 Wall slabs, 58 of them at their original location (partially show below left). Those Wall remnants are the only ones within the government district that are not landmarked.

Above right: The Sculpture Garden in the Tiergarten was designed in 1961, by thirteen artists, one of which was Wagin, in protest of the Wall, built that year. In the background, the dome of the Reichstag is visible.

Above left: A "roadsign" to the *Parliament of Trees* at Schiffbauerdamm.

Opposite: The Soviet soldiers who were killed while storming the Reichstag in 1945 are remembered as "unknown victims."

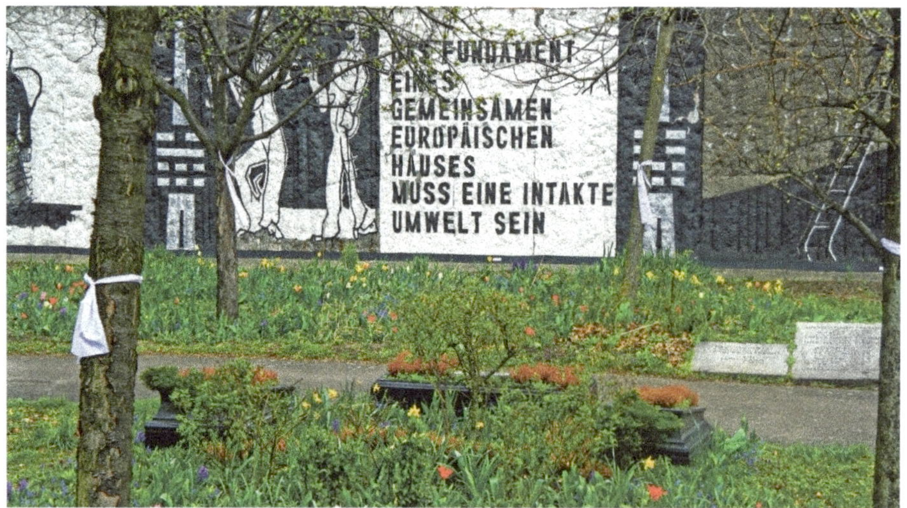

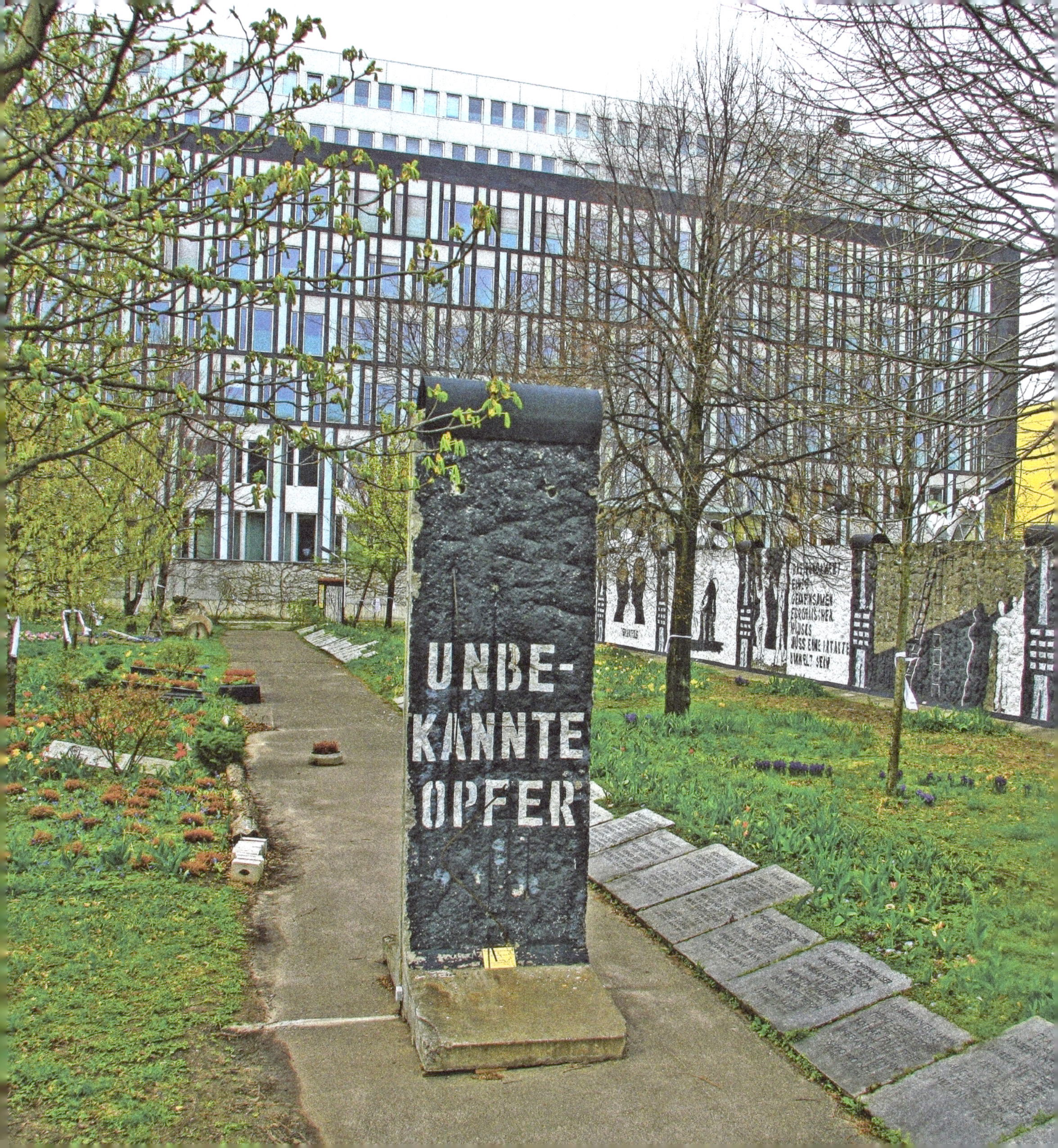

UNBE-
KANNTE
OPFER

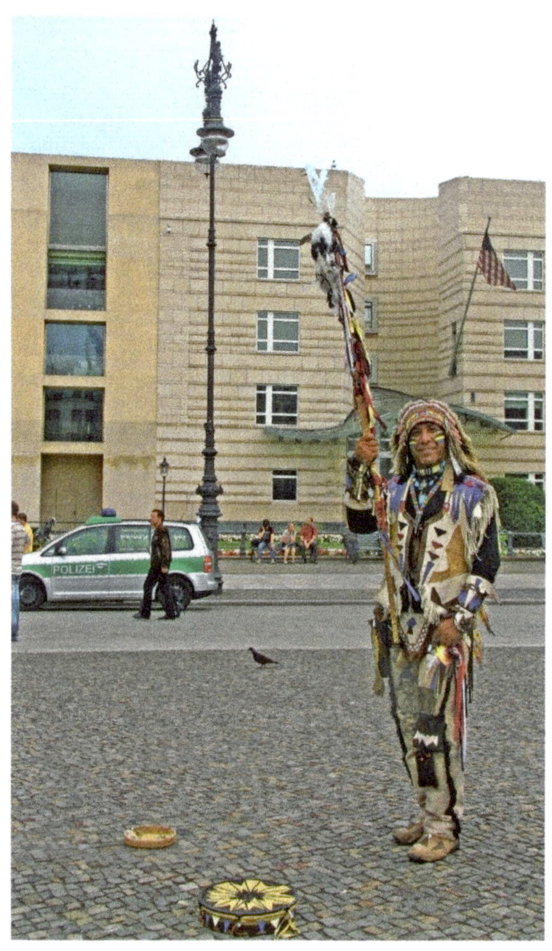 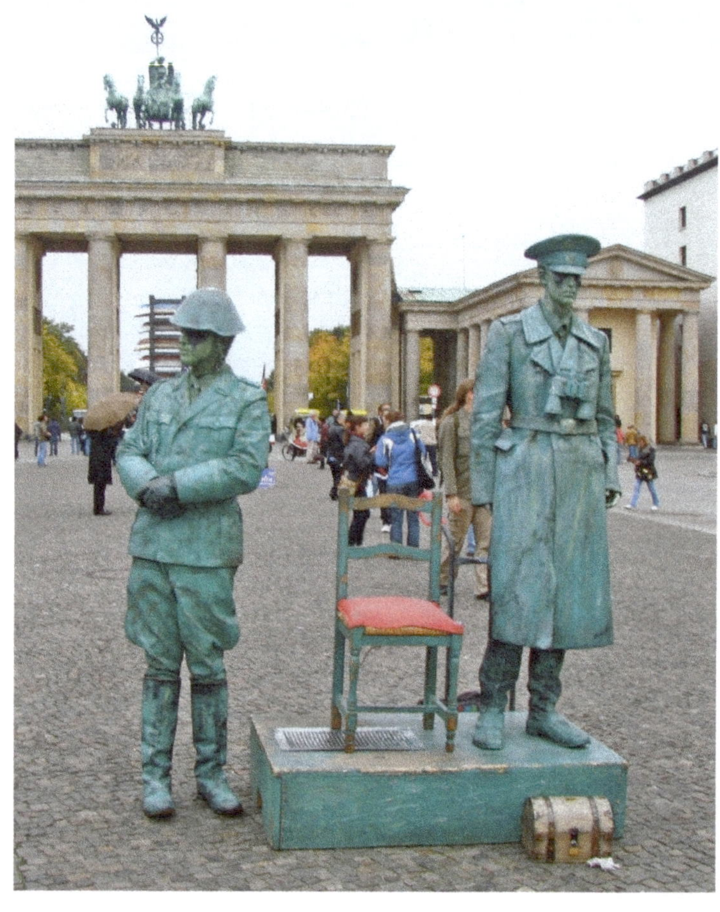

The historic Brandenburg Gate, built in 1791, has been the traditional gateway to Berlin since the era of the Prussian emperors. Prussian kings and princesses rode through the classicist gate, from Schloss Charlottenburg to Unter den Linden and the Berlin Castle. On March 18, 1848, street battles erupted around the gate, when Berliners, yearning for democracy, protested against the king. In 1961, when the Wall was built, the gate was blocked with barbed wire. Soon it became a symbol of the divided city. And when the first border crossings opened in November 1989, droves of West Berliners climbed onto the Wall in front of the Brandenburg Gate and peeked into the East—images that were seen all over the world.

Today, the Brandenburg Gate has been renovated and the area rebuilt, including Pariser Platz east of the gate. Pariser Platz was the site of quite a few embassies until 1945: the French, the British right around the corner, and the American embassy seen in the photo on the left. In front of the building is a visiting Native American musician—one of many street artists who congregate at Pariser Platz, juggling, singing, playing music, or posing for pictures.

The Wall path can only be recognized here by the cobblestone row running through the traffic, barely visible. The area in front of the gate was renamed Square of March 18, in memory of the people killed during the 1848 uprising.

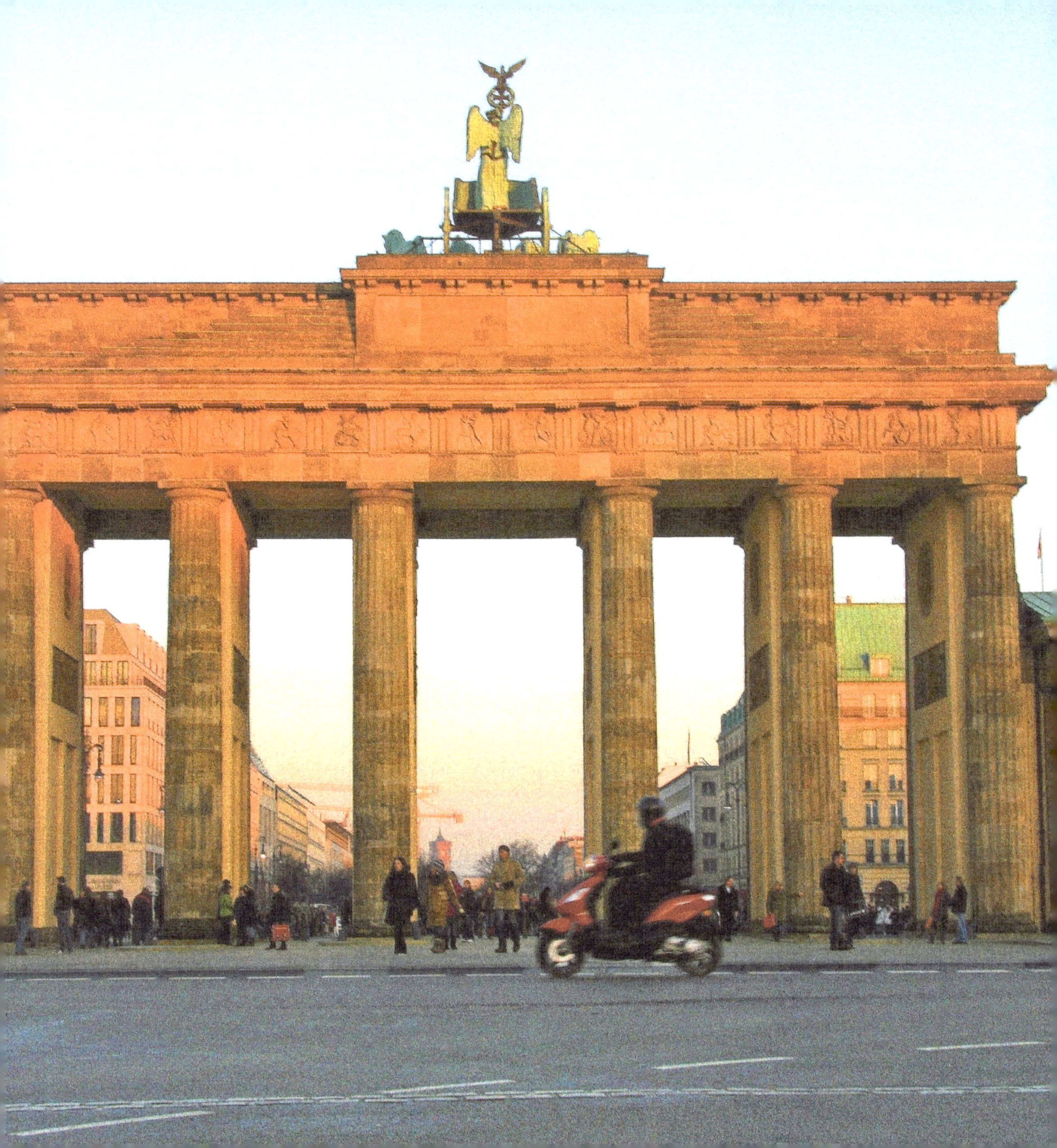

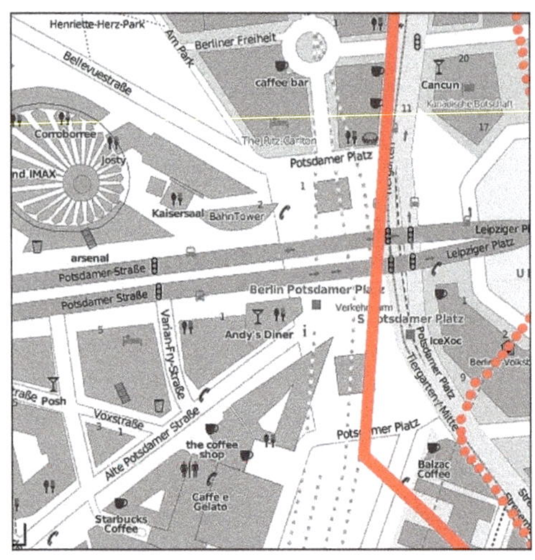

POTSDAMER PLATZ
LEIPZIGER PLATZ

POTSDAMER SQUARE
LEIPZIGER SQUARE

The former heart of Berlin, Potsdamer Platz, was famous for its cabarets, bars, cafés, luxury hotels—like the Fürstenhof and the Esplanade—and the *Haus Vaterland*, with a movie theater and the offices of the movie giant UFA. Germany's first radio broadcast originated here in 1923, from the Vox House. Berlin's first traffic light was installed here in 1924. Potsdamer Platz was destroyed first by Allied bombs in 1943, then by the Wall.

Whatever was left of the buildings in the West was torn down—including the Anhalter Train Station—to make way for an inner-city highway that never came. In the 1980s, Wim Wender's movie *Wings of Desire* (*Der Himmel über Berlin*) was filmed in the shadow of the Wall at Potsdamer Platz. Only two structures survived in this urban wasteland: Winehouse Huth and a small part of the Hotel Esplanade.

Today, three slabs of the Wall are left in their original place here, on the sidewalk near the S-Bahn entrance. This is also where the Berlin Wall Trail starts. Here, visitors can get their passports stamped by "real" border guards (opposite page). There's also a small exhibit with pictures, information, and maps.

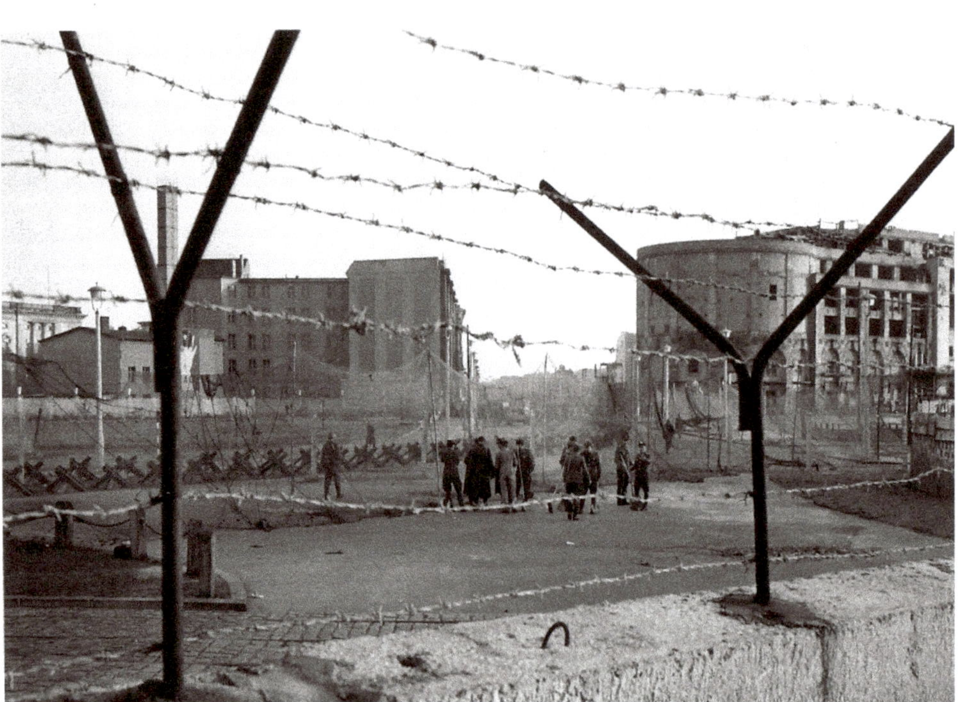

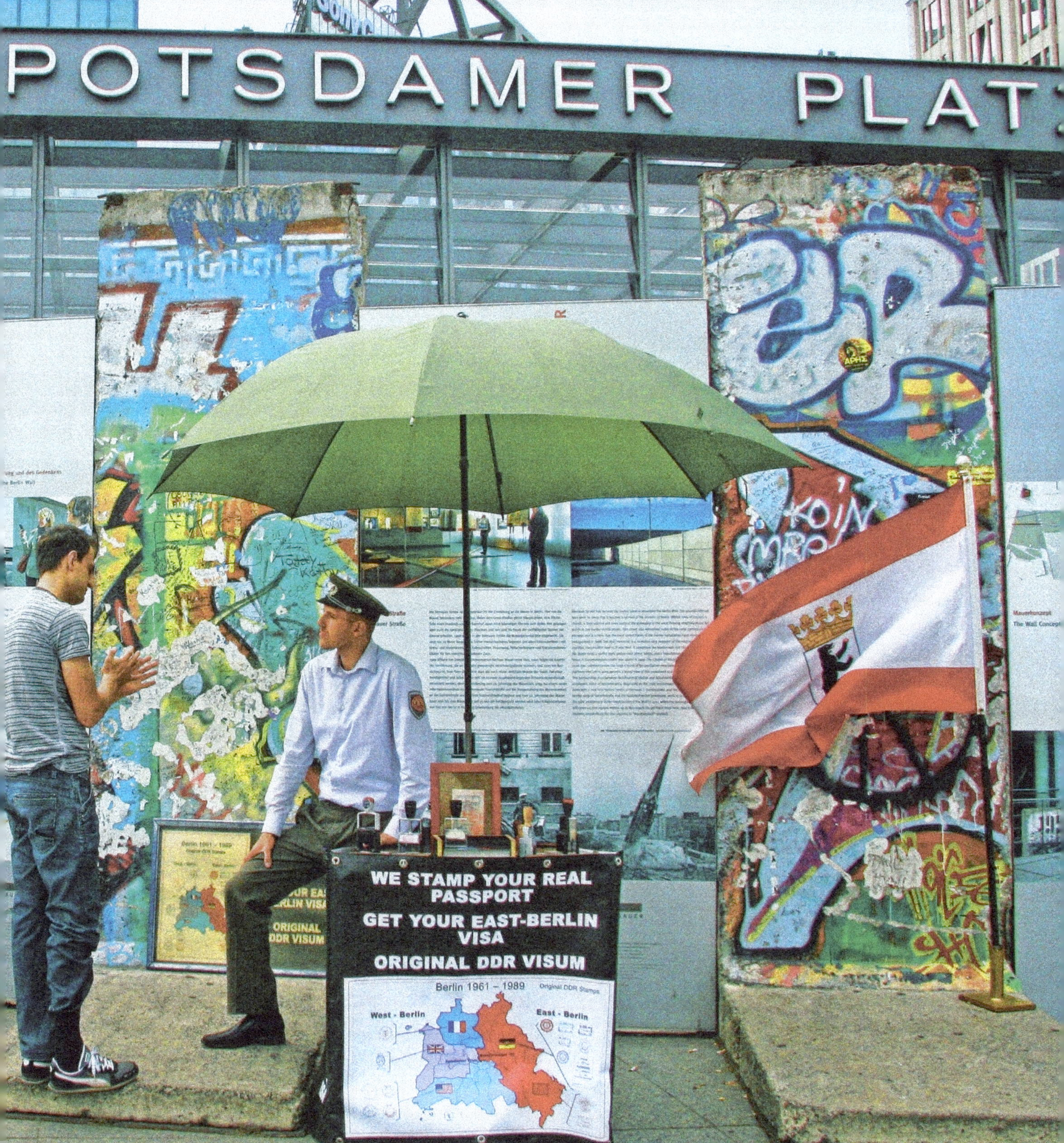

POTSDAMER PLATZ
SONY
WE STAMP YOUR REAL PASSPORT
GET YOUR EAST-BERLIN VISA
ORIGINAL DDR VISUM
Berlin 1961 – 1989
Original DDR Stamps
West - Berlin
East - Berlin

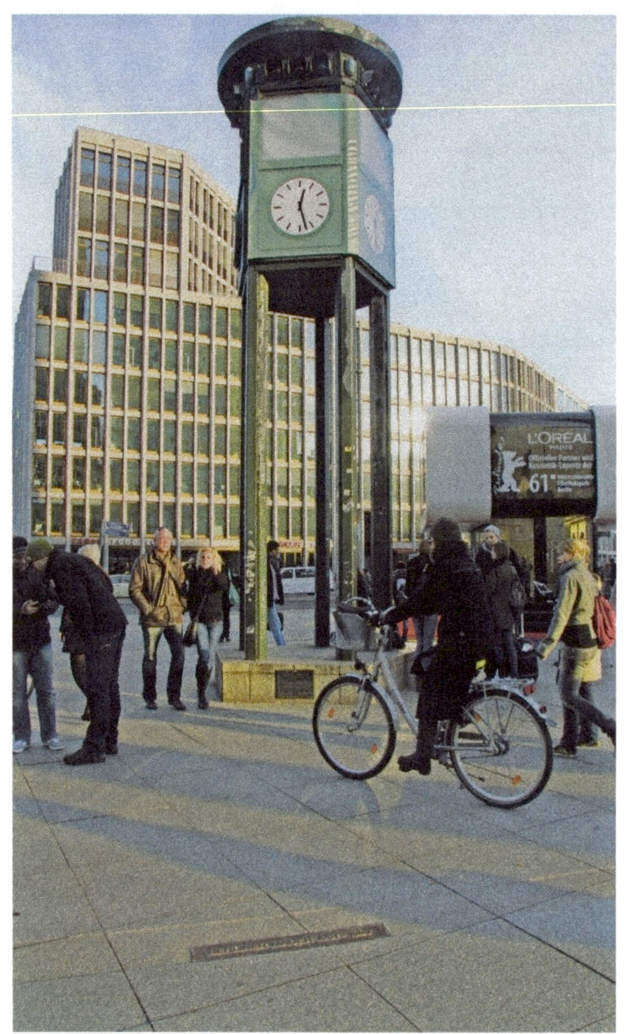

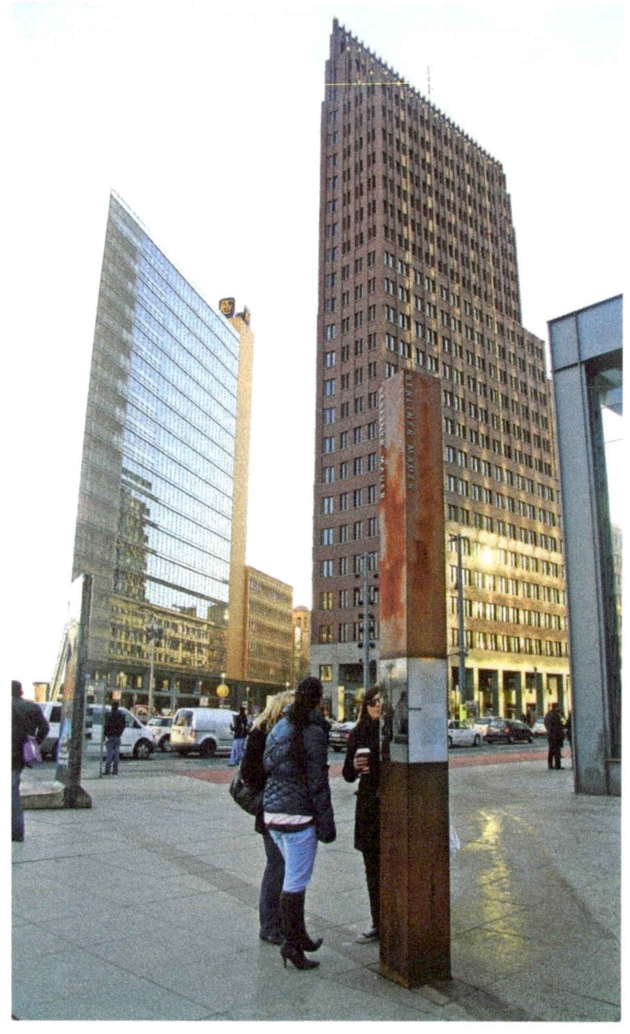

Today, the square is bustling again with pedestrians and car traffic. Sony, Daimler Benz, and other companies have put up skyscrapers. Dozens of movie screens have been added, as well as an IMAX, two musical theaters, restaurants and bars, a casino, a couple of hotels, and a movie museum featuring Marlene Dietrich. The Berlin Film Festival is celebrated here in February, with Brad Pitt and George Clooney walking the red carpet. The photo on the upper left shows a replica of the famous traffic light from 1924 on the sidewalk, which today only serves as a landmark, and a clock (the plaque in front reads: "Berliner Mauer 1961—1989"). The photo above shows a pillar that is the actual beginning of the Berlin Wall Trail—the dark strip in the ground marks the path of the Wall and will eventually turn into the double-row of cobblestones. The skyscrapers in the background were designed by architects Renzo Piano (left) and Hans Kollhoff (right).

Opposite: These kids are enjoying their Berlin visit. In the background, remnants of the Wall, covered in graffiti.

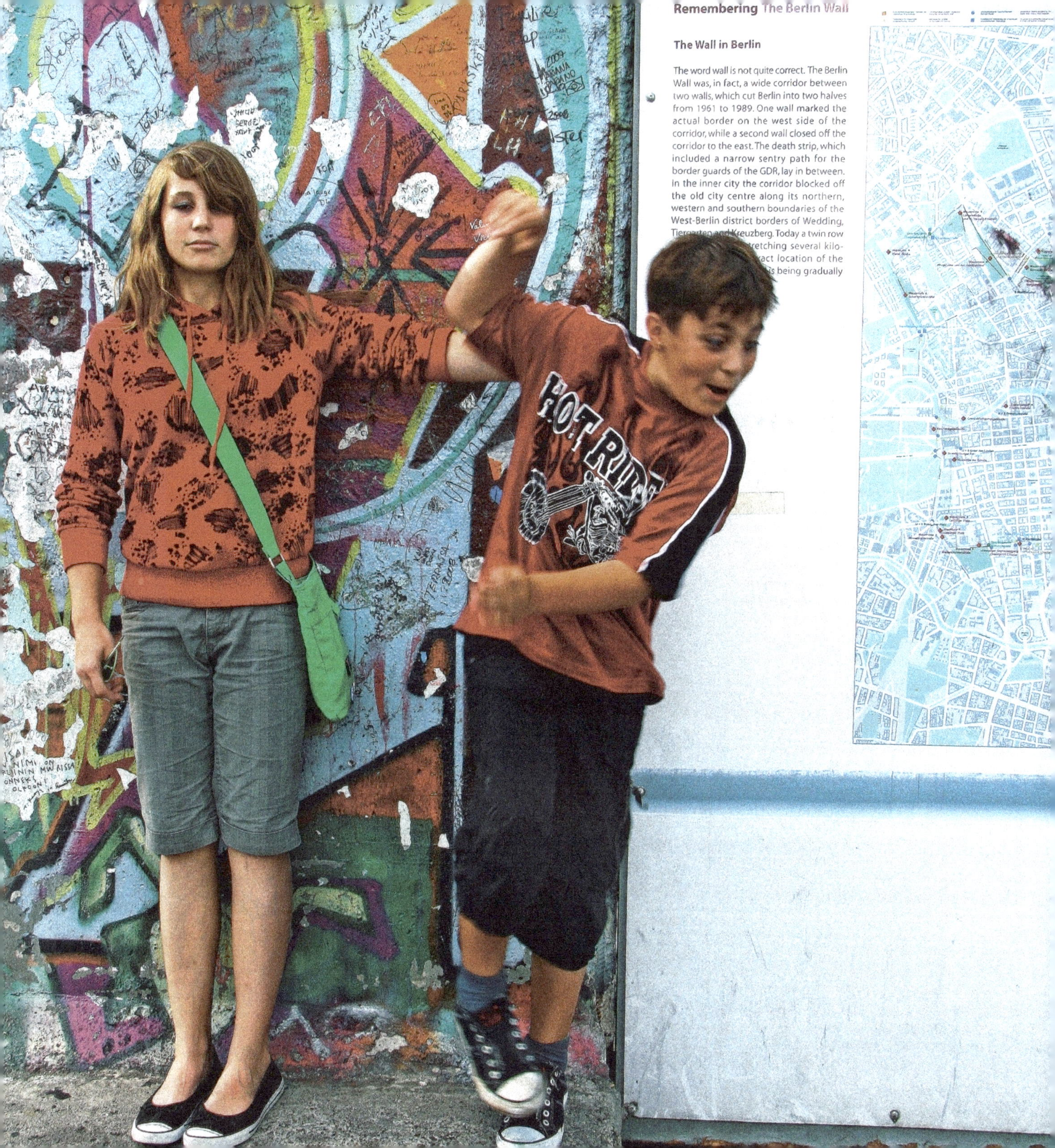

Remembering The Berlin Wall

The Wall in Berlin

The word wall is not quite correct. The Berlin
Wall was, in fact, a wide corridor between
two walls, which cut Berlin into two halves
from 1961 to 1989. One wall marked the
actual border on the west side of the
corridor, while a second wall closed off the
corridor to the east. The death strip, which
included a narrow sentry path for the
border guards of the GDR, lay in between.
In the inner city the corridor blocked off
the old city centre along its northern,
western and southern boundaries of the
West-Berlin district borders of Wedding,
Tiergarten and Kreuzberg. Today a twin row
stretching several kilo-
exact location of the
is being gradually

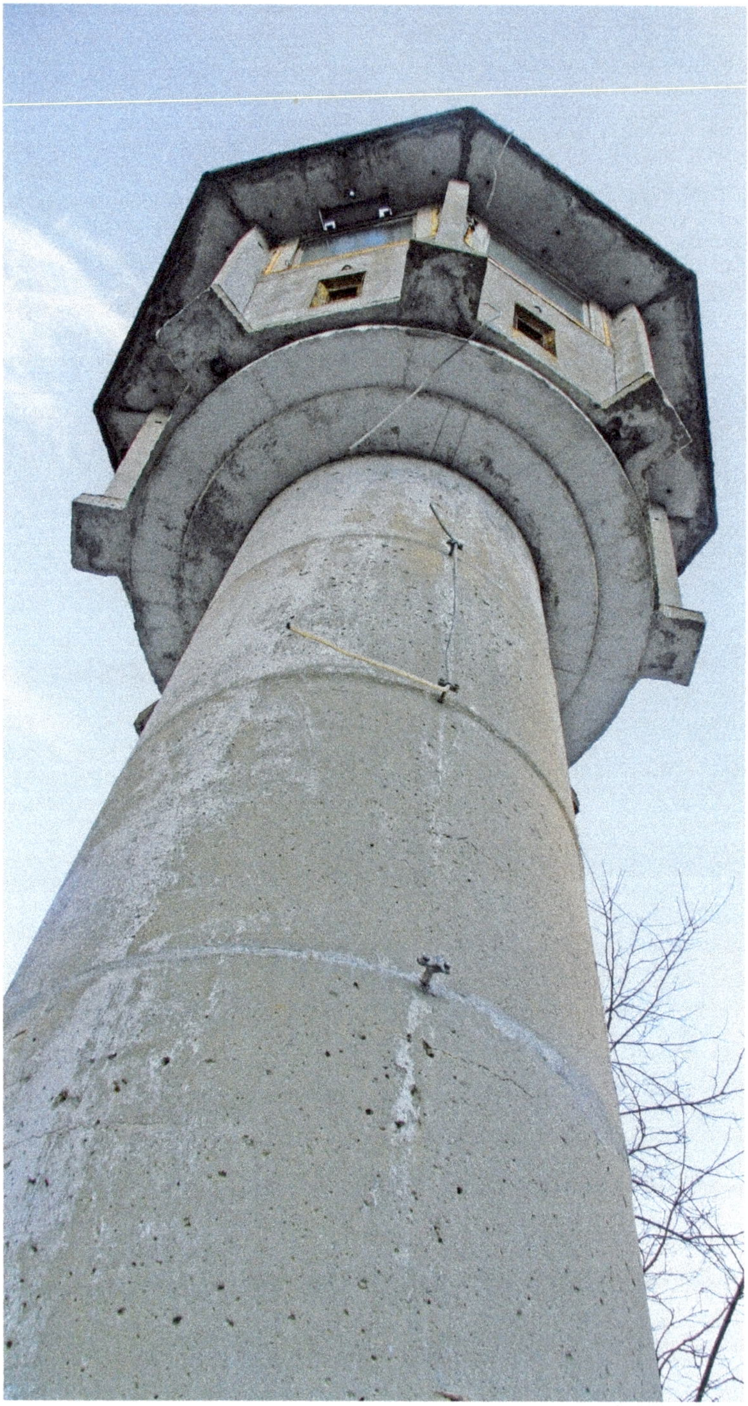

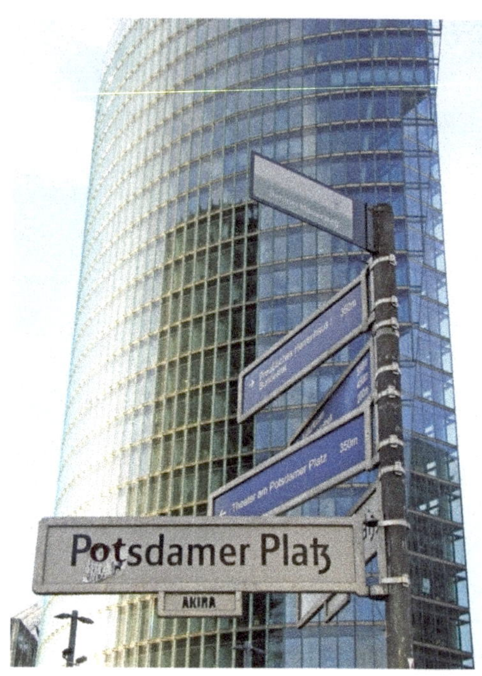

Above: The new high-rise of Deutsche Bahn.
Below: Only six thousand miles to Los Angeles, Berlin's sister city—a reference to the *Berlinale*, Berlin's International Film Festival.
Left: A few hundred yards south of Potsdamer Platz, at Erna-Berger-Strasse, an older guard tower from the 1960s, has been preserved, tiny and lost between the new buildings. It was moved thirty feet from its original location. Recently, it was bought by an artist who plans to open it for visitors.
Opposite: A slab of the Wall at Leipziger Platz, the octagon east of Potsdamer Platz, next to the subway entrance. After the Wall was built, the station was closed, the subway became a "ghost train" that did not stop. Now it's open again.

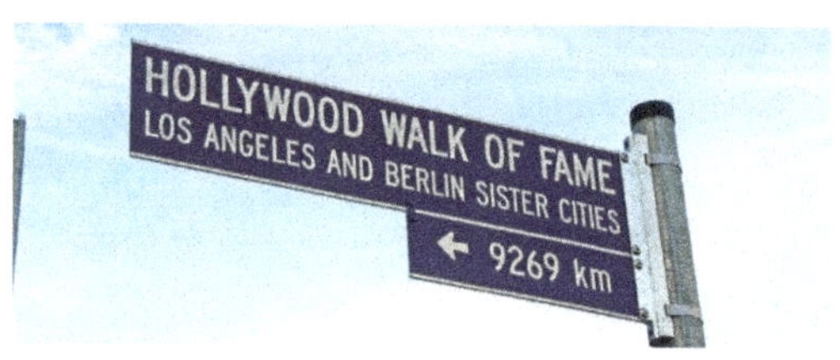

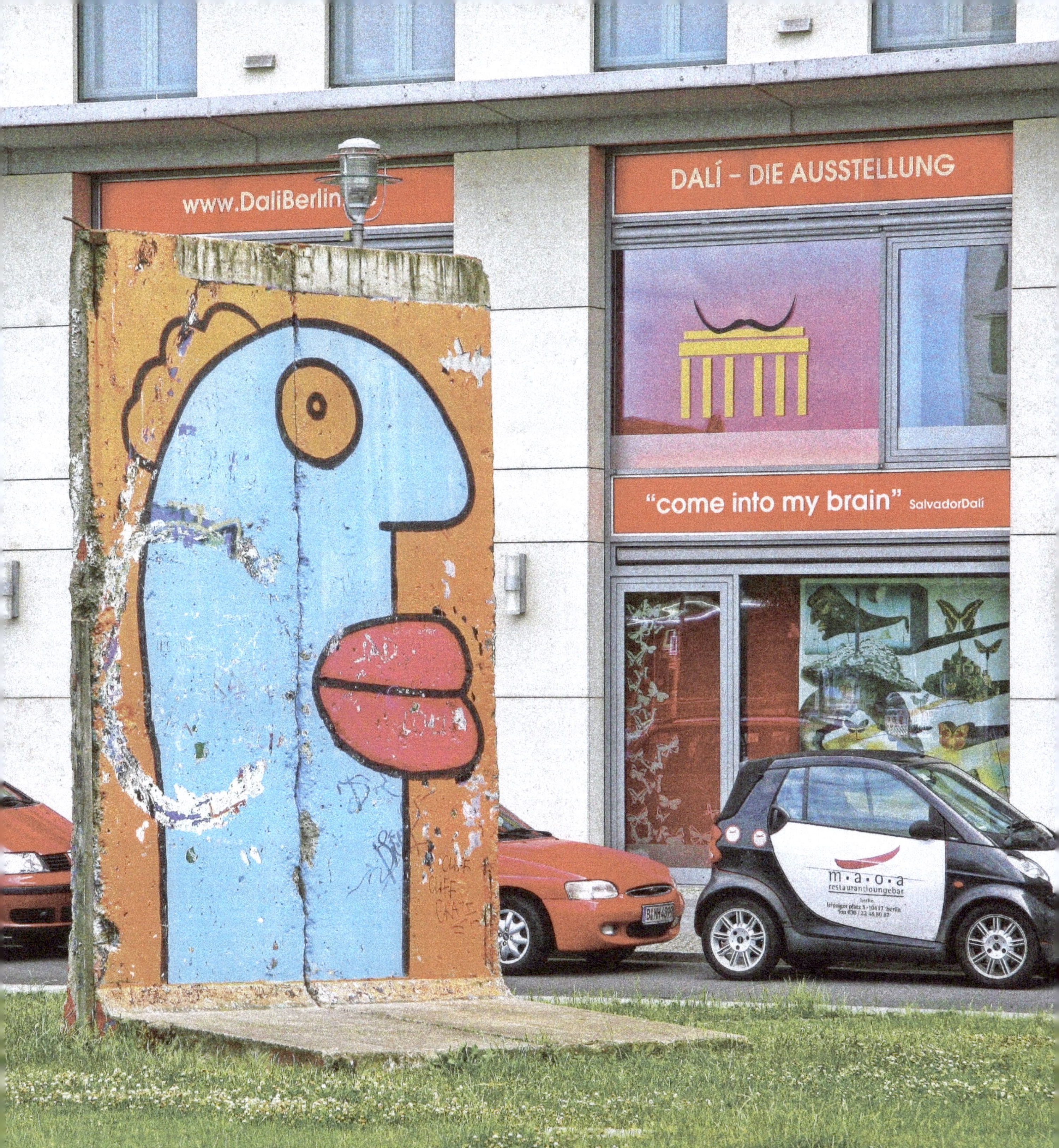

www.DaliBerlin
DALÍ – DIE AUSSTELLUNG
"come into my brain" SalvadorDalí
m·a·o·a
restaurantloungebar

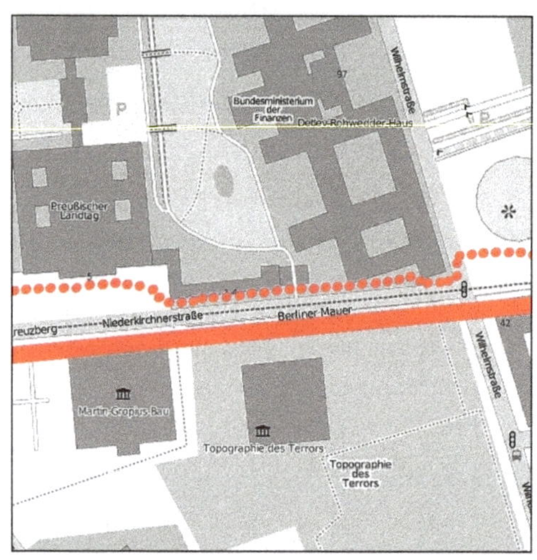

MUSEUM DER TOPO-GRAPHIE DES TERRORS

TOPOGRAPHY OF TERROR MUSEUM

A large stretch of the Wall was preserved along the Topography of Terror Museum. This is the largest remaining section of the inner-city Wall, although much of it has been damaged by *Mauerspechte* (Wall woodpeckers), Berliners who took pieces of the Wall home. This is the darkest place in Berlin's history: the Topography museum is built on the ruins of the former Gestapo and SS headquarters. In the basement, political prisoners and resistance fighters were tortured and murdered by the Gestapo. Among them was an American woman, Mildred Harnack, who was a member of the Red Orchestra resistance group, along with her German husband, Arvid Harnack. They had met in Minnesota.

Today, the remainders have been turned into a museum, with a new building, including a library and an outdoor exhibit. The museum draws hundreds of thousands of visitors every year, from all over the world. Right across the street is the Berlin Parliament, located in the former building of the Prussian diet. This is also where the German Communist Party was founded, in 1919. Nearby, at Ebertstrasse, is the Holocaust Memorial for the six million European Jews that have been murdered.

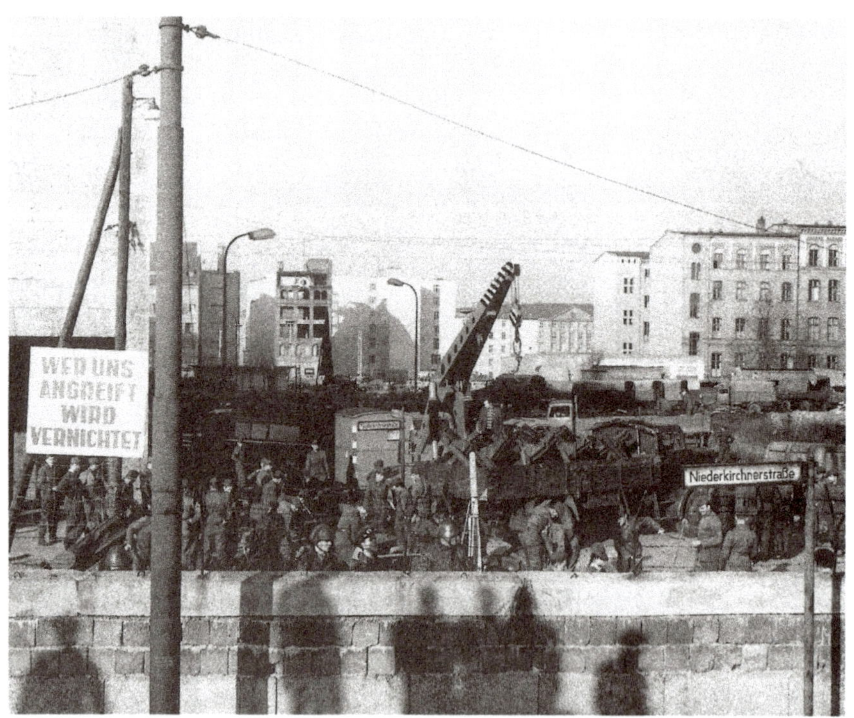

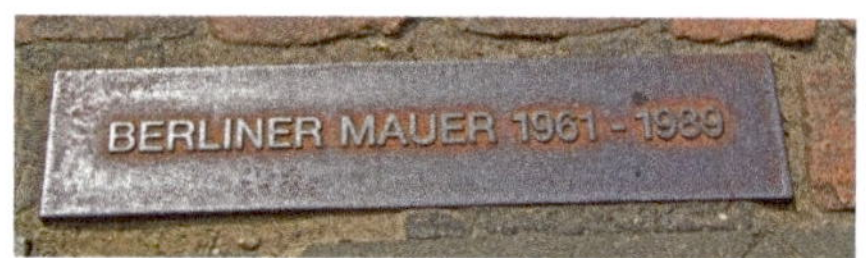

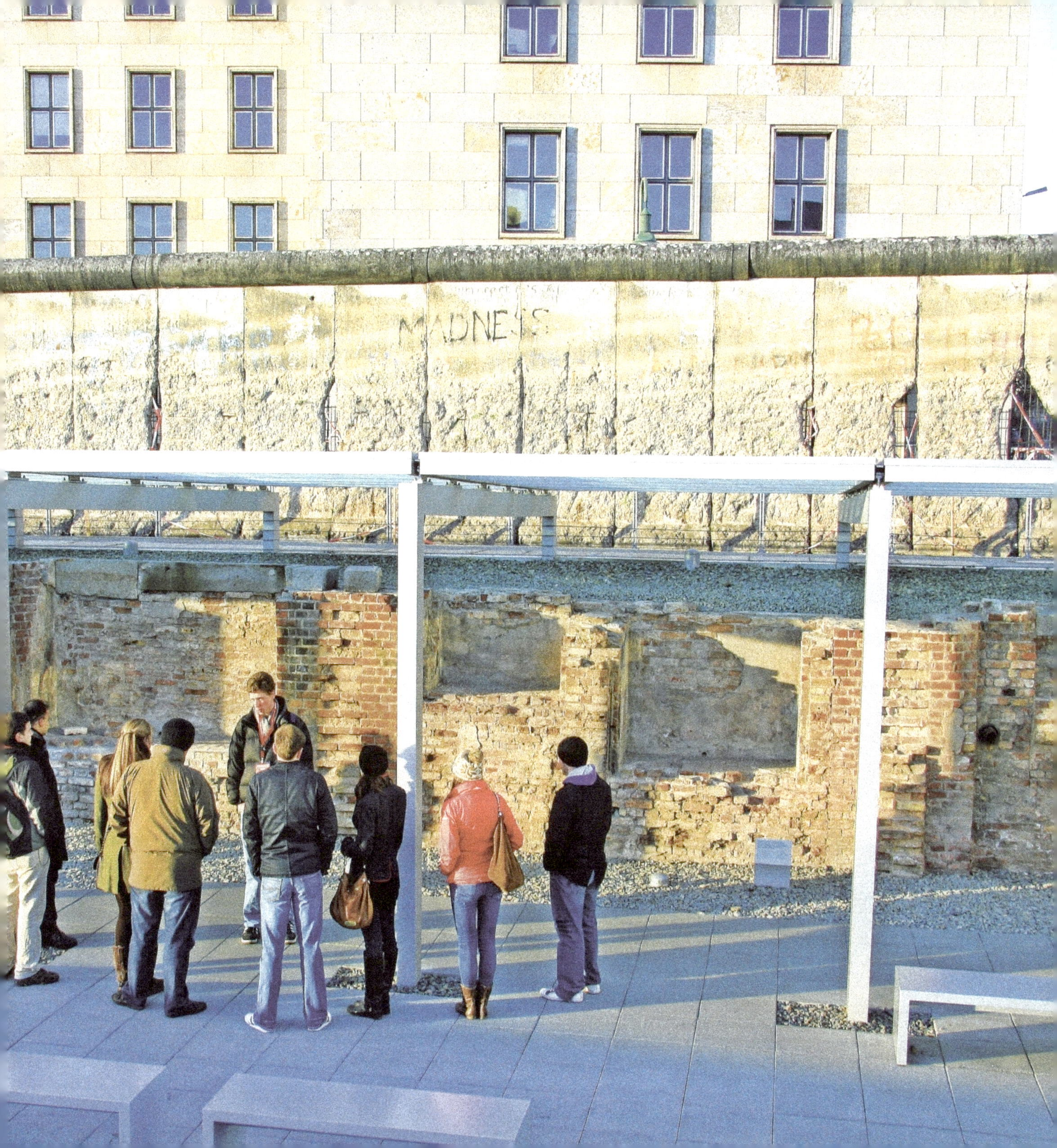
MADNESS

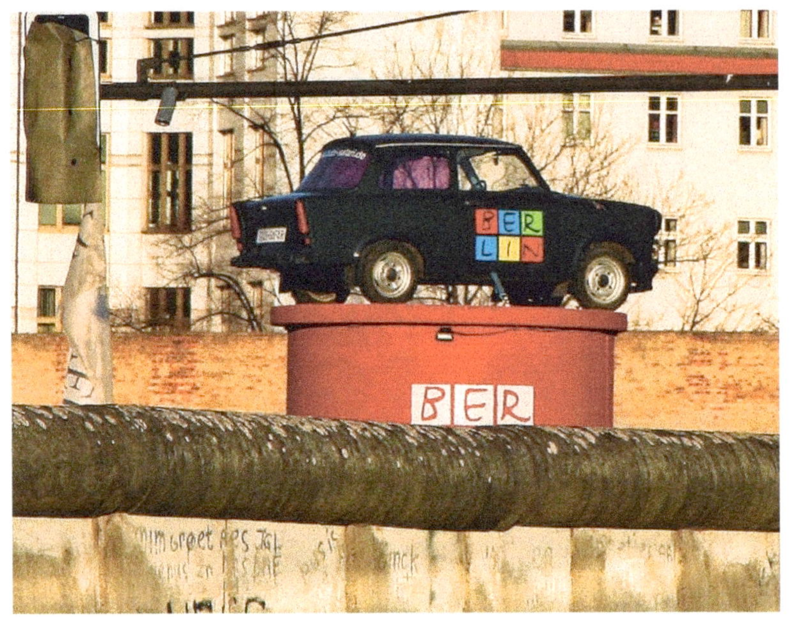

At Wilhelmstrasse, the former mile of Prussian ministries, a rather entertaining remnant of the GDR can be found: Trabi Safari, a venture that rents out Trabants, the tiny Duroplast cars East Germans used to drive—though newly painted, in colors unheard of in the GDR. Visitors to the city (and Berliners too, of course) can book guided Trabi tours.

The lot is surrounded by some leftover slabs of the Wall. Most of them were moved at least a few yards from their original locations—and like the Trabis, they've also been freshly painted. Also to be found on the otherwise vacant lot: a twenty-minute ride on a moored balloon that can carry some dozen people, offering a spectacular view of the city—though not for those with a faint heart.
Opposite: A Trabi formerly driven by the *Volks-polizei,* the people's police of the GDR, which, despite its name, was not all that popular.

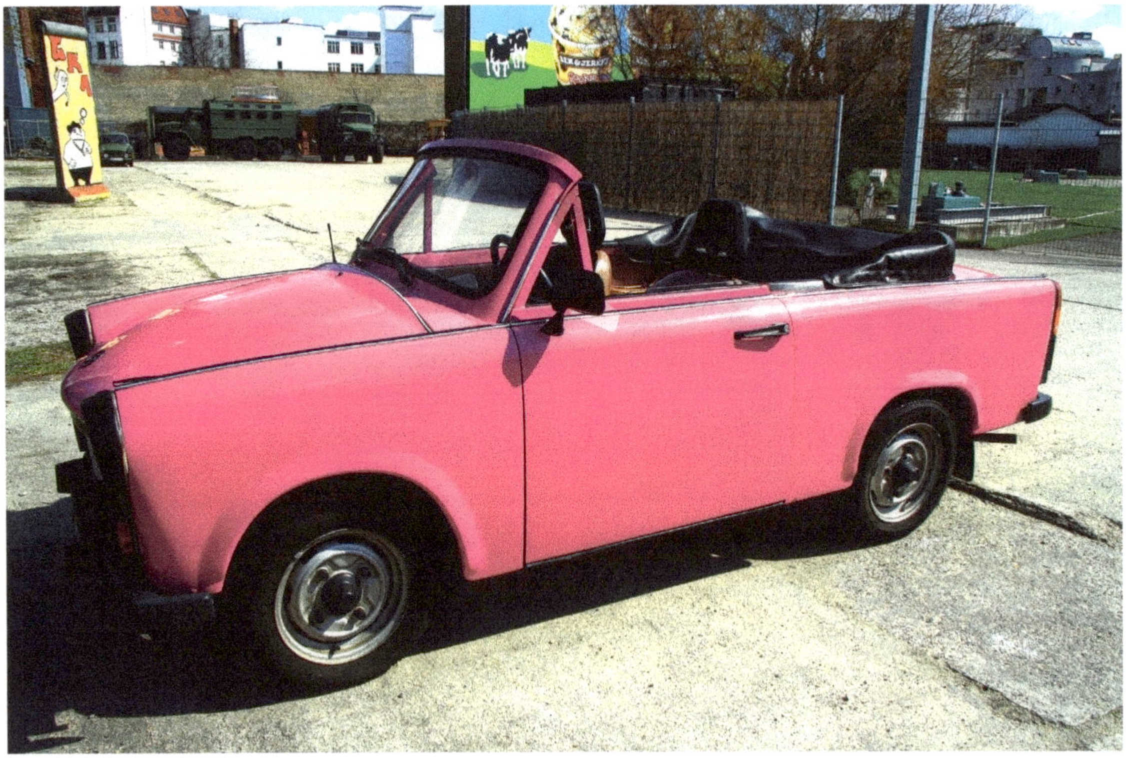

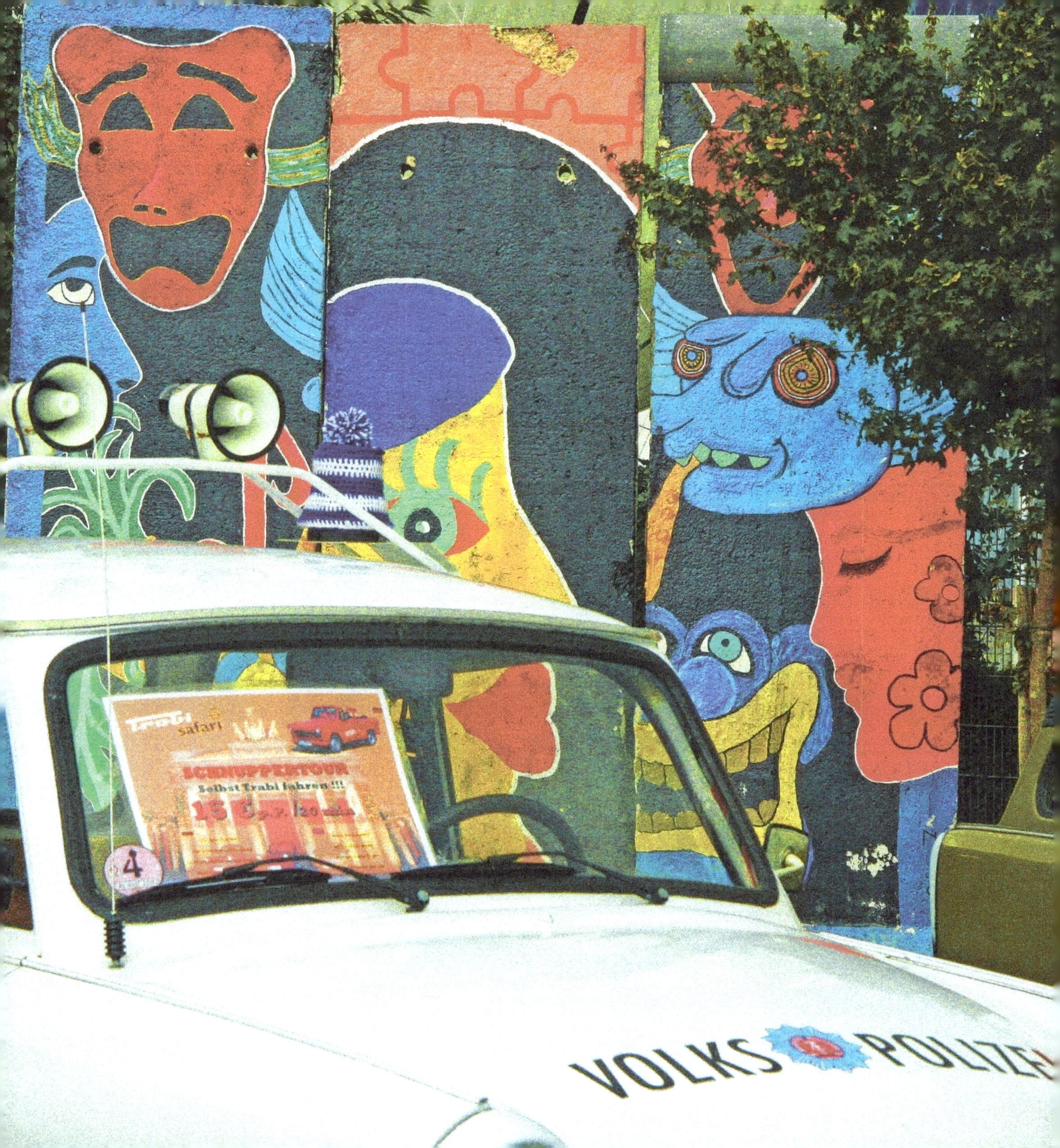

Trabi safari
SCHNUPPERTOUR
Selbst Trabi fahren !!!
VOLKS POLIZEI

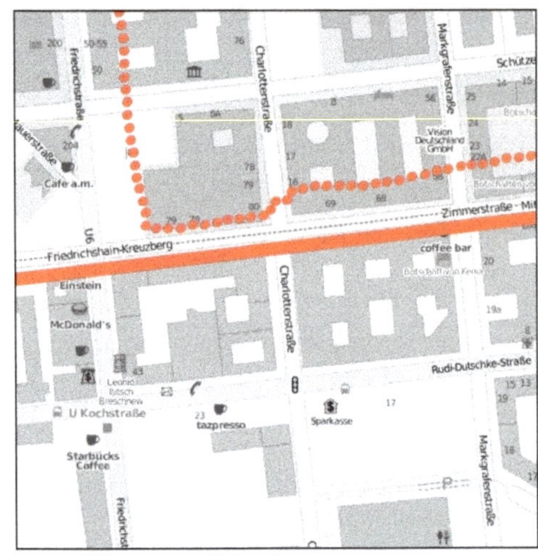

CHECKPOINT CHARLIE
HEINRICH-HEINE-STRASSE

CHECKPOINT CHARLIE
HEINRICH HEINE-STREET

Checkpoint Charlie is arguably the most famous border crossing in the world—which is why spy movies, such as James Bond's *Octopussy*, took place here. And on October 27, 1961, after the Wall was raised, real drama happened at this part of the Wall: American and Soviet tanks faced each other, ready to shoot live ammunition and possibly set off World War III. The US Army checkpoint, located at Friedrichstrasse, was the designated border crossing for foreigners, including American GIs, who faced less controls than West Berliners, so it was also the site of a lot of smuggling.

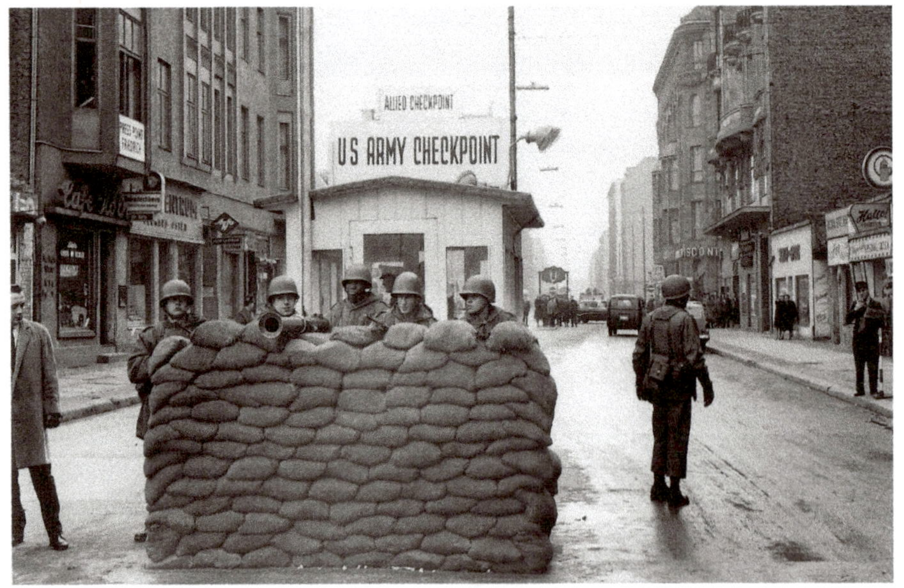

Today, the trademark metal shed in the middle of the street has been dismantled; it was donated to the Allied Museum in Zehlendorf. But since tourists kept asking for it, the area has been turned into a themepark version of its former self. A replica of the metal shed has been put up, with sandbags and "soldiers," really students from an acting school collecting money for their class (or so they claim). For two euros, visitors can get their pictures taken with an American and a Russian "soldier." One of the famous border signs has been preserved here: "You are leaving the American Sector."

Souvenir shops and street peddlers selling Russian dolls, fur hats, and Communist pins line the sidewalks. Most traces of the Wall itself, however, are gone, but not of the Cold War: Kochstrasse, a cross street one block south, was renamed Rudi-Dutschke-Strasse, after an activist of the 1960s who protested the Vietnam War. He was shot by a right-winger and died eleven years later due to these wounds.

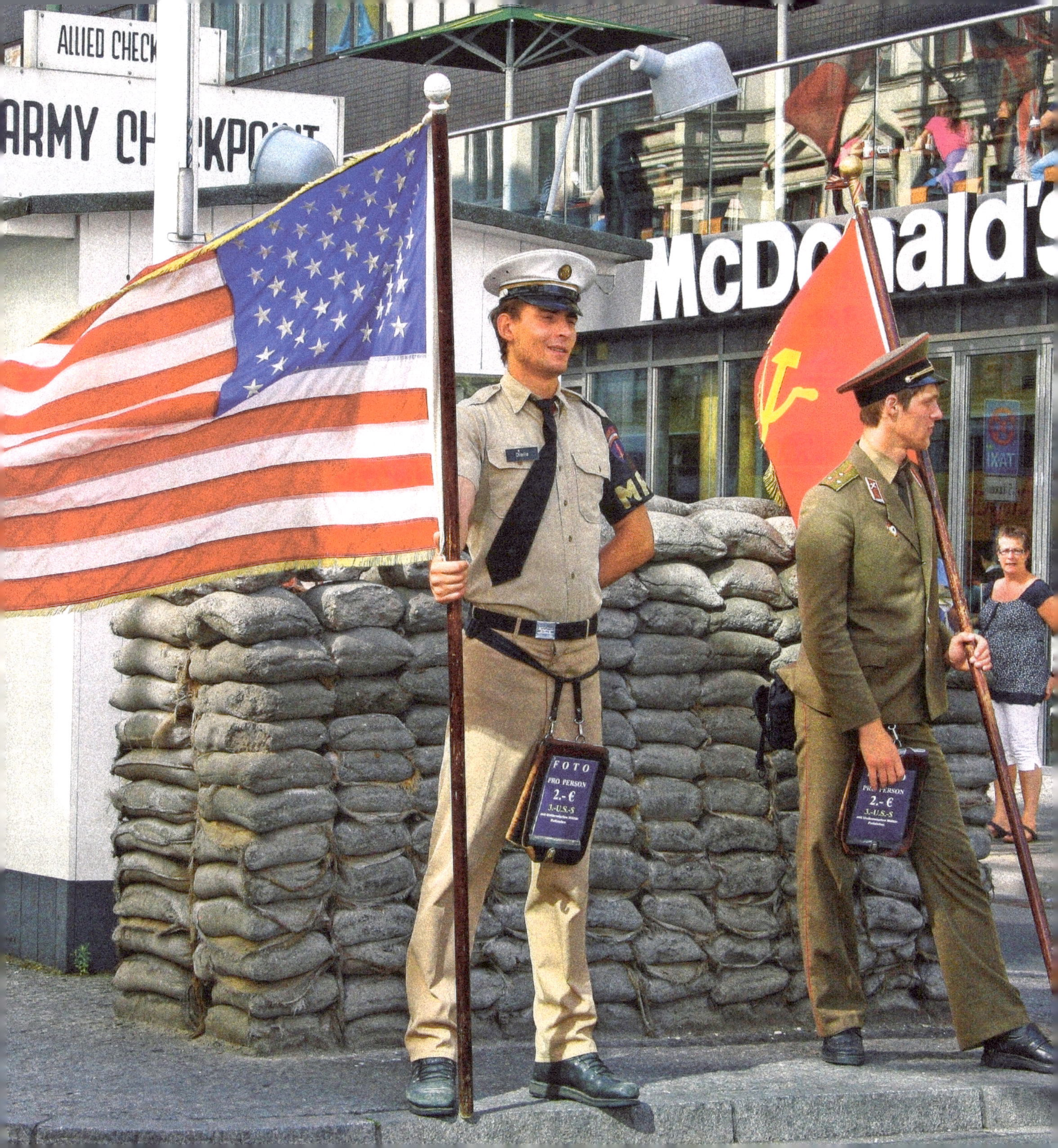

ALLIED CHECK
ARMY CHECKPOINT
McDonald's
FOTO
PRO PERSON
2.- €
3.-U.S.-$
PRO PERSON
2.- €
3.-U.S.-$

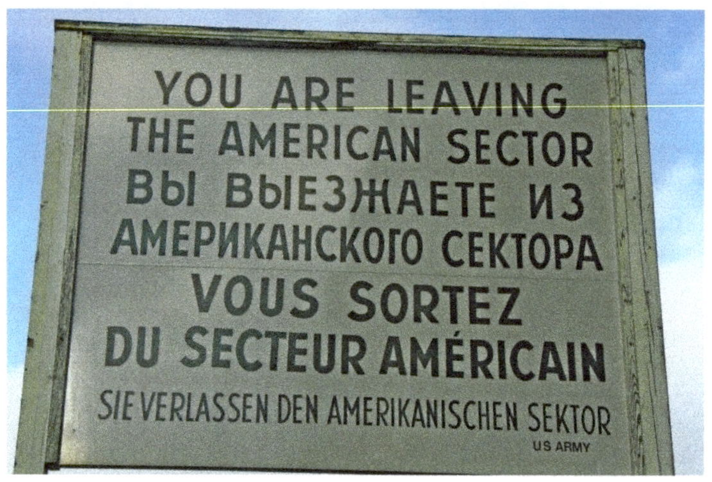

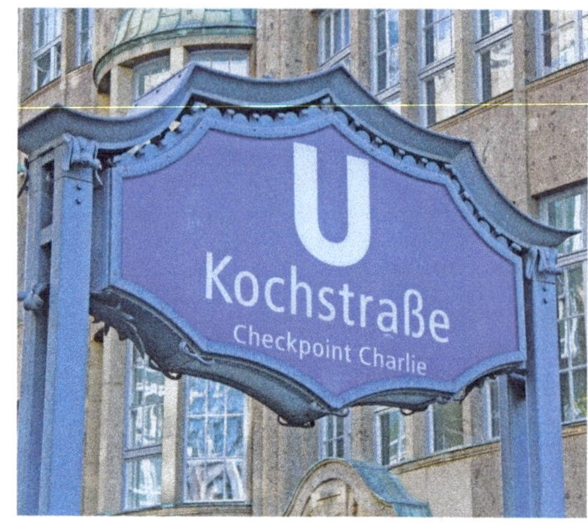

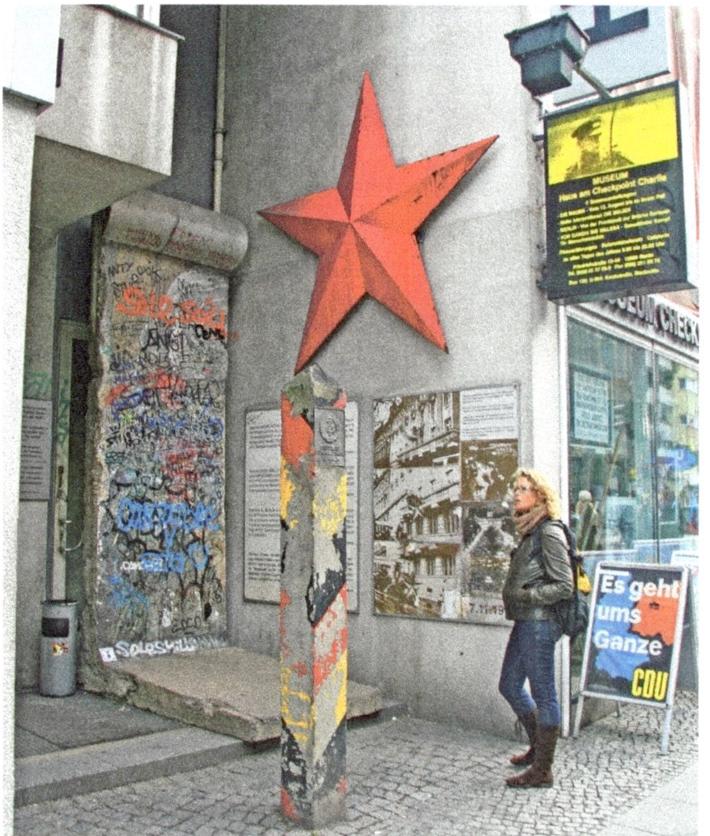

Above: "Checkpoint Charlie" has been added to the name of the subway station.

Left: The Wall Museum is on a corner next to Checkpoint Charlie, at Rudi-Dutschke-Strasse. It features an exhibit about people who tried to flee from the GDR hidden in cars, trucks, trains, and balloons. This slab of the Wall is original but not in its former place.

Zimmerstrasse, running east from Checkpoint Charlie, was the scene of a tragedy that occurred in August 1962: Peter Fechter, an eighteen-year-old bricklayer, wanted to escape, together with his friend Helmut Kulbeik. They tried to climb over the Wall. Kulbeik made it, but Fechter was shot by three border guards. He fell inside the "death strip," wounded and bleeding, and couldn't get up. He screamed, but neither the East border guards, the West Berlin police, nor the American GIs, who were following orders to stand down, would do anything—even though a growing crowd of angry Berliners on both sides of the Wall shouted: "Murderers! Murderers!"

After an hour of screaming, Fechter died. The border guards dragged his lifeless body back into the East. Berliners were so mad that they pelted Allied soldiers' cars with stones. Today, a memorial honors Fechter, in the midst of a newly revived Zimmerstrasse.

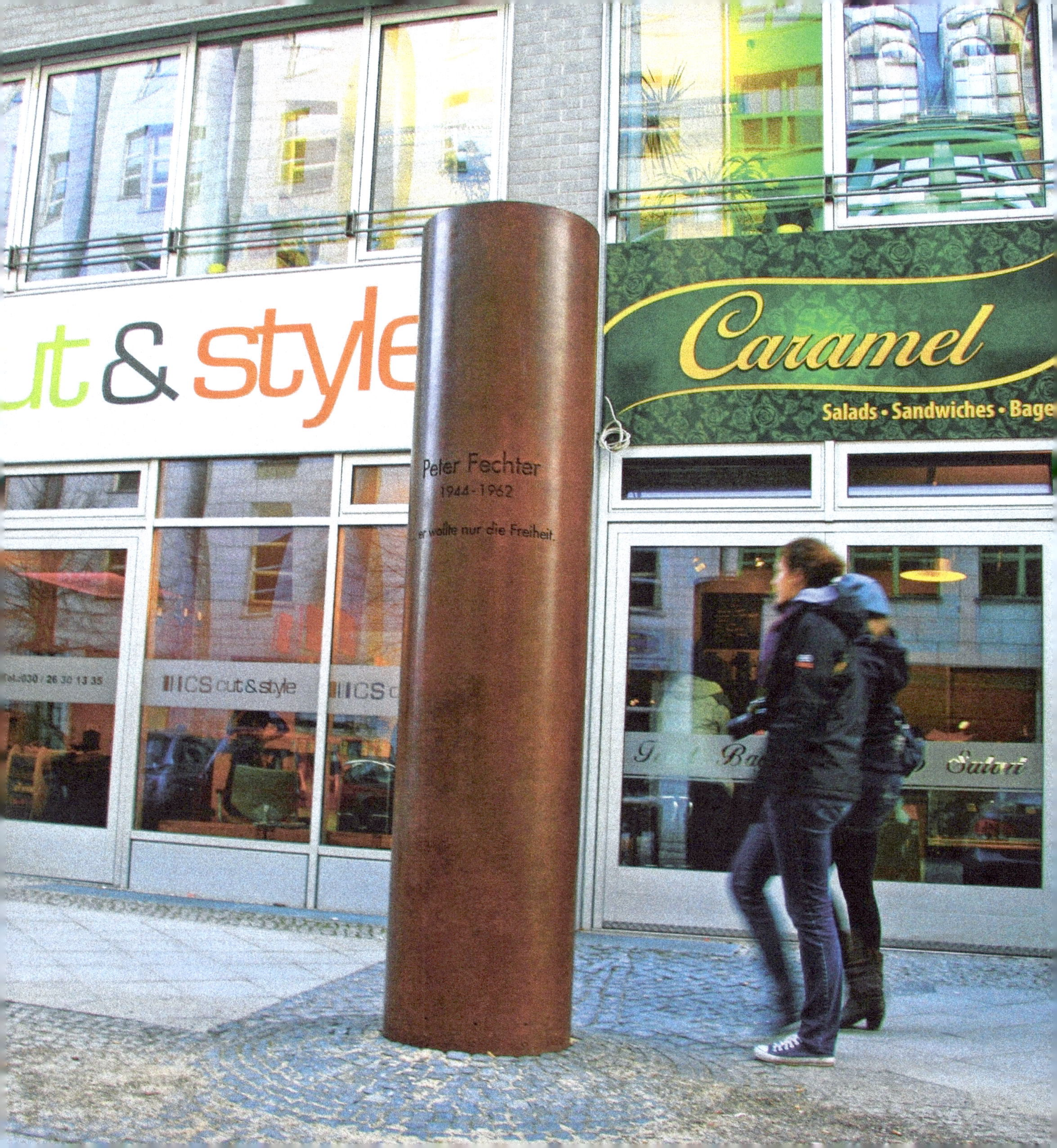
ut & style
Caramel
Salads · Sandwiches · Bage
Peter Fechter
1944 - 1962
er wollte nur die Freiheit.
Tel.030 / 26 30 13 35
IICS cut & style
IICS c

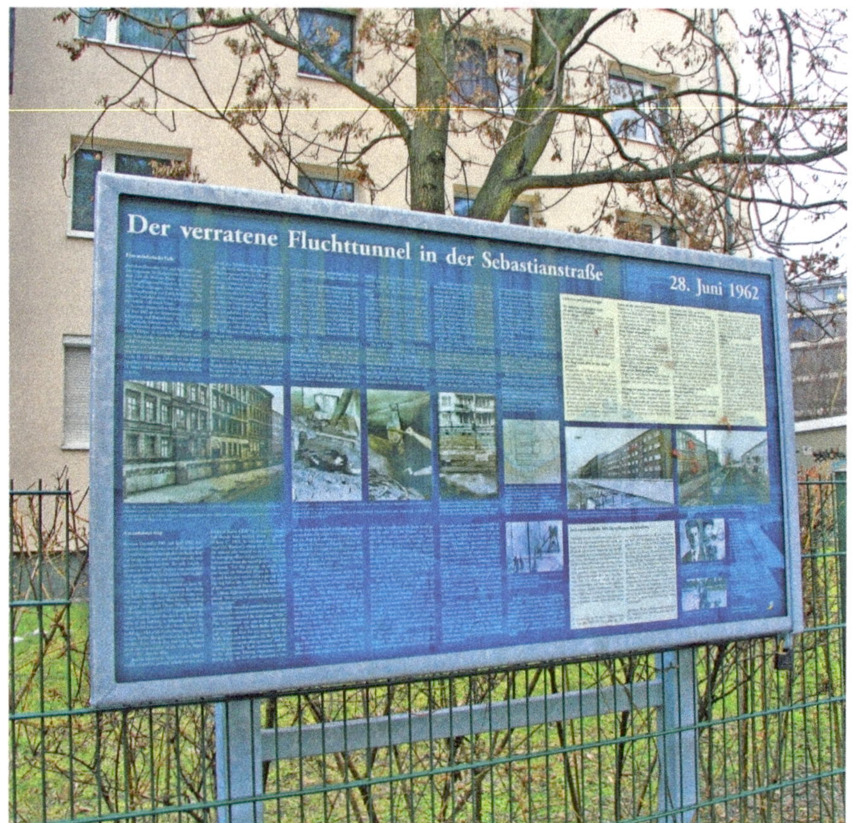

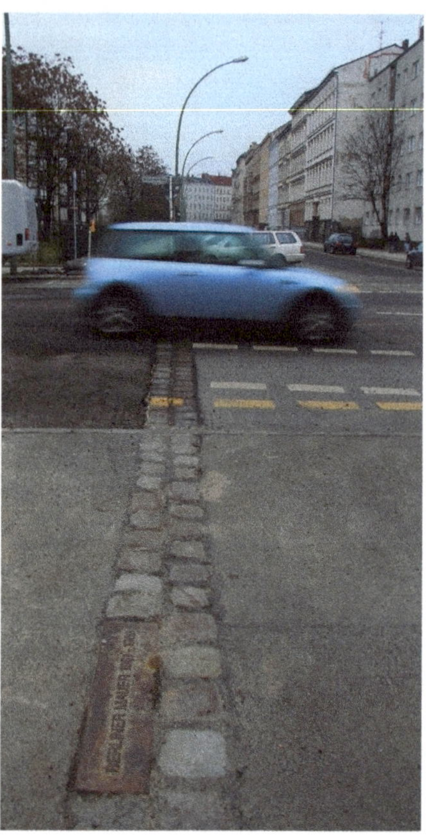

A few hundred yards east of Checkpoint Charlie, at Sebastianstrasse, another tragedy occurred: Siegfried Noffke, a West Berliner who tried to free his wife from the East, was killed. He had met Hannelore in Prenzlauer Berg in the 1950s, but the couple got separated when the Wall was built. Noffke and two friends, who also had girlfriends in the East, dug a tunnel under Sebastianstrasse. The starting point was the basement of a tenement in Kreuzberg, in the western part of the city.

But one of the women they wanted to rescue told her brother about the plan. He was with the *Stasi*. He blew the whistle on the rescue team. When the three men dug their way through to a basement on the eastern side, they were greeted by East soldiers and machine-gun fire. While Noffke's friends survived, he died on the spot. The panel above tells Noffke's story.

Above right: The former border crossing and the Wall trail at Heinrich Heine Strasse, a few hundred yards to the east.

Opposite: The Axel Springer Publishing Company commissioned a piece of art including original slabs of the Wall, though slightly misplaced. The sculpture is called *Border Walker*. Springer, a conservative newspaper company, always insisted that the Wall would fall someday; Springer also has an editorial status of eternal friendship with Israel (and the USA). Oddly enough, Springer built its headquarters in the middle of Jerusalemer Kirchplatz, Jerusalem Church Square, making the square disappear from the city grid forever and blocking a potential Wall opening.

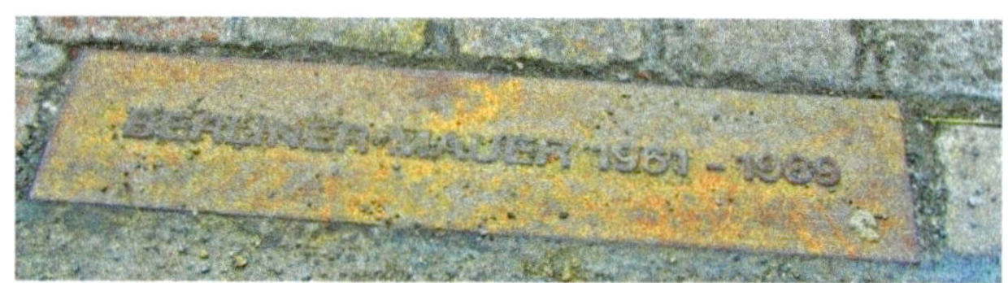

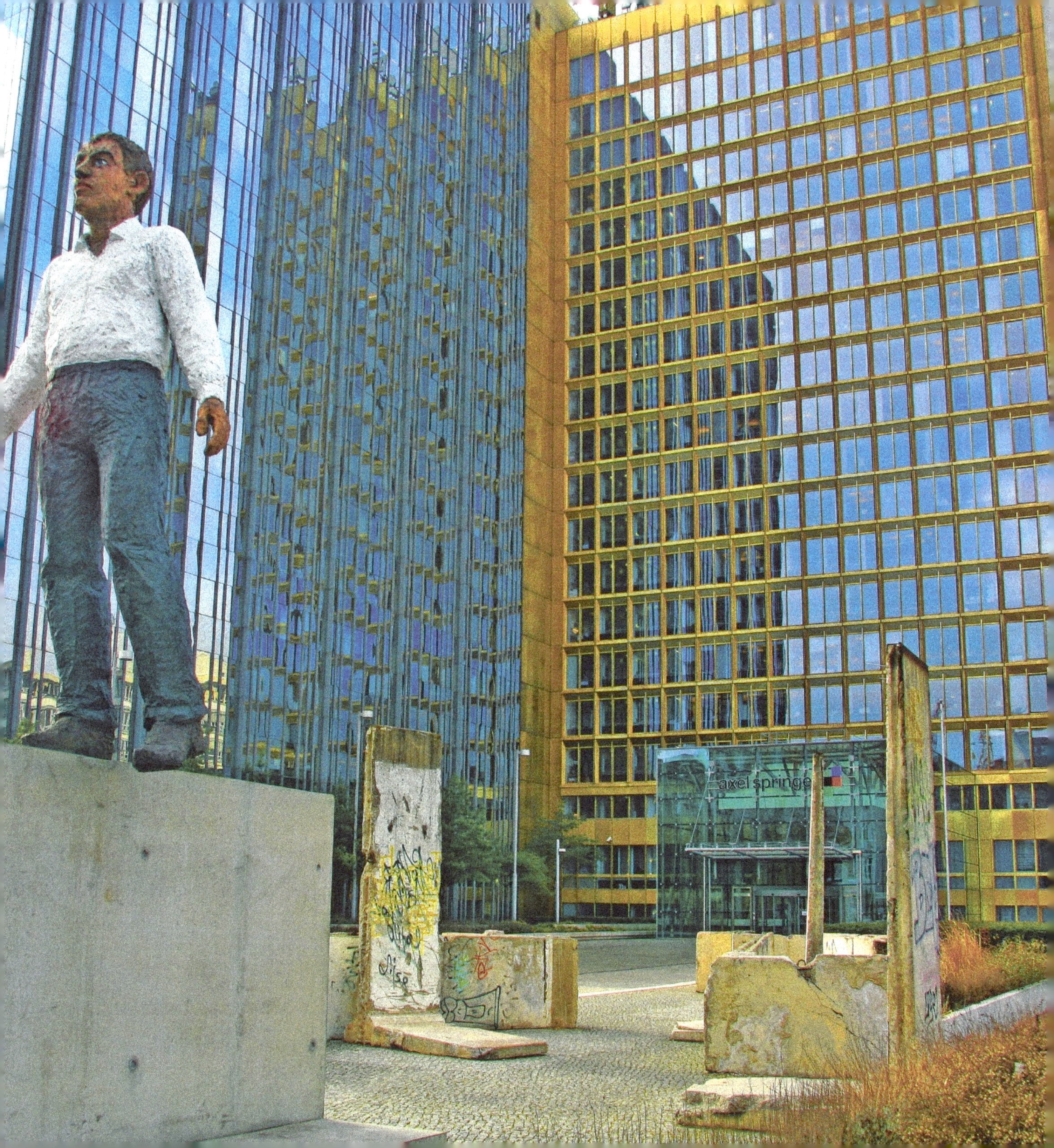

axel springer

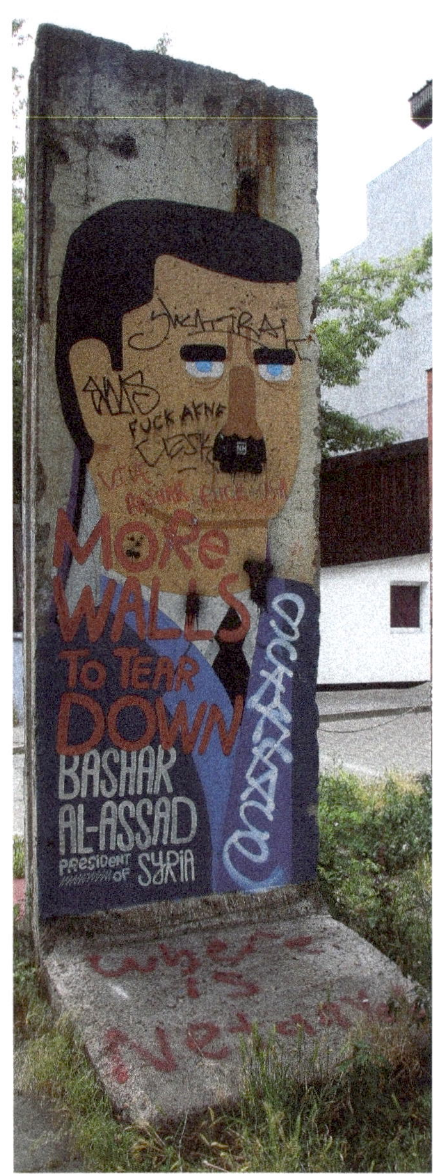

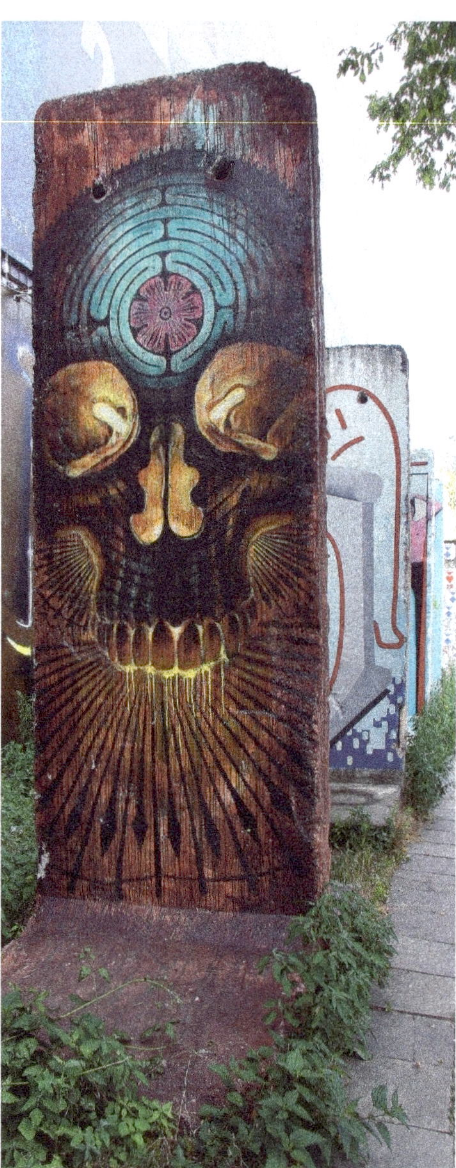

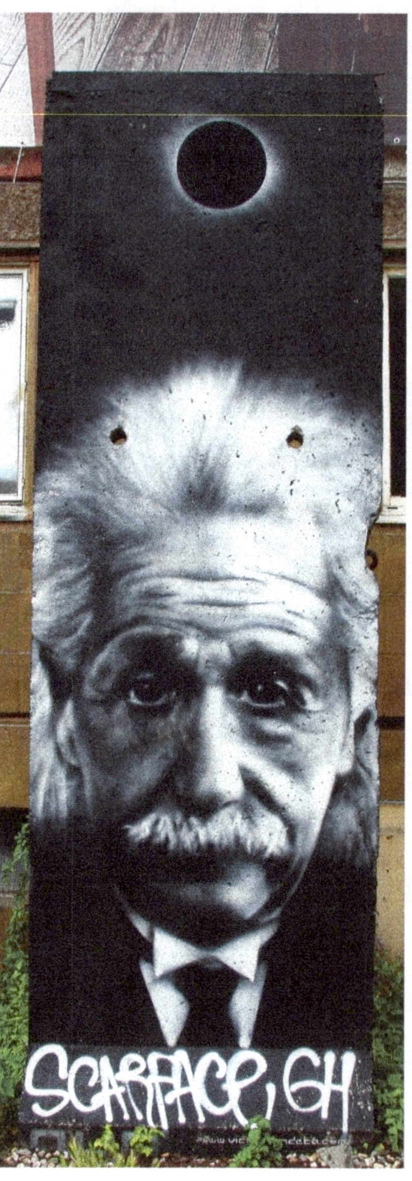

Above: The longer Wall is gone, the more Wall slabs are popping up all over town. Here at Koepenicker Strasse, near the former Heinrich Heine Strasse border crossing, more than a dozen have been put up and painted.

Opposite: Wall slabs at Maerkisches Museum, devoted to Berlin and Brandenburg history and heritage, near the Spree River. The building looks like a medieval castle, but it was built from 1904 to 1908, by city architect Ludwig Hoffmann.

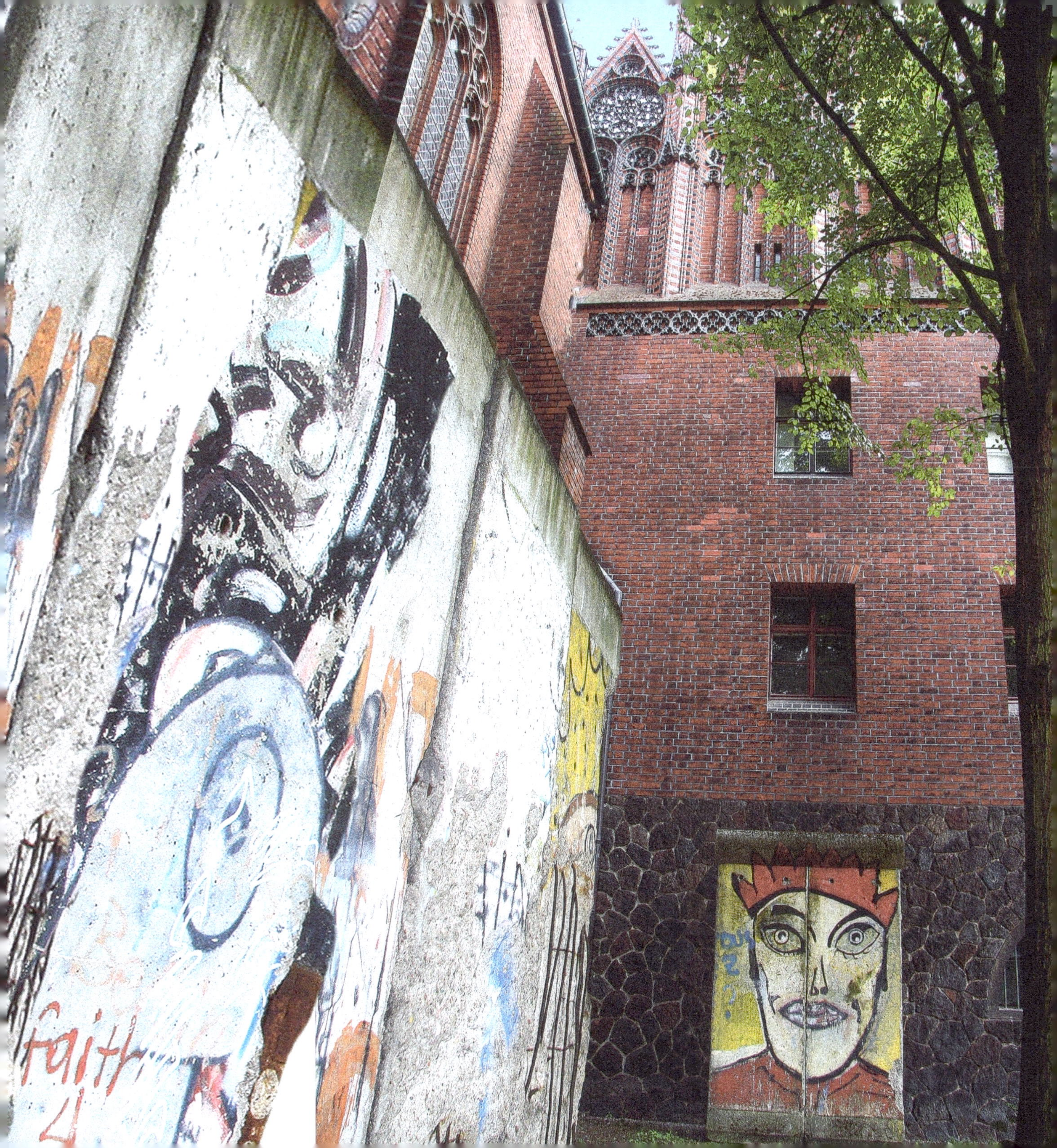

faith

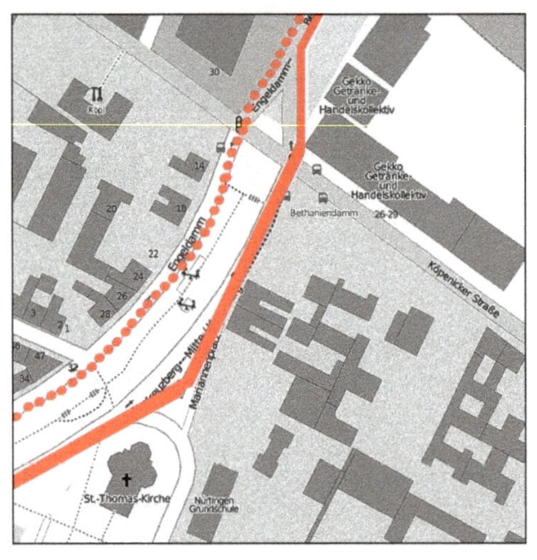

BETHANIENDAMM
THOMASKIRCHE

BETHANIEN BOULEVARD
CHURCH OF ST. THOMAS

Kreuzberg was in the shadow of the Wall for a long time. An alternative lifestyle blossomed here: squatters, artists, musicians, slackers, and draft-dodgers moved in; left-wing political parties such as the Green Party were founded; Turkish families moved into the district abandoned by Berliners who had survived the war, the blockade, and the construction of the Wall. Here, the Wall was covered with graffiti, and East Berlin, the city center, seemed far away.

Today, much of the prewar landscape has been restored. Luisenstädtischer Kanal, a canal from 1852 was turned into a park. Churches like St. Michael and St. Thomas are accessible again. Bethanien, an old hospital occupied by squatters in the 1970s is now the home of Gypsies. The Wall became a green trail between turn-of-the-century houses. And the city center is very close to Kreuzberg now.

Opposite: St. Thomas at Bethaniendamm used to be the largest church in Berlin, with three thousand seats and fifteen thousand members. The community was slashed by the Wall and still numbers only two thousand. In the foreground is an information kiosk for the Berlin Wall Trail. The Wall was where the car is now.

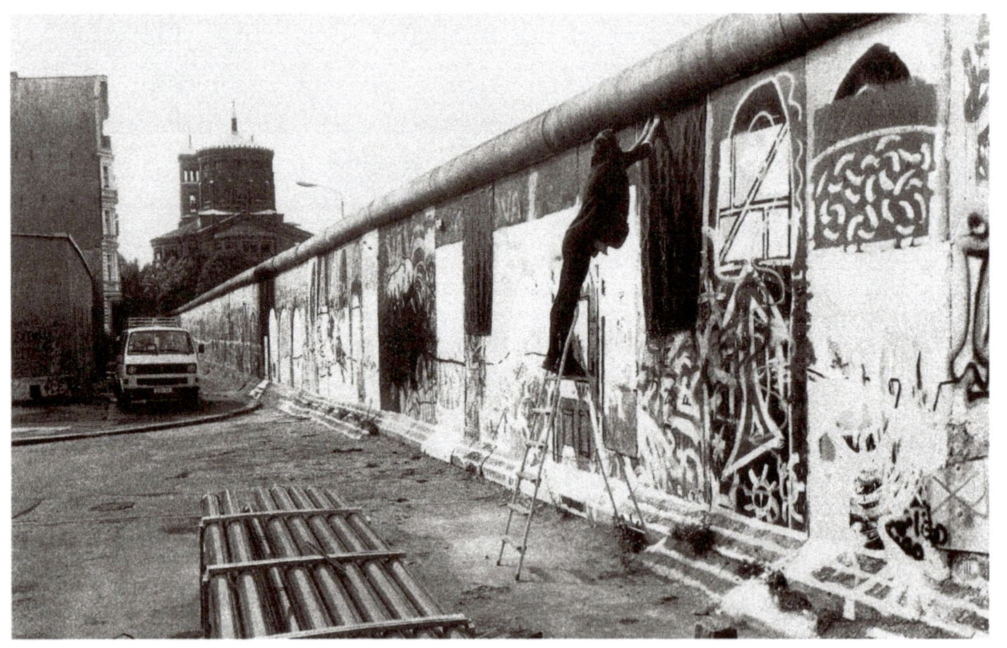

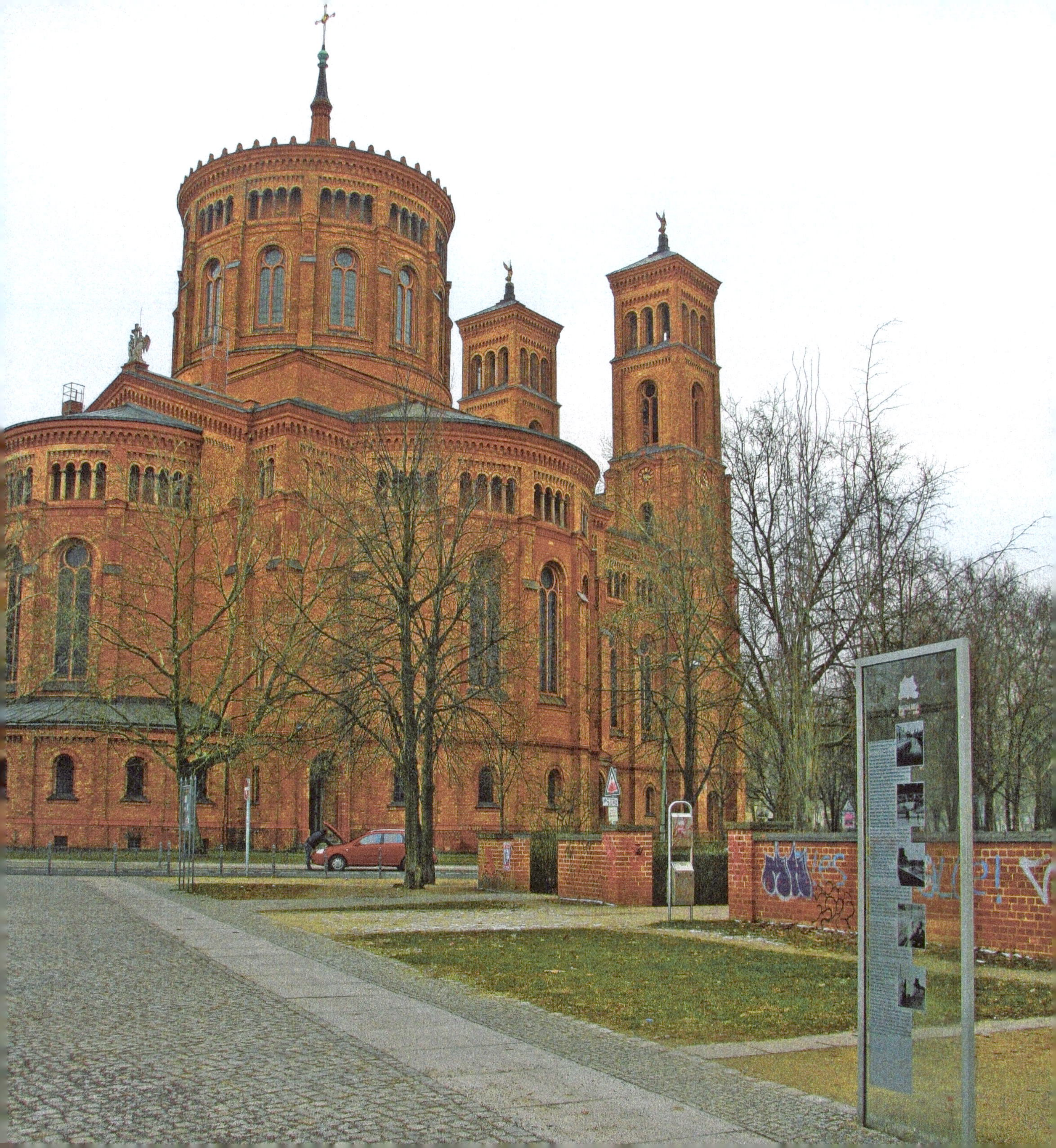

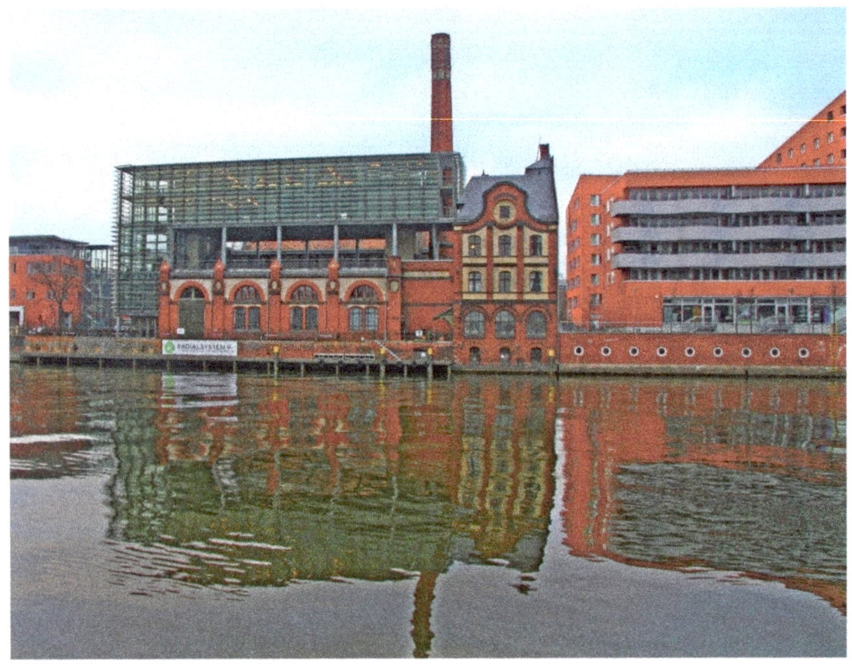

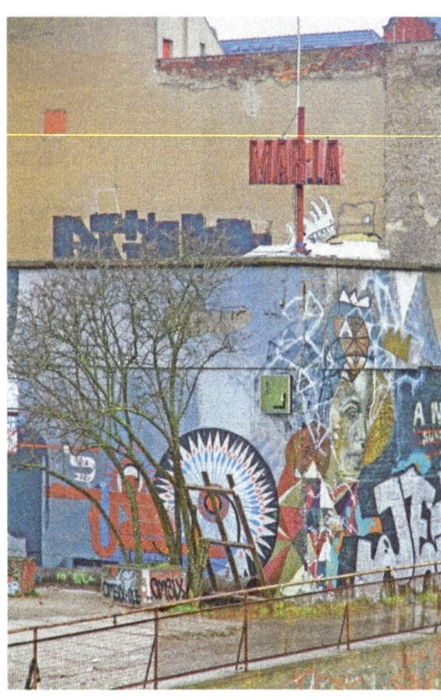

Above: Radialsystem and Maria am Ostbahnhof, two cutting-edge clubs in turn-of-the-century lofts on the Spree River.
Below: The Baumhaus an der Mauer—Wall Tree House—in front of St. Thomas, built by Osman Kalin, a Turkish immigrant, before the Wall fell and on GDR territory.

Opposite: This former 1896 ice factory at the end of Bethaniendamm, near Schillingbrücke, is still guarded by the Hinterland Wall. After the Wall fell, the building was sold. Despite its landmark status and community resistance (like that pictured below), parts of it have been torn down.

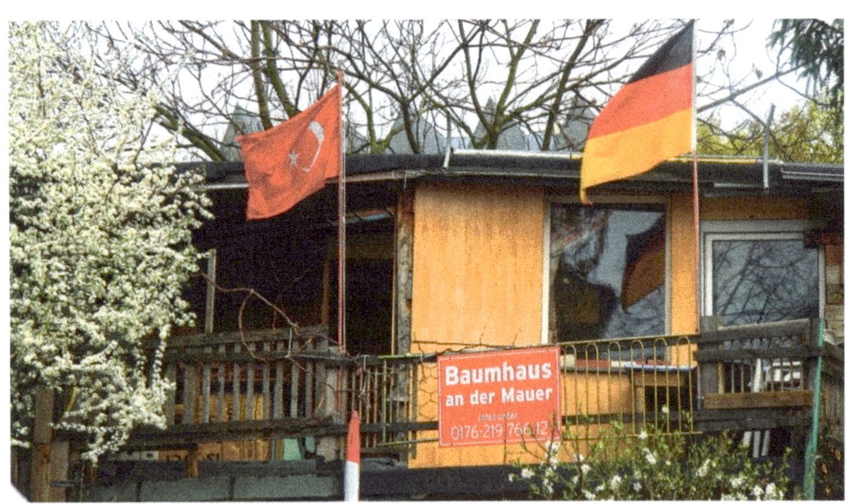

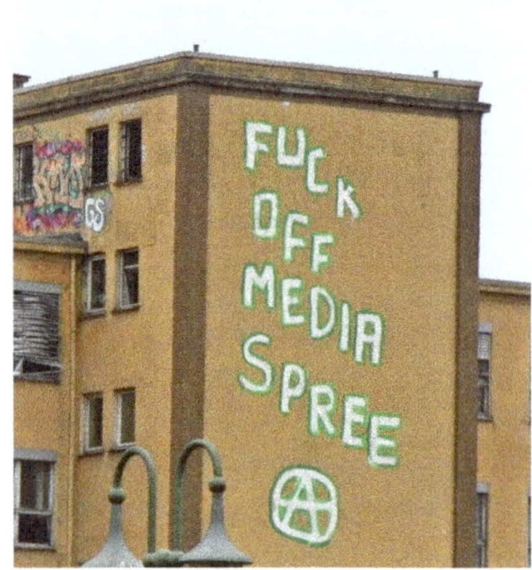

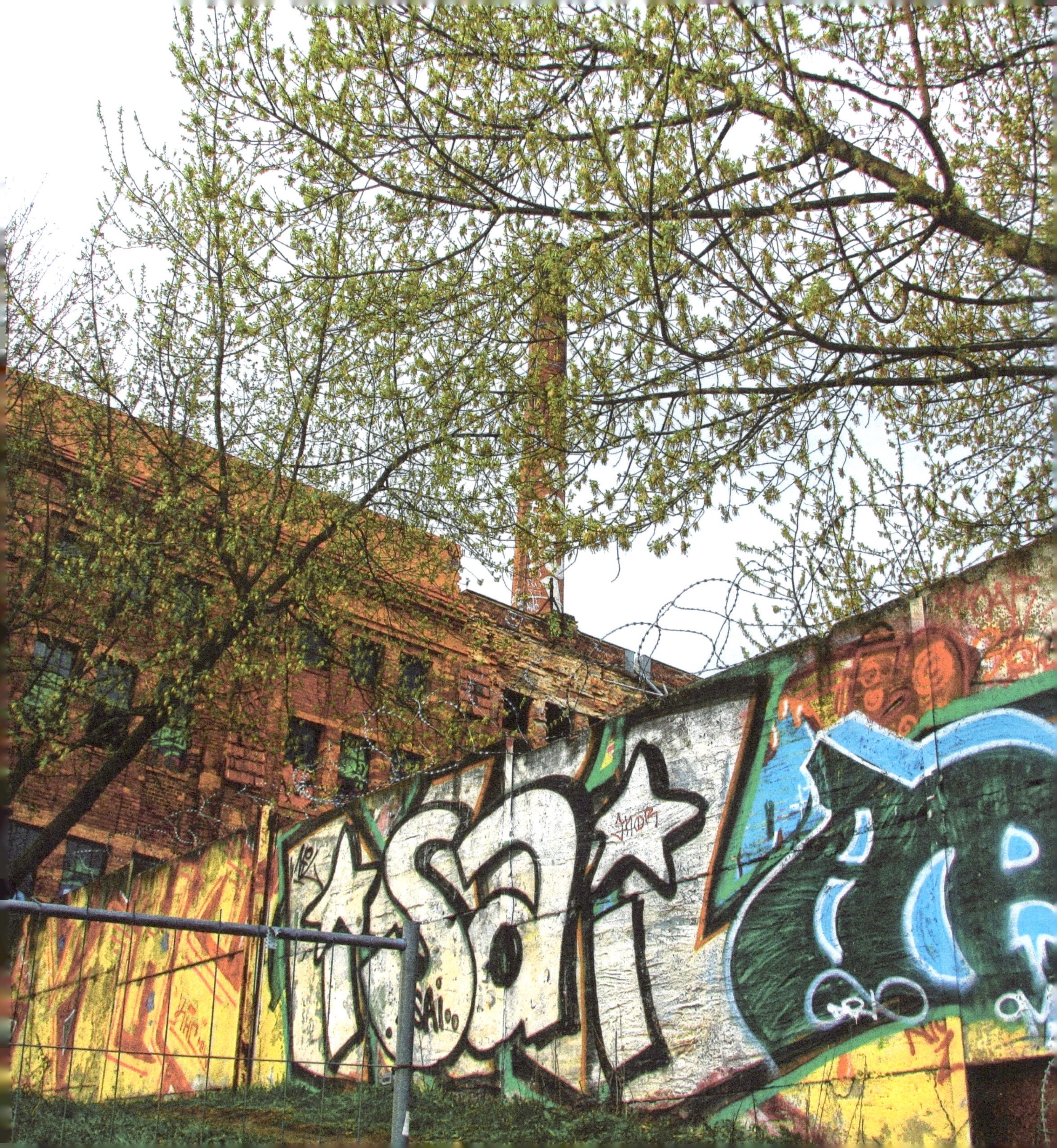

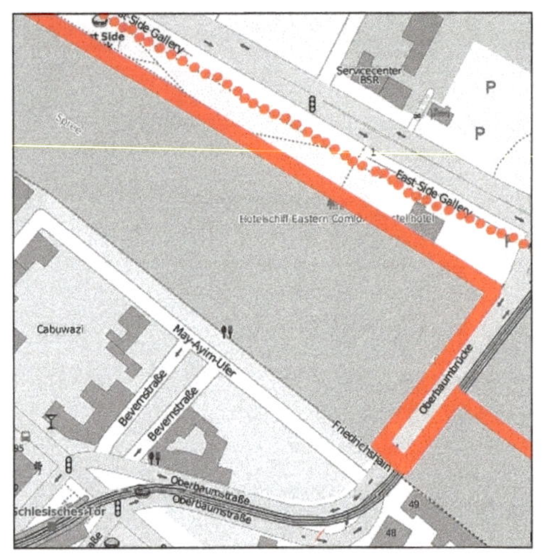

OBERBAUMBRÜCKE
EAST SIDE GALLERY

OBERBAUM BRIDGE
EAST SIDE GALLERY

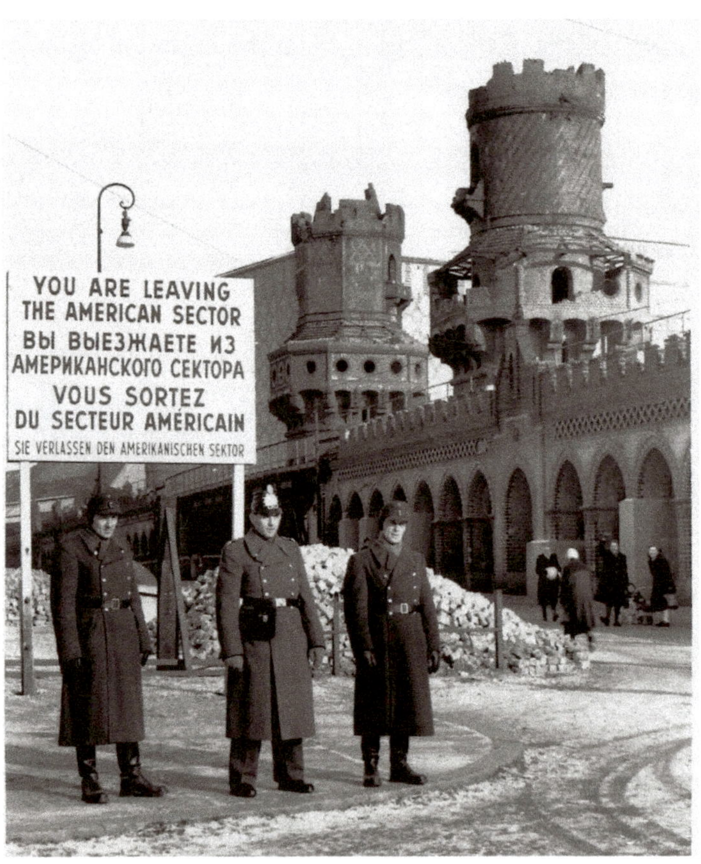

Beginning in 1963, Oberbaumbrücke was the checkpoint for West Berliners (during the two years before that, West Berliners could not go into the East at all). When it opened in 1896, the red-brick edifice was the most beautiful bridge in Berlin, connecting Friedrichshain (East) and Kreuzberg (West). The name came from the 18th century, when an iron-clad pole, *Baum*, closed off the Spree to make sure ships paid customs.

During World War II, the towers were damaged. The bridge was not renovated until 1995, in a multi-million-dollar effort involving architect Santiago Calatrava. A Berlin Bear and a Brandenburg Eagle are emblazoned in copper on top of each tower. The subway that had ended at Schlesisches Tor was refurbished, including Warschauer Brücke (Warsaw Bridge) Station, while another station, Strahlauer Tor (Strahlau Gate), was abandoned. Light-rail tracks were also installed, though the light-rail train itself doesn't cross the bridge yet.

The bridge is also known from the Tom Tykwer movie *Run Lola Run*. Every summer, Kreuzbergers and Friedrichshainers meet on the bridge for a "battle," in which they pelt each other with rotten vegetables. However, the two districts have now been united, the only district in Berlin that is half East and half West. At Oberbaum Bridge, the famous East Side Gallery begins, which runs all the way to Ostbahnhof (East Station), formerly Schlesischer Bahnhof (Silesian Station).

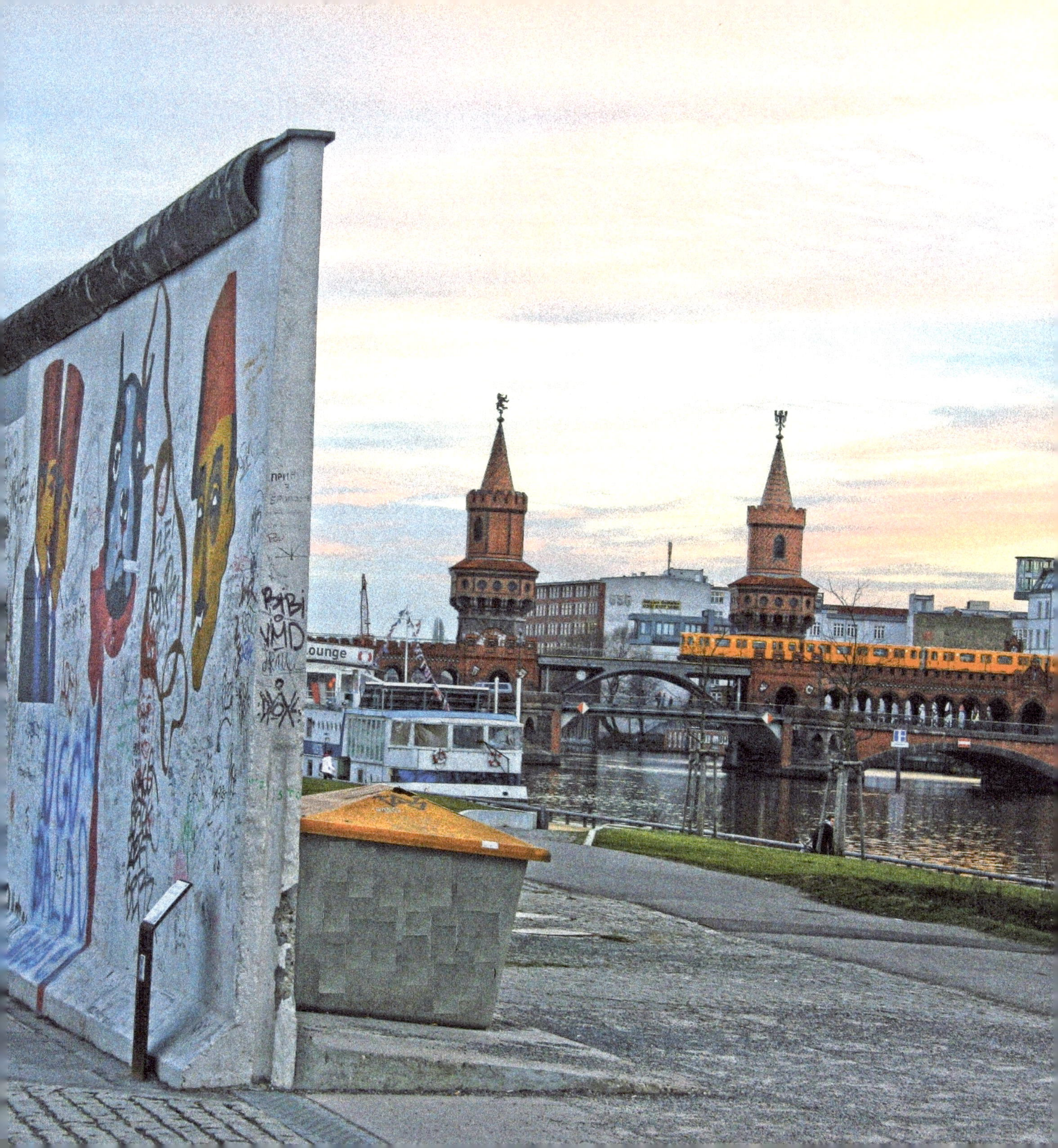

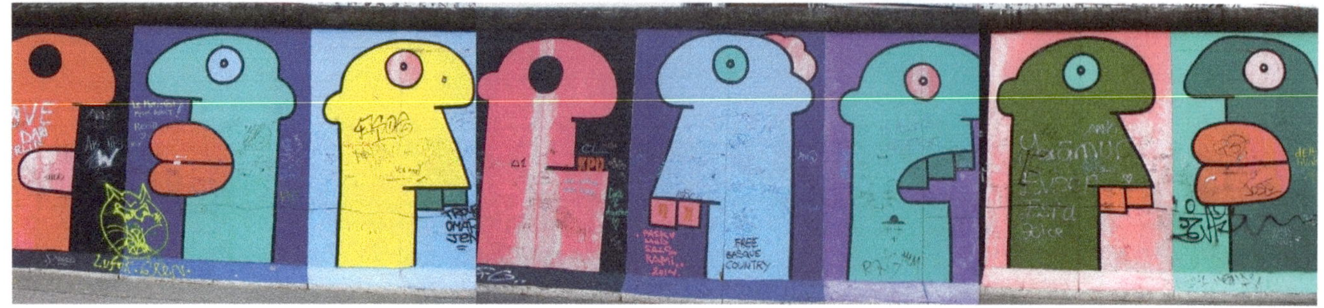

Nearly one mile long, the East Side Gallery is the longest remaining piece of the Wall, albeit only the Hinterland Wall. It runs along the Spree River, which formerly marked the East-West border along the district of Friedrichshain. Only weeks after the Wall came down—with the GDR still in existence—artists from the East and the West decided to paint it. 118 artists were invited.

By 2008, most of their works were weather-worn and damaged by graffiti, so the gallery was renovated at a cost of one million euros. Today, these paintings still attract tens of thousands of tourists every month. The graffiti has returned, however—as one can see above on Thierry Noir's colorful faces, among other places.

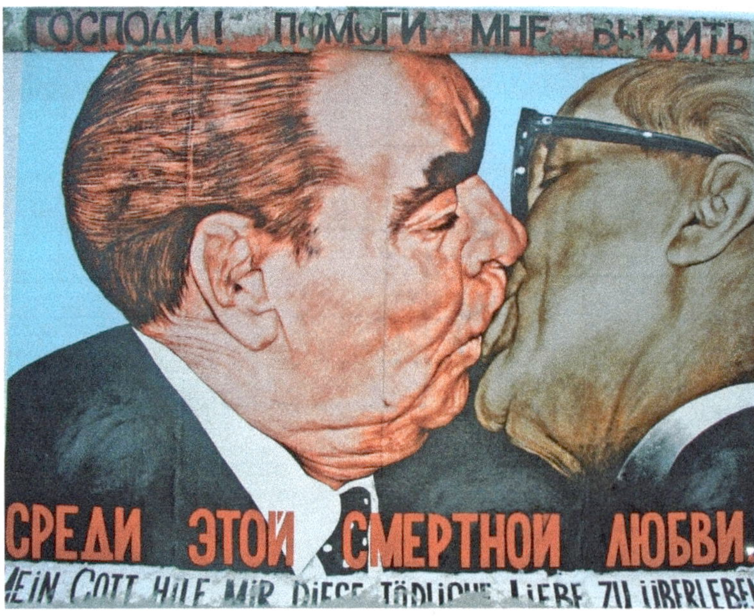

Opposite: Birgit Kinder created this world-famous image of a GDR Trabi breaking through the Wall.

Left: Dimitrj Vrubel painted this kissing couple: Leonid Brezhnev, who was General Secretary of the Central Committee of the Communist Party of the Soviet Union, and Erich Honecker, his East German counterpart.

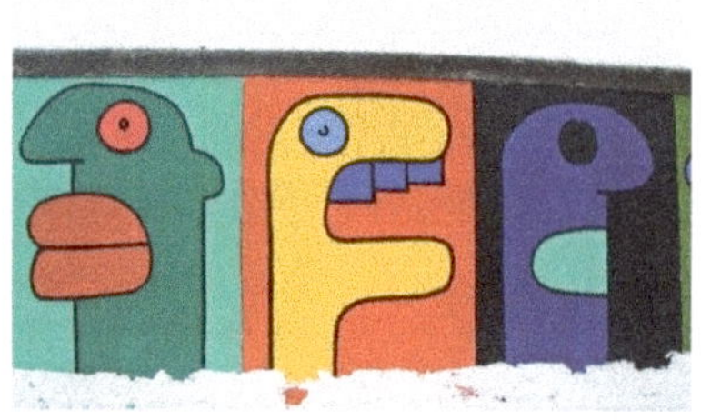

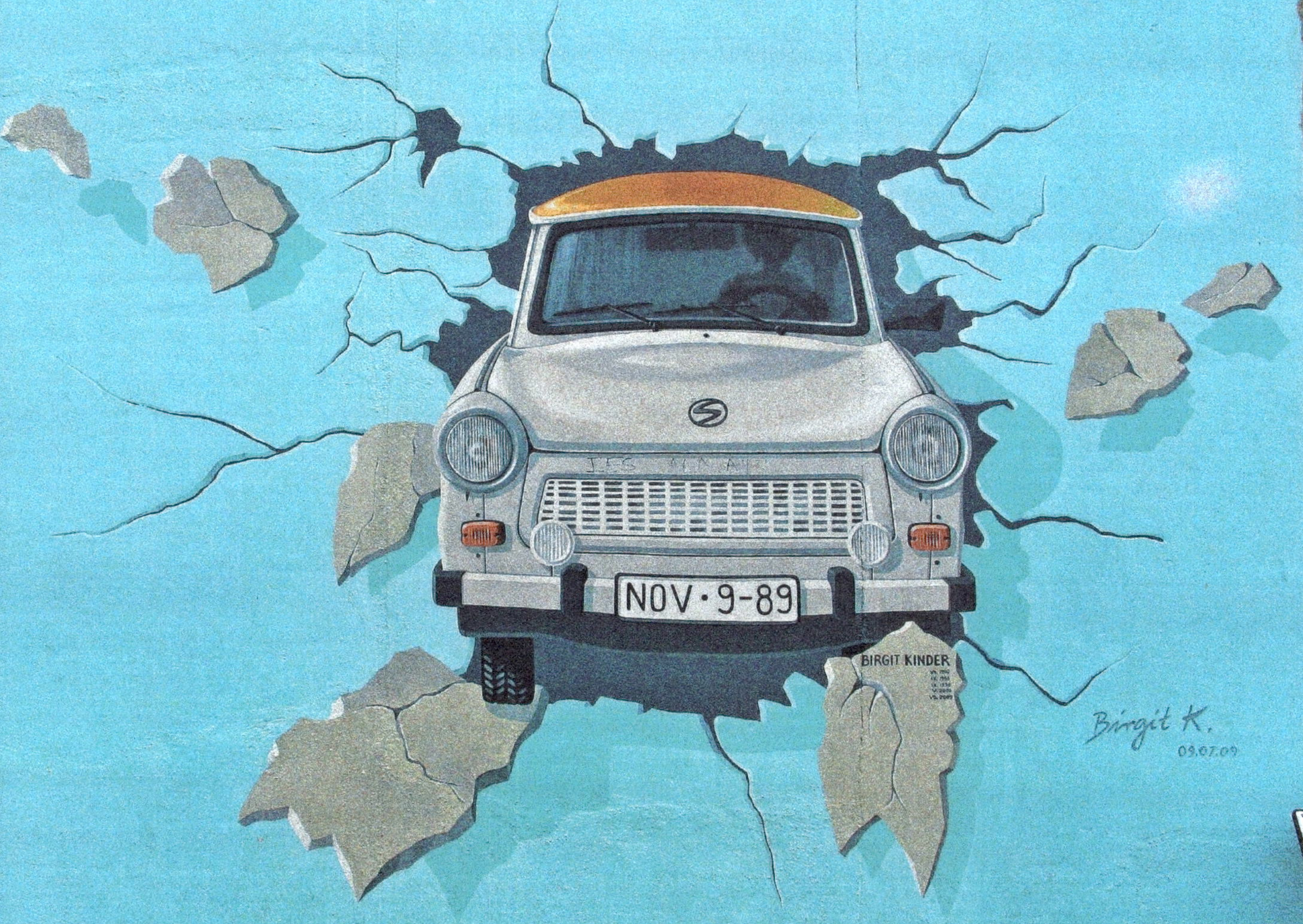

TEST THE REST
NOV·9-89
BIRGIT KINDER
Birgit K.
09.07.09
ww.wandmalerei-berlin.de

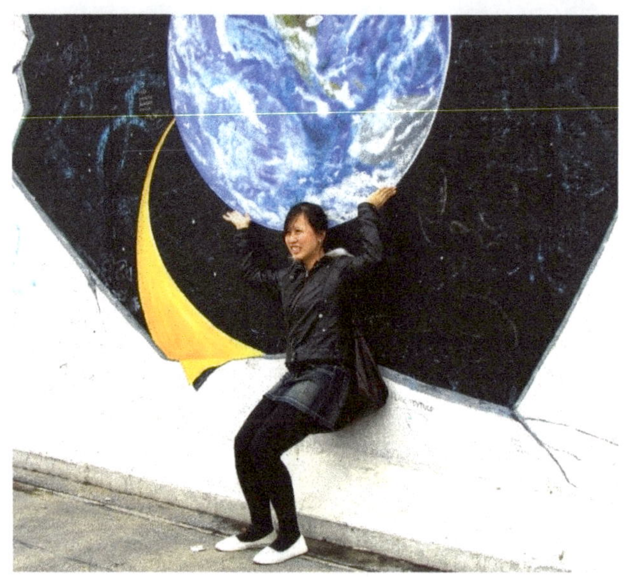

Opposite: This painting by Kani Alavi symbolizes the day in November 1989, when the Wall fell and thousands of people poured into the streets.

Right: This girl is visiting the East Side Gallery from overseas —one of many.

Below: Gerhard Lahr's iconic painting dubbed New York - Berlin - Tokyo.

Next page: Schamil Gimajew's painting, "World's People, wir sind ein Volk," (we are one people), now has a door with love locks attached to it.

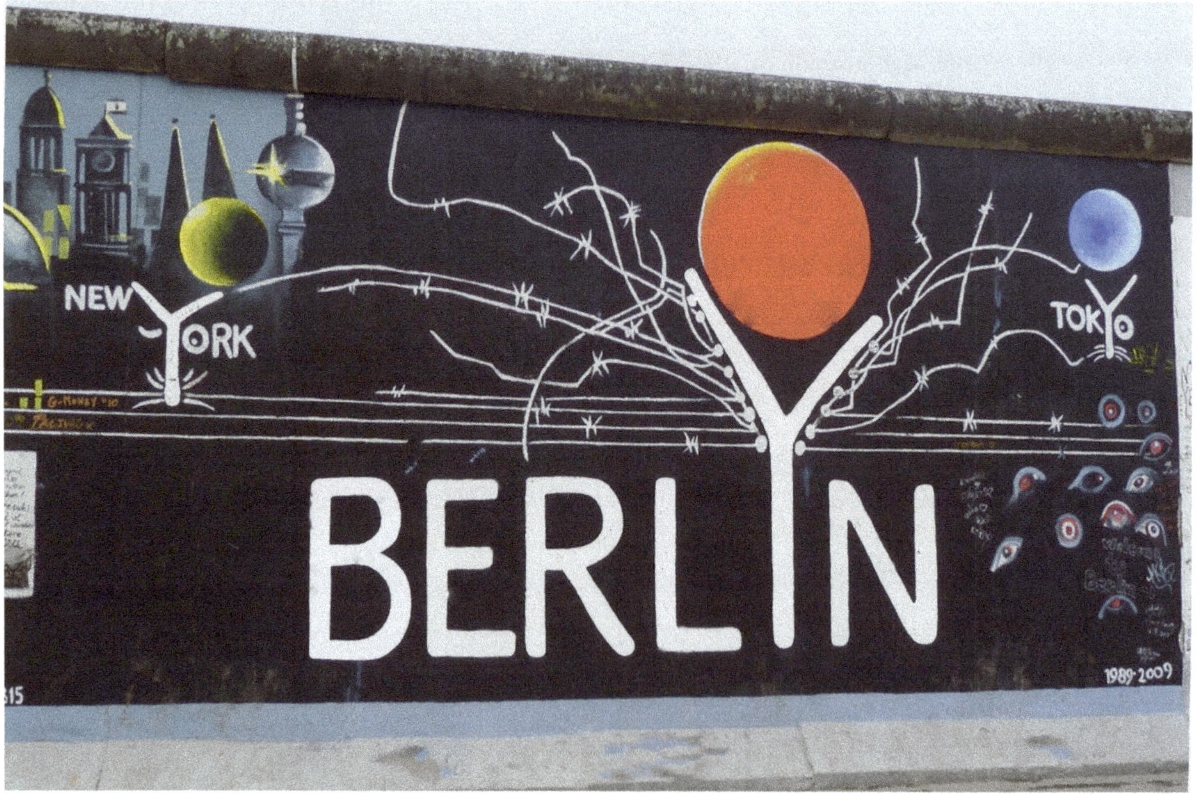

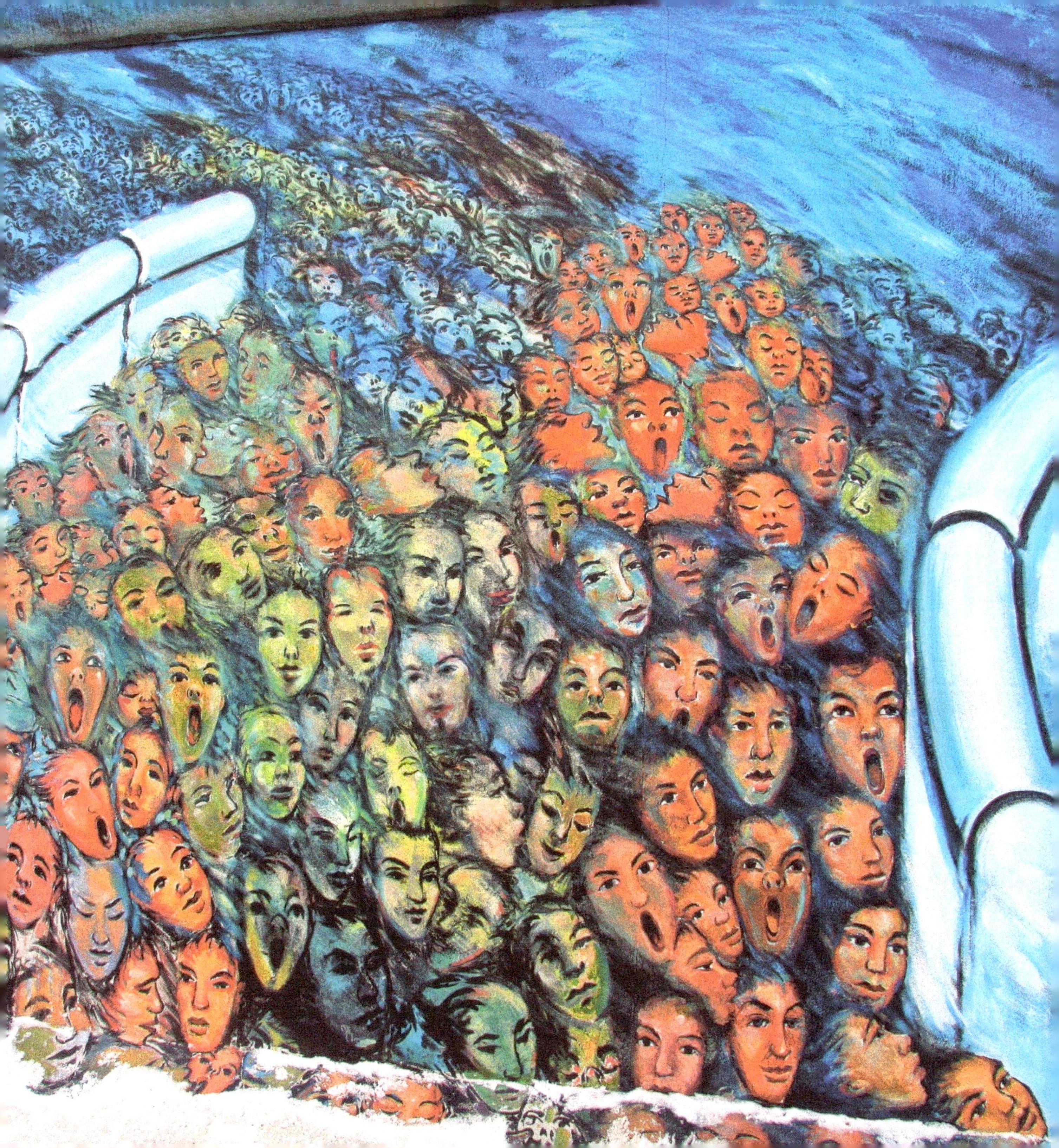

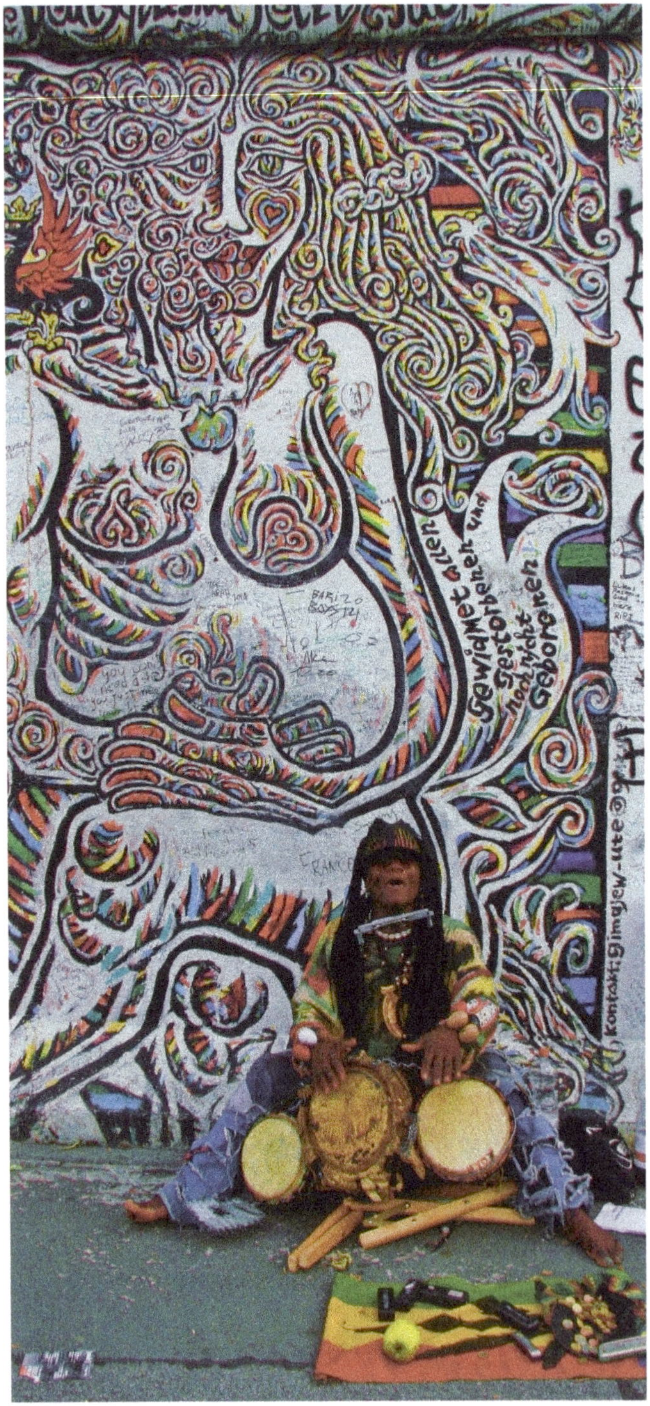

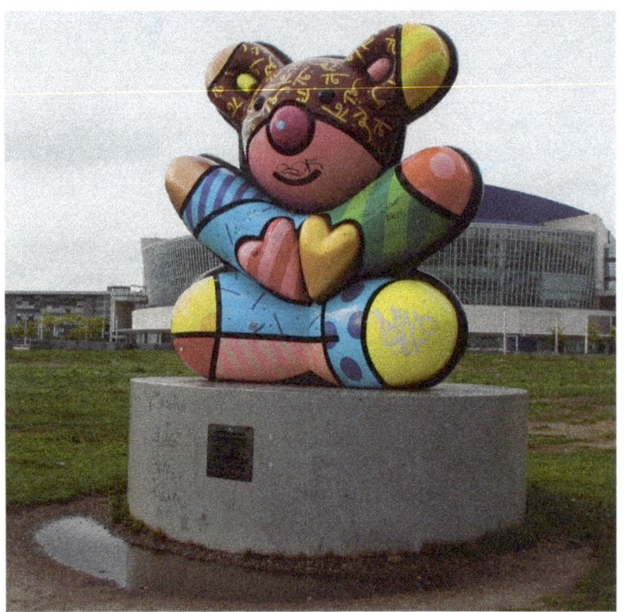

Above: A version of the Berlin bear, right in front of the O2 sports arena across the street from the East Side Gallery.

Left: Schamil Gimajew's painting "Wir sind ein Volk".

Below: This side street is named after Tamara Danz, a famous rock singer in the GDR, who died of cancer in 1996.

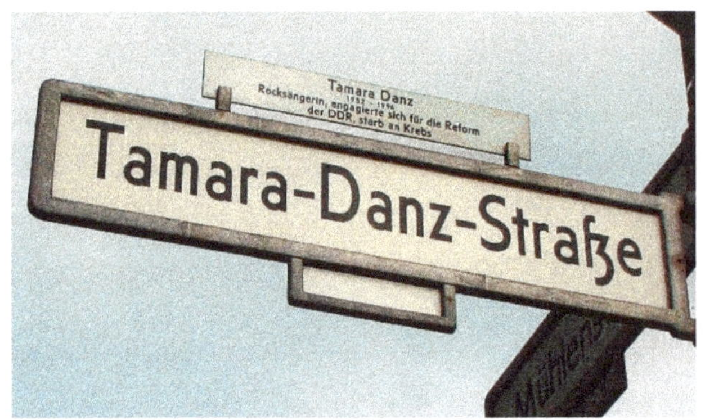

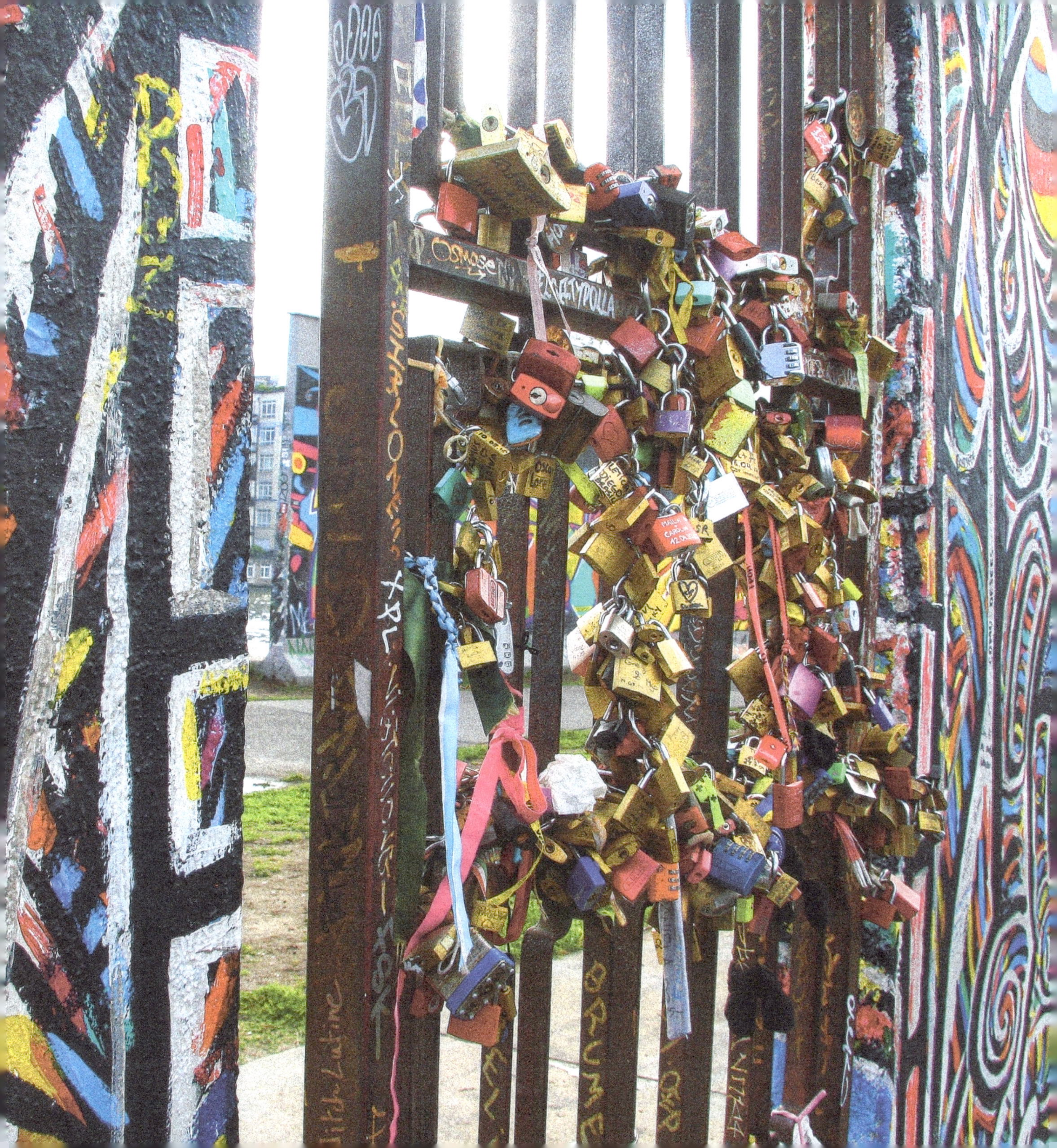

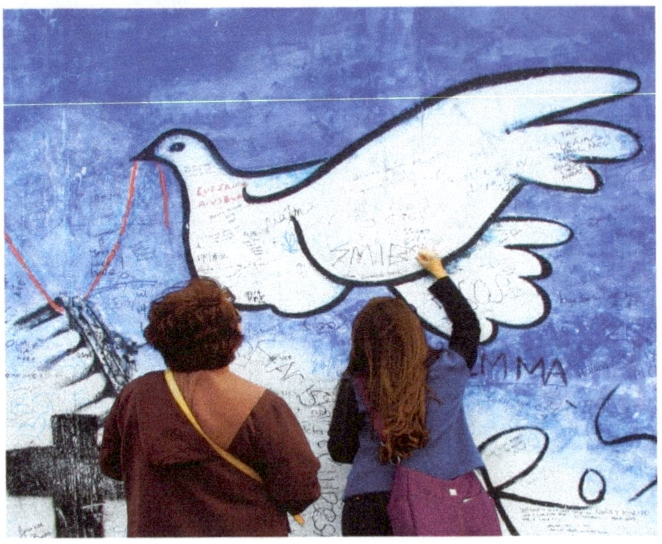

Above: Rosemarie Schinzler's doves of peace bearing the Brandenburg Gate, the symbol of the city. Some tourists cannot resist scribbling all over it.

Below: This picture by Dieter Wien at the East Side Gallery is called „Morning.".

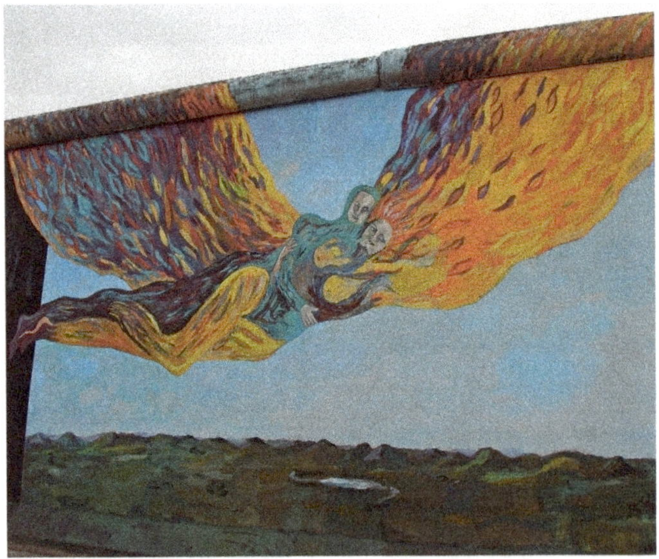

Opposite page: Karina Bjerregaard's and Lotte Haubart's artwork *Himlen over Berlin*.

Below: Zwingli Church in Friedrichshain, at the S- and U-Bahn Station Warschauer Strasse south of Oberbaum Bridge. Today, the church is a museum. The Wall slabs in front of the church have been placed there by the district of Kreuzberg-Friedrichshain.

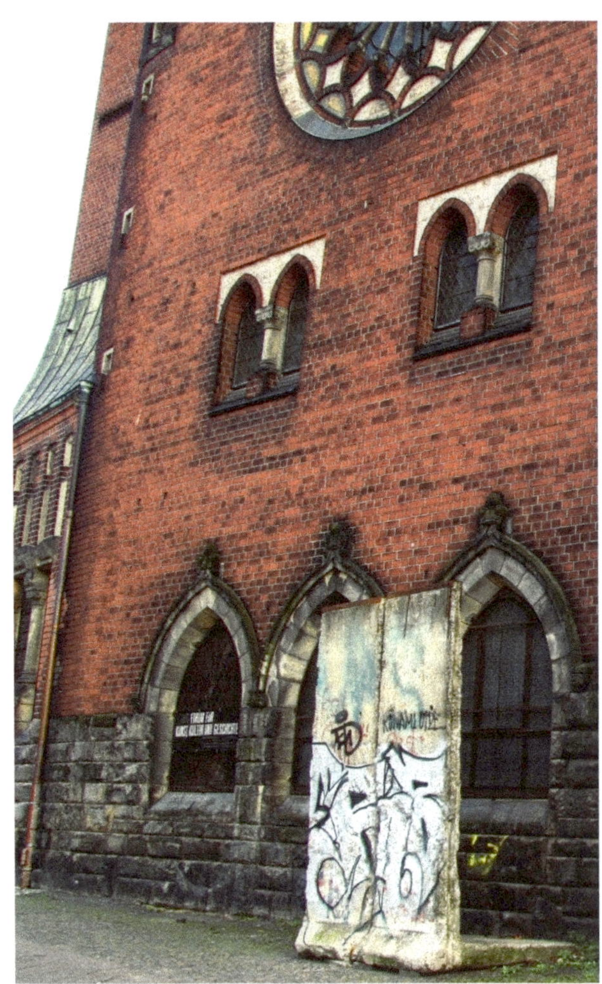

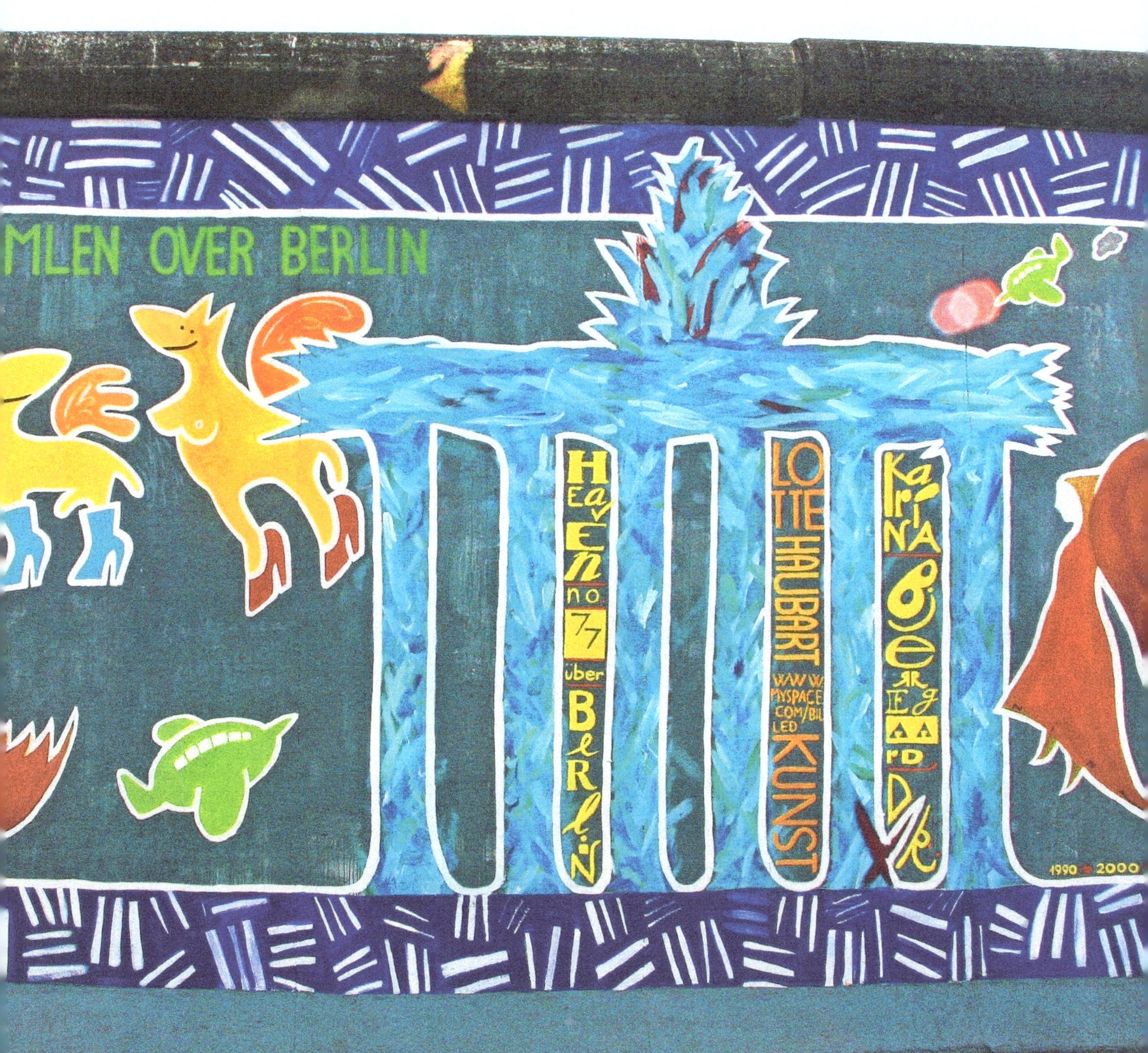
MLEN OVER BERLIN
HeaVEn no 77 über BerliN
LOTTE HAUBART www MYSPACE COM/BILLED KUNST
KarINA Berg D.R.
1990 2000

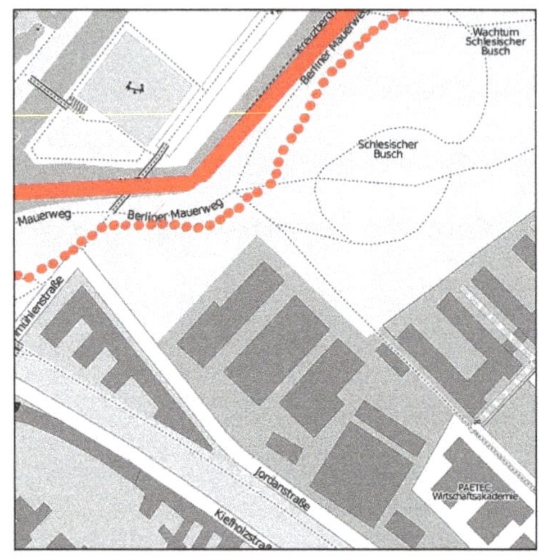

WACHTURM
HARZER STRASSE

GUARD TOWER
HARZER STREET

The Wall ran along the Landwehrkanal, a canal, down to Treptow and the Schlesischer Busch, formerly a forest, now a park. The name recalls the tens of thousands of workers from Silesia who moved into Berlin in the 1900s. The Landwehrkanal is infamous for a historic incident: on January 15, 1919, two people were murdered by the right-wing paramilitary *Freikorps*: the German Marxist Karl Liebknecht, and Rosa Luxemburg, a Polish-Jewish activist, the founders of the *Spartakusbund* and its successor, the German Communist Party. Luxemburg's body was dumped into the canal. An uprising as well as a nationwide strike following the murders were crushed by soldiers and the *Freikorps*; thousands of Communists and Socialists were killed.

The Wall continued along Heidelberger Strasse, Harzer Strasse and Kiefholzstrasse. Here, two children were killed in 1966 by GDR border guards with machine guns: ten-year-old Jörg Hartmann and thirteen-year-old Lothar Schleusener. One of the guards was finally sentenced in 1997, but to only twenty months of probation (the other one had died by then).

Opposite: This lot at Harzer Strasse was part of the Wall and thus was disposessed by the GDR. But after the Wall came down, the West German government refused to give the real estate back; so Joachim Hildebrandt, the former owner, is protesting on this sign against the "Wall injustice" perpetuated in the present.

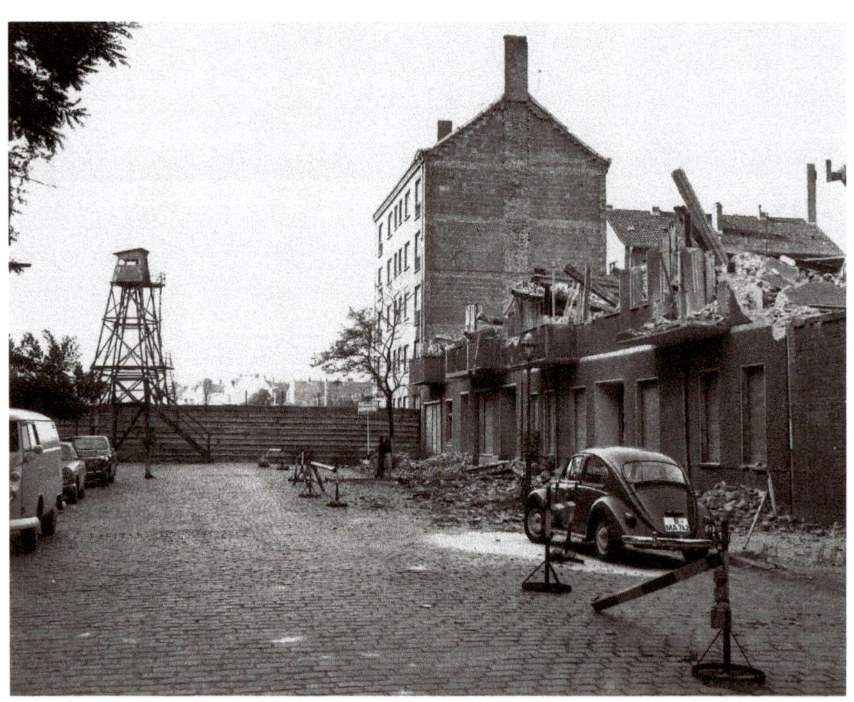

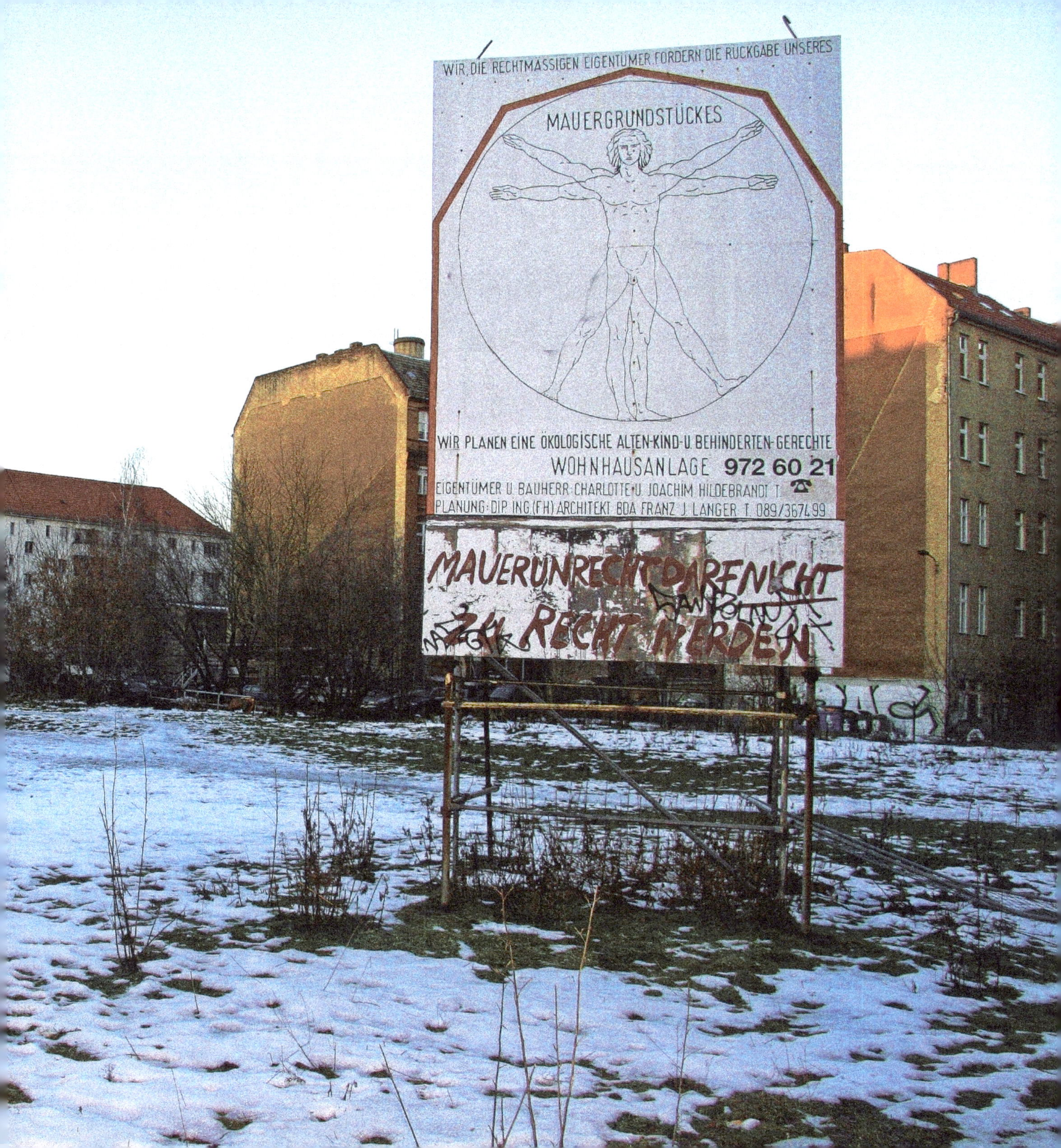

WIR DIE RECHTMÄSSIGEN EIGENTÜMER FORDERN DIE RÜCKGABE UNSERES
MAUERGRUNDSTÜCKES
WIR PLANEN EINE ÖKOLOGISCHE ALTEN-KIND-U BEHINDERTEN-GERECHTE
WOHNHAUSANLAGE 972 60 21
EIGENTÜMER U BAUHERR CHARLOTTE U JOACHIM HILDEBRANDT T
PLANUNG DIP ING (FH) ARCHITEKT BDA FRANZ J LANGER T 089/367499
MAUERUNRECHT DARF NICHT ZU RECHT WERDEN

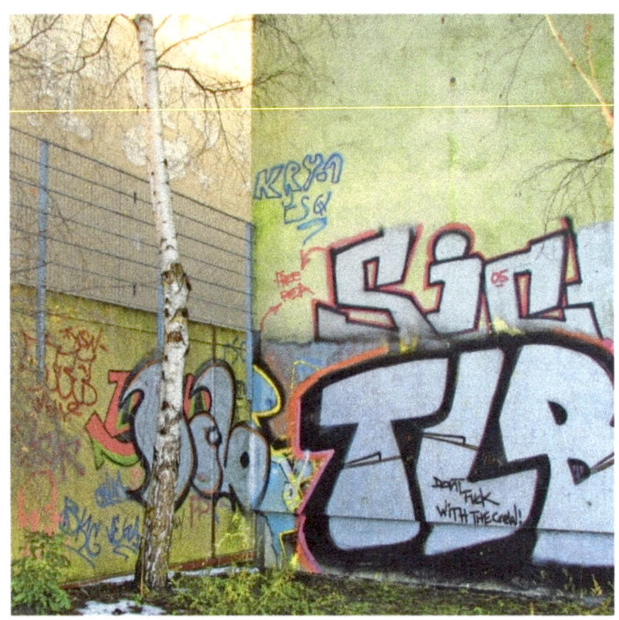

South of Schlesischer Busch, the Wall is gone. At Britzer Verbindungskanal however, a canal for ships between Treptow and Neukölln, one memorial remains. It remembers twenty-year-old Chris Gueffroy, the last Berliner who died at the Wall, in February 1989. Together with a friend, he tried to swim to freedom, but he was killed by ten bullets. He had believed the border guards would no longer shoot at people trying to flee, a fatal mistake. His friend was arrested. His mother was not told what had happened until many days later.

Above: A few parts of the graffiti-covered Hinterland Wall still stand in this schoolyard at Heidelberger Strasse.
Opposite: One of only five remaining guard towers in the park of Schlesischer Busch. In 1990, a group of young artists turned the forty-foot tower into the *Museum der Verbotenen Kunst* (Museum of Forbidden Art), for art that was illegal in the GDR. Today, it features changing exhibits. The tower, accessible during the summer, is landmarked.

Below: These are the photographs of Günter Litfin, Chris Gueffroy, Lothar Schleusener, and Peter Fechter.
Right: The photos of Siegfried Noffke and Ida Siekmann. The photos are from the "Window

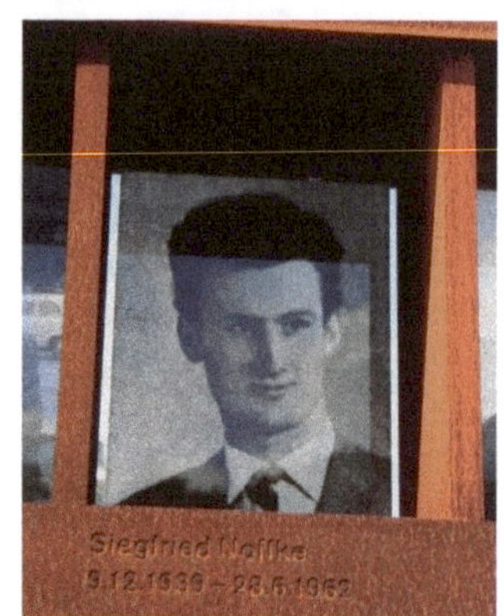

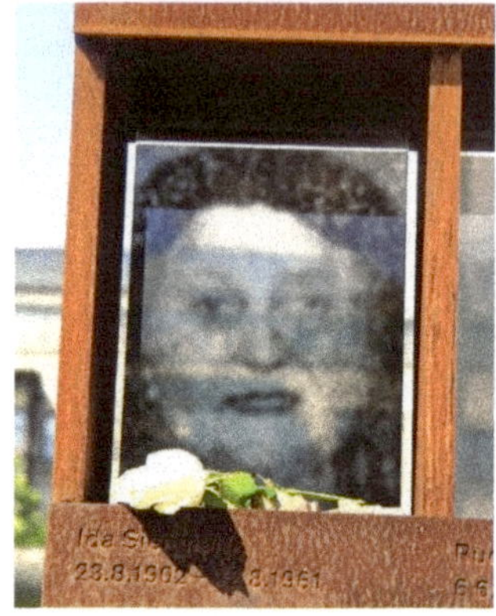

of Remembrance" at Bernauer Strasse. Neither these nor any of the others killed at the Wall will ever be forgotten.

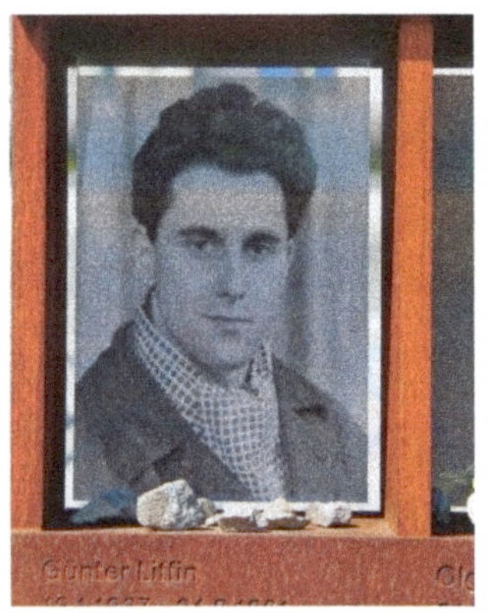

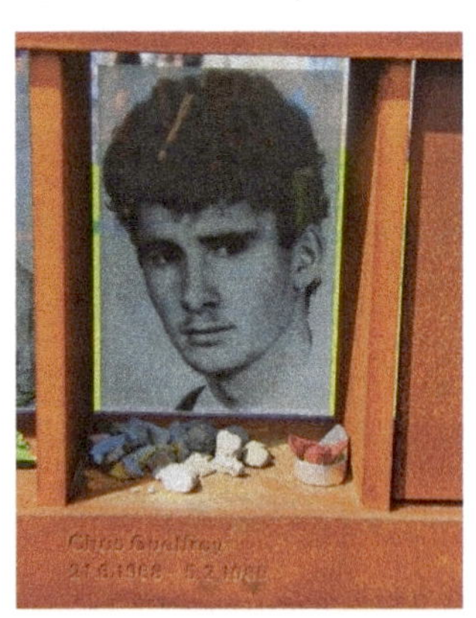

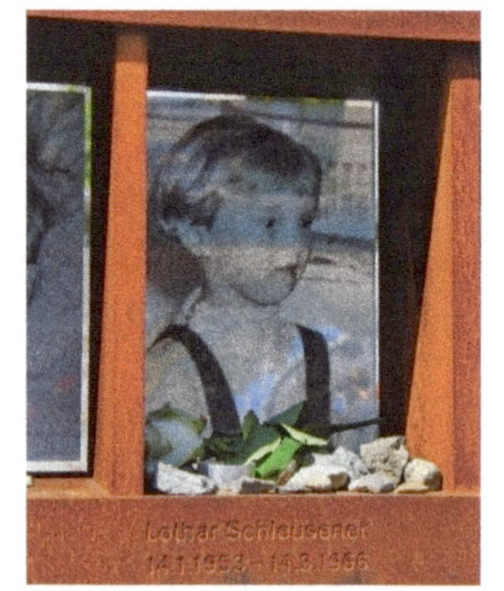

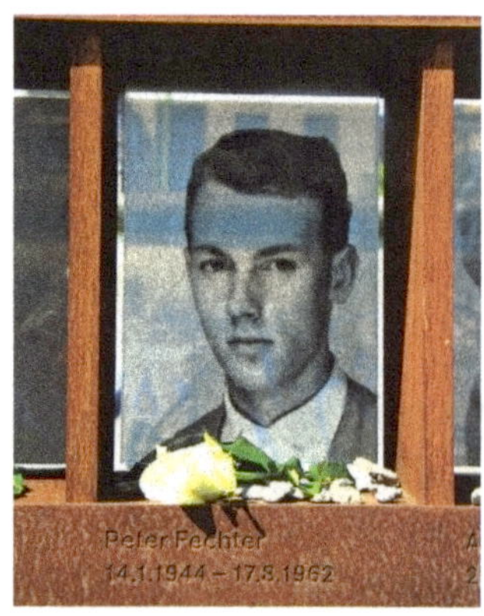

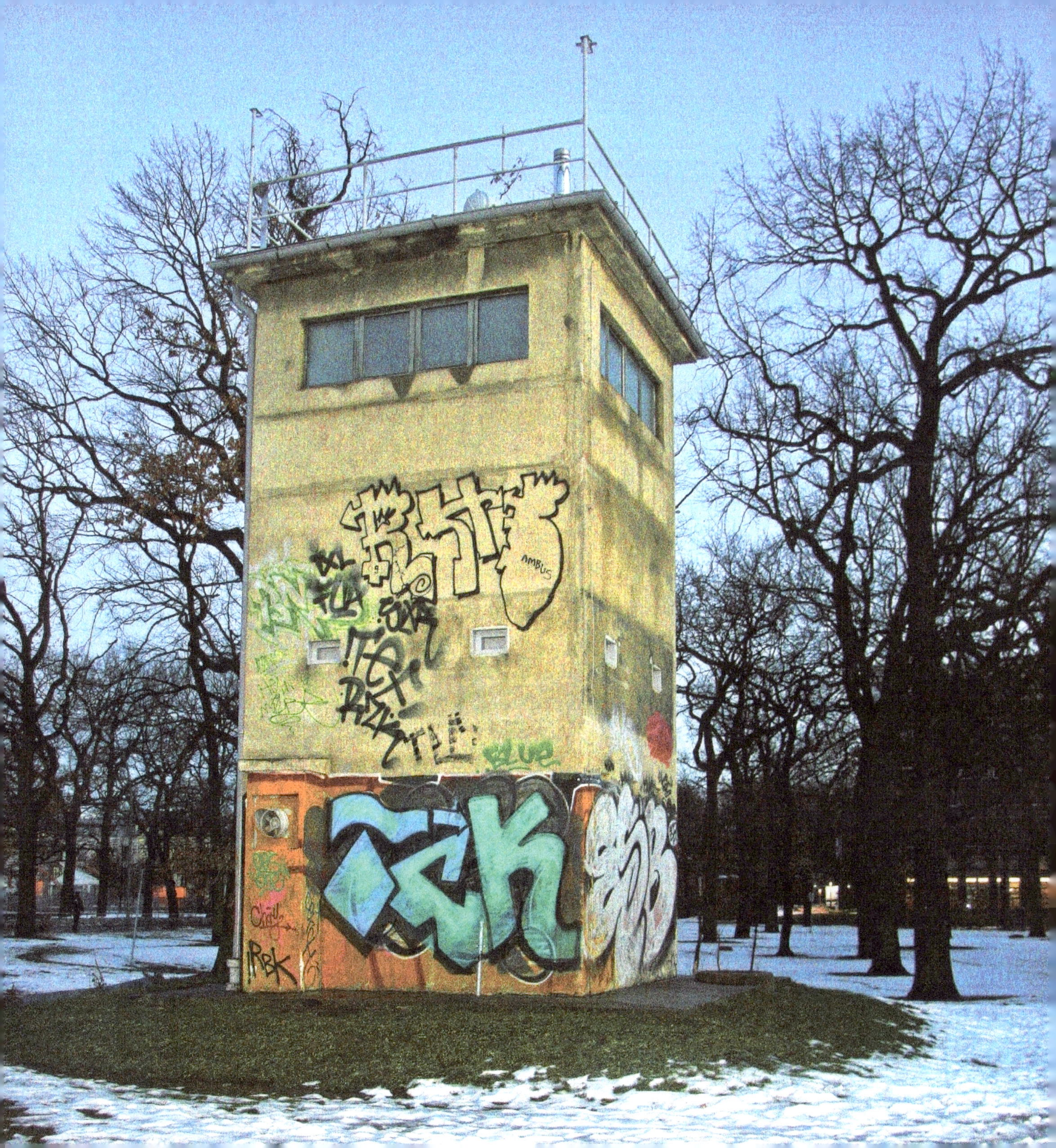

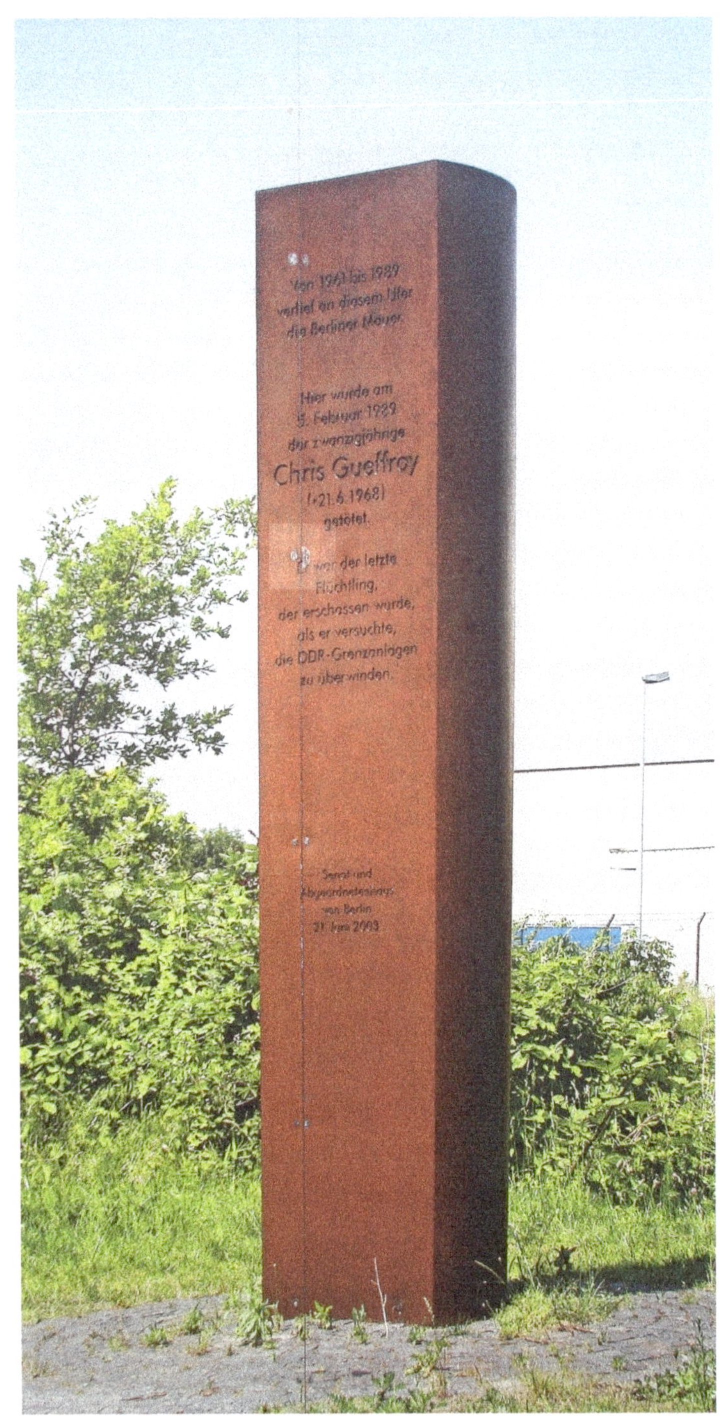

A memorial column devoted to twenty-year-old Chris Gueffroy, who was the last person to be shot at the Berlin Wall.

Berlinica presents

2010–2015 Program

If you subscribe to our monthly newsletter at www.berlinica.com/contact, you will get one of those two e-books below for free.

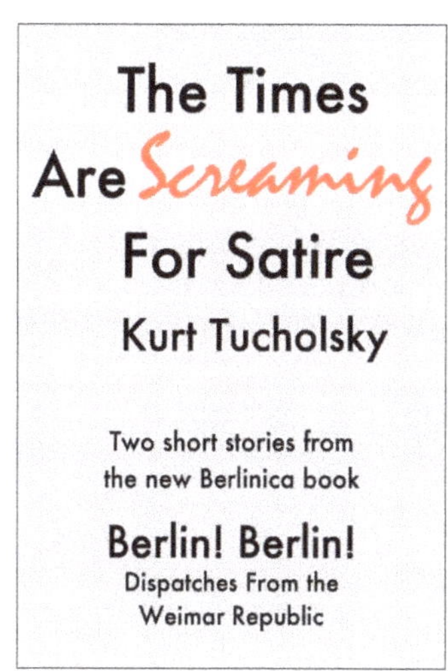

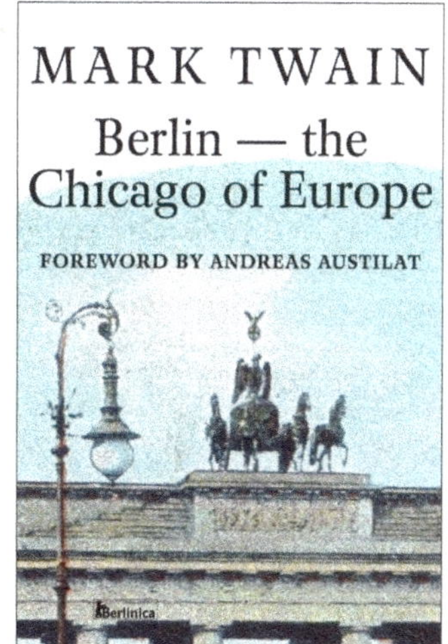

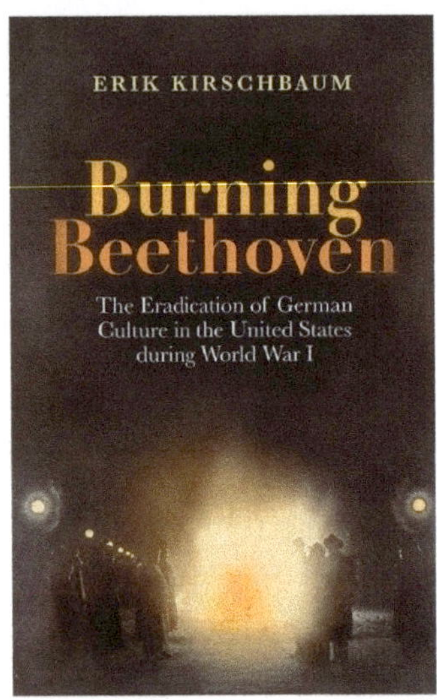

Erik Kirschbaum
BURNING BEETHOVEN
The Eradication of German Culture during World War I
Softcover, 176 pp., $13.95
ISBN: 978-1-935902-85-0

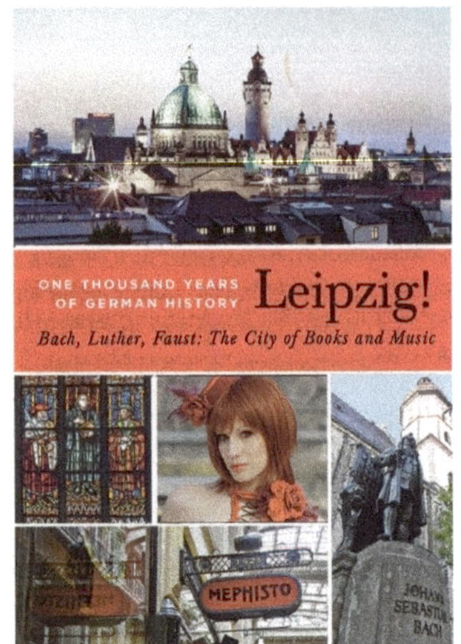

Sebastian Ringel
LEIPZIG!
One Thousand Years of German History
Softcover, 224 pp., $24.95
ISBN: 978-1-935902-58-1

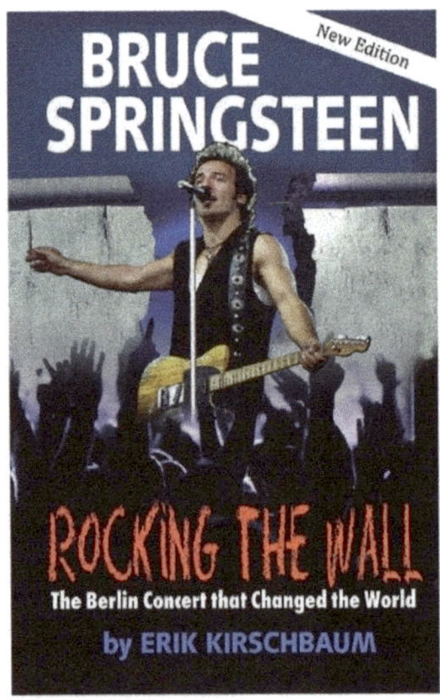

Erik Kirschbaum
ROCKING THE WALL
The Berlin Concert that Changed the World
Softcover, 176 pp., $17.95
ISBN: 978-1-935902-82-9

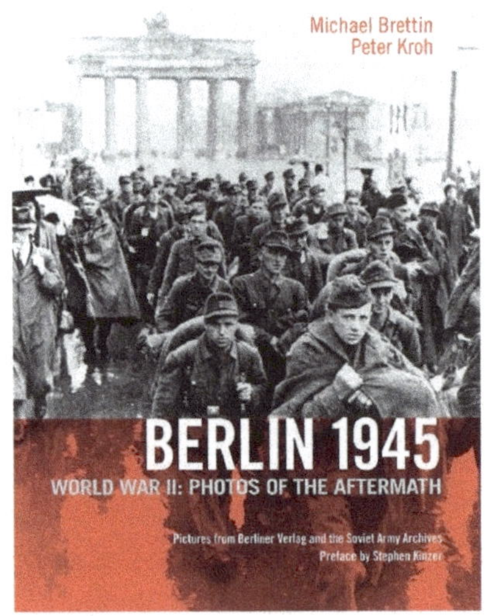

Michael Brettin
BERLIN 1945
Photos of the Aftermath
Softcover, 218 pp., $23.95
ISBN: 978-1-935902-02-7
Preface by Steven Kinzer

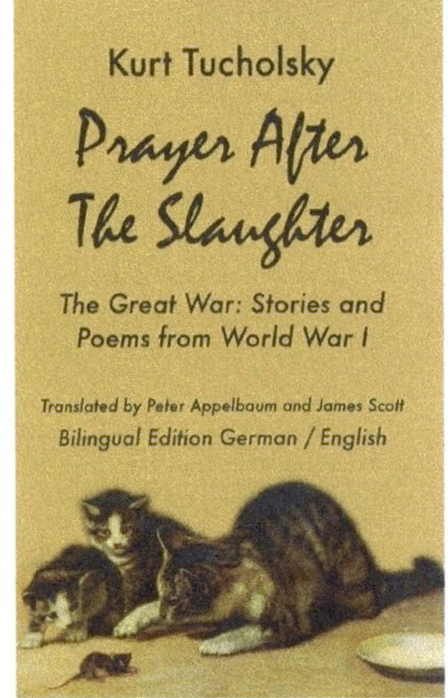

Kurt Tucholsky
PRAYER AFTER THE SLAUGHTER
The Great War: Stories and Poems from World War I
Softcover, 112 pp., $11.95
ISBN: 978-1-935902-287
Bilingual English / German

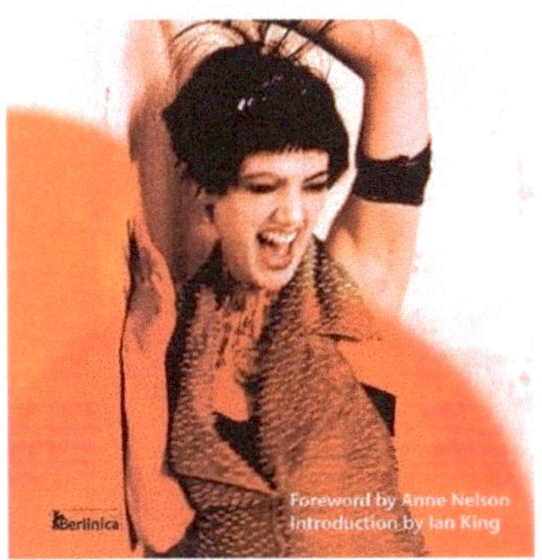

Kurt Tucholsky
Berlin! Berlin!

Dispatches from the Weimar Republic
Softcover, 198 pp., $13.95
ISBN: 978-1-935902-23-3

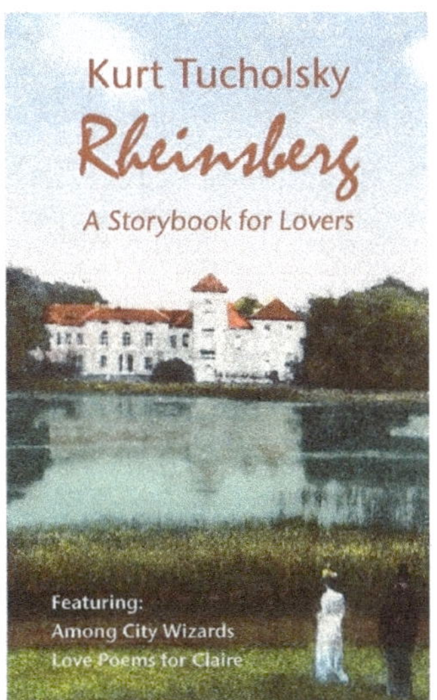

Kurt Tucholsky
Rheinsberg

A Storybook for Lovers
Hardcover, 96 pp., $14.95
ISBN: 978-1-935902-25-6

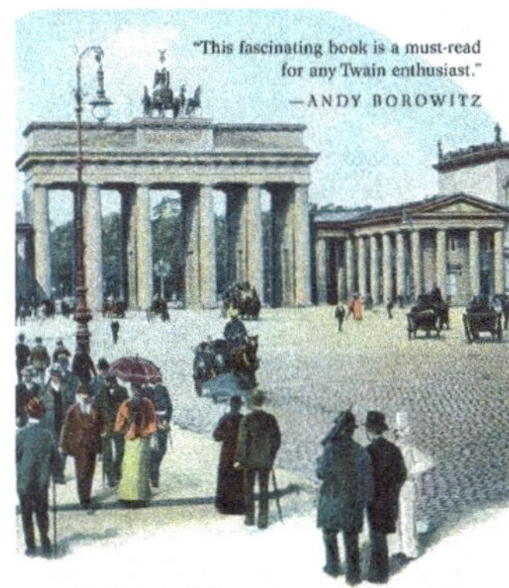

Andreas Austilat
Mark Twain in Berlin

Newly Discovered Stories
Softcover, 176 pp., $14.95
ISBN: 978-1-935902-95-9
Preface by Lewis Lapham

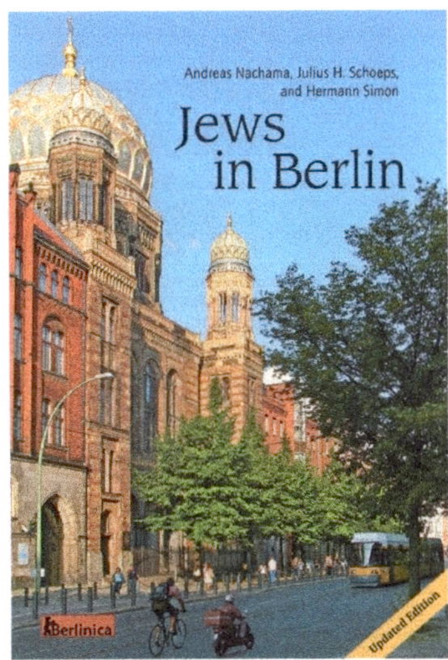

Andreas Nachama
Julius Schoeps
Hermann Simon
Jews in Berlin

Softcover, 310 pp., $24,95
ISBN: 978-1-935902-60-7

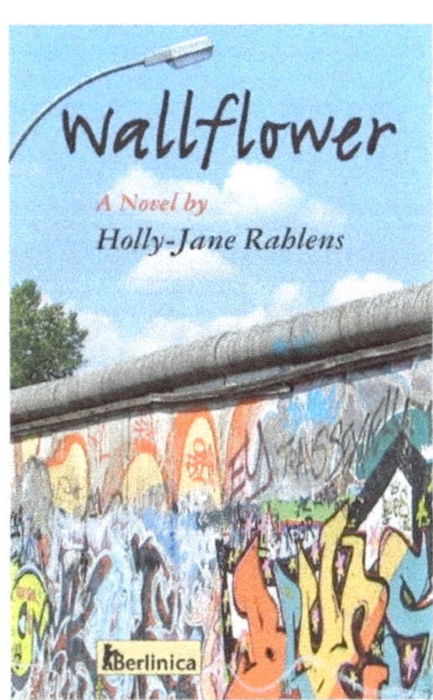

Holly-Jane Rahlens
Wallflower

A Novel
Softcover, 150 pp., $11.95
ISBN: 978-1-935902-70-6

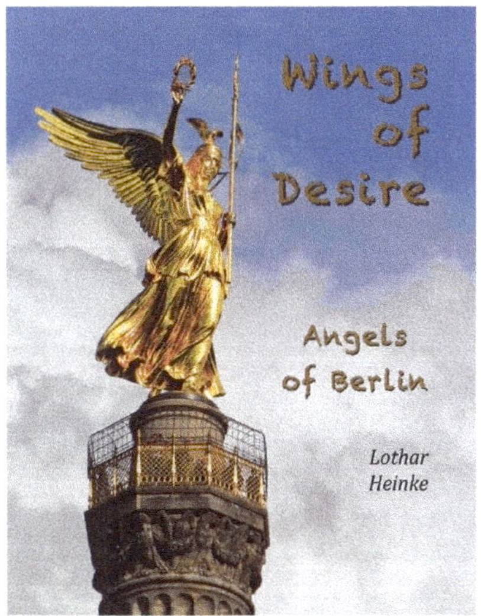

Lothar Heinke
Wings of Desire—
Angels of Berlin

Softcover, Color, 102 pp., $19.95
ISBN: 978-1-935902-18-8

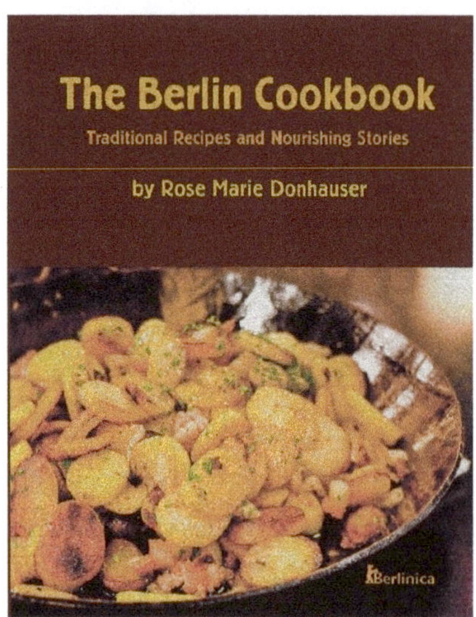

Rose Marie Donhauser
THE BERLIN COOKBOOK

**Traditional Recipes
and Nourishing Stories**
Hardcover, 104 pp., $19.95
ISBN: 978-1-935902-51-5

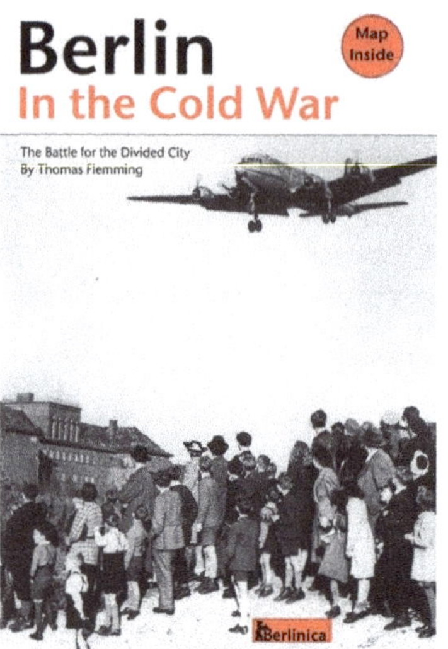

Thomas Flemming
BERLIN IN THE COLD WAR

Softcover, 96 pp., $10.95
ISBN: 978-1-935902-80-5
With a map of Cold War places

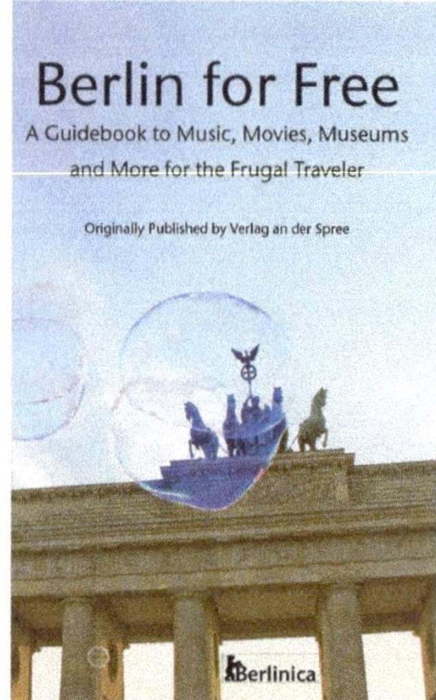

Monika Maertens
BERLIN FOR FREE

**A Guidebook for the
Frugal Traveler**
Softcover, 104pp., $10.95
ISBN: 978-1-935902-40-9

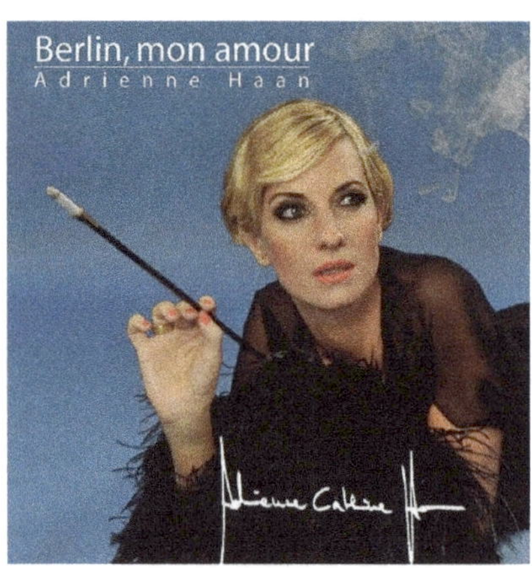

Adrienne Haan
BERLIN, MON AMOUR

Music from the 1920s
Music CD, 1 disc
in English
48 minutes; retail $15.95

Also in German

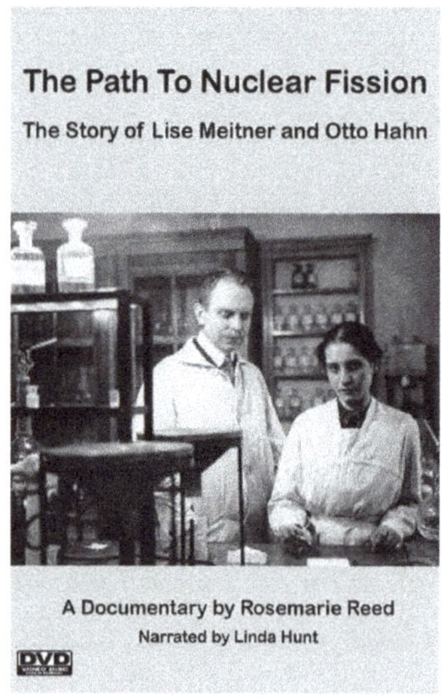

Rosemarie Reed
THE PATH TO NUCLEAR FISSION

English/German (subtitled)
Run time: 81 minutes; $19.95

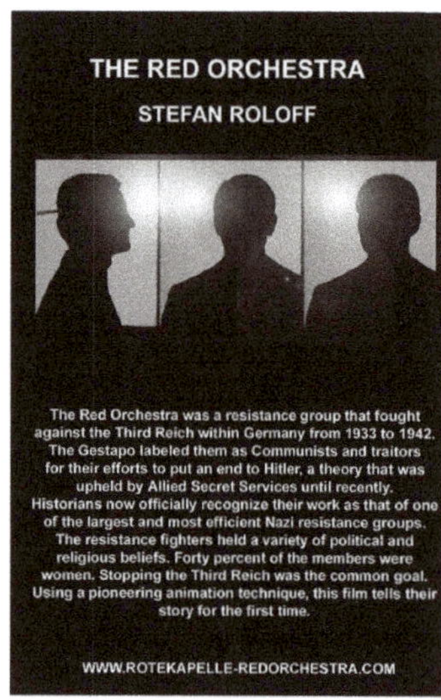

Stefan Roloff
THE RED ORCHESTRA

Die Rote Kapelle
English/German (subtitled)
Run time: 57 minutes; $24.95